Cognitive Behaviour Therapy in Sport and Performance

Many sport and performance psychologists worldwide practise cognitive behaviour therapy (CBT) as a therapeutic and applied practice approach. But no textbook currently offers a blueprint to understand and use CBT in sport and performance settings.

Cognitive Behaviour Therapy in Sport and Performance: An Applied Practice Guide builds upon a tangible foundation for the practice of CBT and related techniques in sport and performance contexts. This new book presents key points to help students and practitioners bring CBT into the sport and performance context. We focus on the 'what is' and the 'how to'.

Drawing upon the latest research and a wealth of applied practice experience, this easy-to-use guide takes the reader through each step of the CBT process with case examples, plain instructions, and worksheets to maximise the quality and depth necessary for effective CBT practice.

As an applied guide, this book educates undergraduates and postgraduates in sport and performance psychology (and all its variants). This book is an instrumental guidance material for sport and exercise psychology students but also invaluable as a practice guide for performance psychology trainees in applied practice placements and as a refresher primer for established professionals.

Paul McCarthy, PhD, leads the taught doctorate in Sport and Exercise Psychology at Glasgow Caledonian University, UK. He is a BPS chartered psychologist and a HCPC-registered sport and exercise psychologist.

Sahen Gupta is a Lecturer in Applied Sport & Exercise Psychology at the University of Portsmouth, UK. He is nearing completion of his Doctorate in Sport and Exercise Psychology and his Chartered status with BPS and HCPC (April 2023). He focuses on CBT, resilience, and athlete development for mental health and high performance. He is the Founder of Discovery Sport and Performance Lab, working to implement sport psychology across multiple countries and cultures.

Lindsey Burns, PhD, is an Assistant Professor in Psychology at Herriot Watt University, UK. Lindsey is a Chartered Psychologist with the British Psychological Society and a HCPC practitioner health psychologist.

Cognitive Behaviour Therapy in Sport and Performance

An Applied Practice Guide

Paul McCarthy, Sahen Gupta, and Lindsey Burns

Routledge
Taylor & Francis Group
NEW YORK AND LONDON

Designed cover image: Shiyamek Dasgupta

First published 2023
by Routledge
605 Third Avenue, New York, NY 10158

and by Routledge
4 Park Square, Milton Park, Abingdon, Oxon, OX14 4RN

Routledge is an imprint of the Taylor & Francis Group, an informa business

ISBN: 978-1-032-22858-7 (hbk)
ISBN: 978-1-032-22856-3 (pbk)
ISBN: 978-1-003-27451-3 (ebk)

DOI: 10.4324/9781003274513

Typeset in Times
by KnowledgeWorks Global Ltd.

Contents

List of Figures

List of Tables

Section I

Background

1 Introducing Cognitive Behaviour Therapy

Cognitive behaviour therapy (CBT) focuses on how people think and act to help them manage their emotional and behavioural issues. Emotional and behavioural issues are common in sport because the trials of training, competition, and the media spotlight, for example, mean athletes periodically think and act contrary to their needs. All athletes learn to navigate these emotional and behavioural issues on their own or with support from support staff in developmental years. The sport psychology practitioner/sport psychologist (referred to throughout this book as a practitioner) is one of them. Practitioners help athletes to address emotional and behavioural issues using a therapeutic modality, such as CBT. Like any therapeutic method, CBT seems puzzling initially, but with a helpful guide, we can learn the basics of CBT, how it works, and how it works best. Learning the practicalities of CBT allows practitioners to practise with confidence, knowing and understanding the theory and methods that drive this mode of intervention.

CBT comprises three components: cognitive, behaviour, and therapy. Cognitive is the mental actions/processes of acquiring and understanding information. For example, an archer noticing and interpreting the direction of wind before nocking an arrow. Behaviour encompasses the external reaction to our environment as what we overtly do. To illustrate, the archer notices the wind via their cognitive processes and then adjusts their stance to counteract it and hit the bullseye. Finally, we apply psychological methods to adjust cognitions, behaviours, and emotions via regular personal interaction. For instance, the archer consults you, the practitioner, to understand distractions and fears when the wind picks up, stimulating self-doubt. You apply the key principles of CBT you have learned and practised from this book (remember we often apply CBT principles in sport without the 'therapy' tag or the 'therapy setting').

What is CBT?

Aaron Beck developed CBT in the 1960s and 1970s as a therapeutic approach and a lens through which to view human behaviour. A scientist at heart, he developed a structured, short-term, form of psychotherapy that helped clients solve current problems by modifying dysfunctional thinking and behaviour (Beck, 1964). Beck called it 'cognitive therapy'. Since these early days of cognitive therapy, researchers and practitioners have added the behaviour arm to create CBT. With the CBT approach, we can examine how individuals understand themselves, other people, and the world. We start with understanding how people think, which influences how they feel.

DOI: 10.4324/9781003274513-2

Feelings influence their physical or body reactions. These combine to affect how individuals behave. This chain reaction occurs in a helpful or an unhelpful way. To illustrate, if I think I am not good enough to practise CBT, then this thought makes me feel nervous because I feel I do not know what to do. This feeling manifests as tension in my body and my body feels tight and clenched throughout a therapeutic session. These thoughts, feelings, and sensations cause me to be less than the capable practitioner I know I can be. This example is a negative chain reaction; however, it could be a positive chain reaction. To illustrate, I think I am not good enough to practise CBT but I have and can use therapist micro-skills to help my client. This evidence makes me feel calmer knowing that I know what I am doing. I relax, breathe well, and my body feels normal. Together, although they may cause me to be wary that I may not be the best CBT practitioner in the world, I support my client to the best of my ability.

The premise of CBT is simple, but the complexity of human behaviour makes its execution intricate. Clients often start a session unaware of their thoughts and how these thoughts affect behaviour unhelpfully, much like driving a car unaware that you have a flat tyre. When the client realises this link between their thoughts and actions, they can stop and change their thoughts, which will change feelings, physical reactions, and behaviours. Similar to realising, the tyre is flat, causing the wobbly steering, stopping the car, and changing the tyre. For human behaviour and human lives, each individual has their unique experiences, beliefs, personality, and existing patterns of thinking which prevent the person from easily replacing the flat tyre with a new one. Properly applied, CBT allows the individual to bypass all these difficulties by altering their unhelpful patterns of thinking and replacing them with a new, more helpful version. CBT is a *psychotherapeutic* modality informed by a body of theory which guides performance-oriented interventions. Before we proceed into the specifics of CBT theory, here are certain foundational principles of understanding to keep in mind.

'We don't see things as they are, we see them as we are' – Anaïs Nin

This quote encapsulates a cornerstone of CBT, derived from Stoic philosophers. We can trace the origin to Epictetus and Marcus Aurelius on the importance of psychological control (i.e., that our thoughts and our beliefs are in our control, whereas events of life are out of our control). This is central to the idea that our thoughts and core beliefs influence our emotions and behaviour. Events themselves do not trigger nor dictate emotional reactions and our behaviour. For example, being put on the transfer list of your club despite maintaining a steady performance is out of your control. But its interpretation as an attack on your self-image or self-respect is a judgment you have made about it. For more on the link between CBT and Stoic philosophy, see Robertson (2018).

Modern CBT theory has extended this idea that emotions and behaviour are a simple consequence of our thinking. One can tweak one's emotions and actions by changing one's thinking; however, it is more likely that any event (e.g., negative feedback from a new coach) is intensified by the unhelpful pattern of thinking, which interferes with helpful thought patterns (e.g., *'s/he thinks I am not good enough; I will never be selected'*). CBT helps clients to recognise that this type of thinking is the flat tyre and works to develop alternatives (e.g., *'I need to sit down with him and figure out an action plan to develop'*) which stem from the CBT premise that there are multiple ways of thinking and seeing an event.

'I am a part of all that I have met' – Alfred Lord Tennyson

In CBT theory, thoughts (and beliefs) play a key role in interpreting and perceiving events in the environment. Meaning-making is holistic, not in one direction. Thoughts are not the only contributors to interpreting the environment. Thoughts or cognitions interact with physical reactions, emotions, and how the individual is interacting with elements in their environment. This point is crucial when we apply CBT principles to the sporting environment, which is rather different from a counselling room.

Elements in the environment, such as critical teammates, discriminatory behaviour, high emphasis on outcome, and financial pressures, among others, can influence the thoughts of the individual. These elements can be structural (larger organisational level) or interpersonal (people in the environment). These elements can influence the thoughts, and by extension, emotions and behaviour in an interaction cycle. Greenberger and Padesky (1995) outlined five major interconnected components: thought, emotion, physiology, behaviour, and environment.

Let us look at our example, the athlete who receives negative feedback from the coach in a cutthroat competitive team (environment), sees himself as incapable and 'not good enough' (thoughts), feels down, gloomy, frustrated (emotion), withdraws from taking risks during play, and being creative which was a signature advantage of his gameplay (behaviour) and is anxious with poor sleep before selection days (physiology). A fundamental change in one of these elements can eventually lead to a positive change in other elements. For example, if the thought processes change to 'need to work on my game', 'talk to the coach and learn', it will lead to a challenge appraisal generating a better engagement in a competitive environment, positive emotional experience in sport and return to homeostasis in physiology.

We shall keep these two fundamentals in mind before addressing the next key point, outlining the theory behind CBT. As a reflective learning exercise, we encourage you to think about similar high-stress or 'high-pressure' situations you have experienced which can prepare you for a test or for the Olympics, or even overcoming a setback. Try to fathom what 'thoughts' you had. Try to isolate your emotions in that situation, then reflect on whether the thoughts and emotions affected your behaviour. Since CBT is a theoretical system founded on general life patterns, it will apply in various situations. Research has indicated that when we apply CBT in our own life situations, it enhances our familiarity with and fluency in CBT skills as a practitioner (Bennett-Levy & Lee, 2014).

Reflective Exercise

- Isolate a situation for yourself (e.g., flipping an omelette or stepping up to take a penalty or sitting down to write an essay).
- Try to understand what 'thoughts' you had (e.g., *'I do not want to mess this omelette up'*, or *'I want to put it in the right corner'*, or *'I am going to be so bad at this, I do not understand this topic'*).
- Isolate your emotions in that situation. Be specific. For example, instead of saying *'I was feeling down'*, try to be specific. Were you feeling sad, lonely, disappointed, devastated, or a specific emotion?
- Try to identify if your behaviour was affected by your thoughts and your emotions.

What is the theory underlying CBT?

Before we dive into the theory underlying CBT, we need a note on flexibility. Imagine there are three practitioners in the world of sport. The first practitioner works with a male youth tennis player; the second supports an international women's rugby team full-time, and the third is a researcher on coach-athlete relationships and only works with coaches in providing psychological support. But in their busy working lives, the fundamental questions they ask, the relationships they form, and the social context they are in guide their formulation, theoretical referencing, and interventions. Psychology and, by extension, sport psychology, as a science faces a similar situation. Every practitioner would be (or should be) united in their shared goal to understand and promote psychological factors of high performance, while promoting mental health and well-being. Therefore, there needs to be flexibility in applying the theory of CBT to guide practice because only then will the theory of CBT and the methods of practice to be outlined in this book be closer to the daily trials and often messy realities in practice (see Sections II and III).

CBT is based on an information processing model. Think of a computer, which boots up and processes information. In human beings, this information processing about ourselves, others, and the world are determined by our levels of thinking. According to CBT theory, there are three broad levels of thinking (see 'Levels of Cognition', Chapter 3). The deeper into the levels one goes, the more the level of thinking influences one's behaviour.

Level 1: Negative automatic thoughts

For ease, we refer to negative automatic thoughts as negative NATs. NATs are involuntary (i.e., they arise in an individual's mind when they are experiencing distress). They are also situation-specific. Remember how the environment leads us to react to certain thoughts? NATs are a prime example. For instance, imagine you are the archer who lost her previous medal final because of a strong wind and is about to fire an arrow with a strong gust blowing. Her NAT is likely to be, *'Not again, the wind will cost me here again'*, generating an emotional reaction. Individuals are more aware of how they feel (emotions) rather than their NATs (thoughts) (Beck & Beck, 2011). NATs are the most explicit and most easily accessible pattern of thoughts if one is using CBT. You could think of it as the topsoil of the individuals' cognitive reactions, which can be easily accessed by digging with CBT-based questioning (we cover such questioning types and examples in Chapters 3–5).

Level 2: Underlying assumptions

The next layer below the NATs comprises our underlying assumptions and rules for living. These underlying assumptions set the standards we live by and expect and provide guidelines which determine how we behave. These assumptions result from our learning throughout our developmental years and often stay hidden beneath. They are difficult for individuals to be aware of and articulate. Let us look at an example. Imagine a player who received negative feedback from his coach. The negative reaction that followed in his thoughts, emotions, and behaviours was likely because of the triggering of his underlying assumptions such as *'If I play well, the coach values me'* or *'If I receive negative feedback, it means I'm hopeless'*.

Now, keep in mind we all have such underlying assumptions. It takes some reflective activity and self-awareness work for practitioners to uncover their own underlying assumptions as well. These underlying assumptions are usually like a switch because they occur in *'If… then…'* much like 'if I press the switch, then the light will come on'. Other examples are characterised by *'must'*, *'should'*, *'have to'*, and similar rigid pressure indicators. Beck et al. (1985) outlined that most underlying assumptions focus on (1) competence (e.g., 'I am what I do and succeed at'); (2) control (e.g., 'I am capable if I get out of this slump on my own'); and (3) acceptance (e.g., 'No one appreciates me for who I am, only what they want me to be'). Underlying assumptions make up the subsoil in human cognition. It takes intensive work, a bigger shovel and more time to access, and be aware of and articulate these underlying assumptions. We cover these in depth and how to initiate them in applied practice in Section II.

Level 3: Core beliefs

Core beliefs are thoughts, opinions, and assumptions that we hold about ourselves ('self'), other people ('others'), the surrounding environment ('world'), and the future ('future'). CBT theory indicates that these core beliefs dictate our patterns of thinking, much like a computer. We internalise these core beliefs from early experiences, and they lie dormant until a relevant life event activates them. These core beliefs determine the thought-emotion-physical reaction-behaviour chain that we have highlighted previously. For example, a child who saw a parent lose a sporting career because of an injury when he used to attend matches when he was little internalises the belief that injuries are career-ending.

Now imagine there is an issue with your computer causing it to malfunction. Usually, this happens because of a hardware issue or a computer virus. For human beings, a similar negative reaction is caused by anything which causes us psychological distress, the now grown-up football player tears his anterior cruciate ligament (ACL) and has a core belief of *'injuries are career ending'* and/or *'I am unlucky and can never catch a break'*. When we experience such distress, the core beliefs are triggered or activated and our thinking becomes rigid and distorted (*'I will never play again'*). Our judgements become absolute and overgeneralised (*'it happened to my dad, and he never played again'*) which affects the underlying assumptions of *'If I never play again, then what am I?'* or similar. Our thoughts and beliefs fix like concrete, unable to change and adapt to situations (*'Doesn't matter what treatment I get, it's over'*). When waiting in the physio room for the final diagnosis, the footballer will dwell upon supposed bad luck and how things never work out, causing a negative emotional spiral which might lead to NATs such as *'Everyone will forget me'* or *'My life is down the drain'*. Core beliefs are the bedrock and often take a long-term intervention to access and intervene.

Such distorted thinking after experiencing distress stems from deeper dysfunctional or unhelpful core beliefs that get activated, causing most psychological difficulties (Ledley et al., 2011). This leads to the underlying assumptions taking remote control of thoughts which determine emotions and ultimately behaviour. More frequent NATs bubble up into the individual's mind, causing a downward spiral. (Tip: If you are explaining these links to an athlete, tumbling down the stairs or sliding down a ski slope on one's bottom flailing are handy metaphors). Working at level 1 (i.e., NATs) provide immediate relief because they allow the individual to control the seemingly unending tsunami of NATs assaulting their mind. This early intervention at the NAT level is standard for CBT before digging deeper into the underlying assumptions and core beliefs for lasting change.

How do the levels work?

Although every individual and their presenting problem/issue can be subjected to the three-level examination, it is unnecessary that every situation needs work at all three levels. But the levels interact and influence each other, ultimately influencing a person's thoughts, emotions, and behaviour. Short-term CBT work can focus on being aware of situations causing NATs and modifying them, which can lead to the individual recognising some of their more obvious underlying assumptions and attempting to control them. Longer-term work includes isolating the negative core beliefs and working to change them. In such cases, cognitive restructuring techniques and belief modifications (in CBT interventions chapter later) can be applied but we must take care to ensure stability of the modified belief across situations and moments of high psychological distress. Think of it like injury rehabilitation. Once the healing is done, the stability of the healed body part needs to be checked in low-intensity training, high-intensity training, and then return to competitive sport to prevent re-injury. A similar process (if differently executed) is employed with CBT.

In a CBT-based session or intervention, the plan is to help clients gain awareness and understanding of how they think, feel, and behave. This uncovering is facilitated by helping them identify situation-specific (environment specific) thought patterns, emotional reactions, physiological indicators, and behaviours. Training this awareness is the first step in helping the client identify this chain that starts with thoughts arising from a situation and ends up influencing their behaviour and performance. We use various techniques which we will outline later. This is central to the CBT proposition that cognitive change (i.e., change in thought/thinking patterns) is central to the ultimate human change process of emotional processing, experiencing events differently and modifying behaviour (Clark & Steer, 1996; Beck, 2020). We will be specifically discussing the Cognitive Model in a later section of this book (Chapter 3, Key Point 11).

Reflective Exercise

- Reflect on the influence any environment (e.g., your office, the training ground, your bed) has on your thinking. For example, when I attend the gym, I think I will look stupid in front of the 'experts'.
- Reflect on how an environment and the thought reaction to it makes you feel. For example, when I walk into my home office and see my desk littered, I get angry at my pet for ruining the start of my day.

Why choose CBT?

The evidence base for CBT extends comprehensively to include research on outcomes of CBT, client factors, therapist factors, relational factors, technique, and practice factors. Since the first outcome study in 1977, over 2000 outcome studies have shown the efficacy of CBT for psychological problems, medical problems with a psychological component, and psychiatric disorders. Several meta-analyses and reviews of

CBT attest to its value. We normally consider efficacy (i.e., what works in controlled research trials) and effectiveness (i.e., what works in everyday clinical practice) when exploring whether CBT works. In sport and performance settings working with athletes, teams, and backroom staff, practitioners focus intensely on the effectiveness of CBT because all involved seek a performance and well-being advantage.

In the cognitive model, when an athlete, for example, learns to evaluate thinking realistically and adaptively, their unpleasant emotions and maladaptive behaviours decrease. To illustrate, if you were experiencing a low mood, struggled to concentrate at training, and were unselected for a game, you might register an automatic thought 'I can't do anything right' with an associated reaction of feeling sad (i.e., emotion) persuading you to withdraw effort in training (i.e., behaviour). A practitioner specialising in CBT would help you examine the validity of this thought. You might conclude you had overgeneralised, and you do many things well even when you feel low. This insight propels more functional behaviour (e.g., preparing your best effort for training) and prepares you for the thoughts (i.e., cognitions) that are likely to arise in training. We can generate positive automatic thoughts (e.g., I can do a great many things well), underlying assumptions (e.g., If I keep at it, I know I can improve), and core beliefs (e.g., I have strengths and weaknesses just like all other athletes).

What are the treatment principles?

Like all good models of therapy, the goal pursued encourages clients to be their own psychologist to help themselves recognise how they think, feel, and behave, and then engage the requisite tools to change maladaptive cognitive and behavioural patterns. CBT occurs in the spirit of collaborative empiricism through a structured, problem-focused process. Collaborative empiricism refers to a collaborative therapeutic relationship between the client and the practitioner to work together to identify maladaptive cognitions and behaviours, question their validity, and revise where necessary. The first step here means defining problems and developing skills to manage these problems. CBT is problem-oriented, emphasising the present, to improve the client's current state of mind. The client and practitioner attend to goals, tasks, and bonds. Goals represent what the client wishes to achieve by the end of the therapeutic support. Tasks reflect the work the client and practitioner do together to achieve the goals. Bonds refer to the therapeutic alliance upon which the goals and tasks unfold. CBT works through a structured and time-limited process and includes cognitive, behavioural, and physical techniques. We go into how to apply these in Section II of this book (Chapters 3–7).

Cognitive techniques

A critical position in CBT involves understanding the client's view, how the client came to think, feel, and behave this way, and adjusting these thoughts and actions by exploring their underlying assumptions to generate more adaptive ways to think, feel, and act. One way to achieve this goal is through guided discovery and a feature of guided discovery is the Socratic method – a cornerstone of cognitive therapy. The most common strategy is the Socratic question. Socrates, a philosopher living in Athens around 400 BC, drew on a unique approach using questions to guide his students towards a conclusion without direct instruction. In this way, we lean on our knowledge to form opinions and generate possibilities to act upon. The fundamental premise here encourages the client to question their current outlook and cultivate new outlooks.

Behavioural techniques

Behavioural techniques or experiments represent planned experiential activities undertaken by the client between therapy sessions. These activities might be experimental or observational, stemming from the formulation of the problem to gather new information for the client and practitioner. The client might test an existing belief about themselves or road test a new, more adaptive belief or offer new information to the ongoing formulation. We can conceptualise behavioural experiments as ways to gather evidence to test hypotheses arising from unhelpful thoughts. Behavioural experiments move from thoughts in our heads to action and observation, generating new evidence and prospects.

Physical techniques

In sport and performance settings, physical techniques, such as relaxation and controlled breathing, complement the cognitive and behavioural collection above. Within the CBT model, alongside cognition, emotion, and behaviour, we have physiological responsiveness, which is one of the interacting systems in the model. In stressful performance environments, athletes experiencing anxiety often disclose the physical tension they feel, which fits as part of the maintenance cycle for anxiety, for example. Athletes can moderate this elevated arousal with specific relaxation exercises which work best within a CBT approach. Here's an example of a maintenance cycle for anxiety about sport performance. An athlete might feel that she needs to keep on practising as much as possible to feel ready for competition. This rumination triggers anxiety and the associated physical symptoms such as muscular tension, light-headedness, and a racing heart. Feeling this way, the athlete's skill execution falters and she thinks that she's nowhere near ready and needs to practise even more which triggers thoughts she will never get it right and so struggles to attend to the task at hand which generates more anxiety, and the cycle maintains itself.

CBT in sport today

Reviewing the literature on service delivery in applied sport contexts presents firm evidence of the use and value of CBT for therapeutic change among athletes, coaches, and teams. When we scratch beneath the surface of this assertion, relatively few studies exploring the efficacy and effectiveness of CBT in sport contexts materialise. This position presents a portentous case on one hand because our evidence-based practice is deficient but there is an opportunity to learn from decades of research and practice in other professional domains (e.g., clinical, counselling psychology) and benefit from their expertise.

Most researchers and practitioners in sport and exercise psychology are more familiar with psychological skills and psychological skills training rather than the cognitive-behavioural approach from which they originate. Applied sport psychology books, whether intended for academics or laypeople, include five psychological skills, sometimes referred to as the 'canon' including relaxation, self-talk, goal setting, imagery, and concentration. These psychological skills interventions come directly from classical CBT (see Meichenbaum, 2014) and we mould them around sport performance issues. To make sense of where we are with CBT in applied sport psychology, we ought to begin by examining the roots of CBT.

If we consider CBT to incorporate several related therapies – a family of therapies blending cognitive and behavioural elements – then we could include rational emotive behaviour therapy (REBT; Ellis, 1957), cognitive therapy (CT; Beck, 1976), schema therapy (ST; Young et al., 2003), and acceptance and commitment therapy (ACT; Hayes et al, 2012), among other approaches, in the sport context. So, why CBT in sport? Most interventions in sport psychology target cognitions or behaviours that allow regulation of the mind for high performance. CBT formalises this process into a therapeutic modality delivered to athletes, under controlled conditions, in a relational context to help athletes improve what they think, feel, and do. We know some of the 'change' for the athlete depends on the quality of the working alliance that CBT prioritises. Through a structured psychotherapeutic modality, CBT processes outlined in this book explore the 'what' of CBT in sport and 'how' to use it. There is currently much 'what' information (e.g., what is imagery, what is an imagery script, what is an imagery protocol) but much less of the 'how' information. The 'how' information integrates the 'what' information. For example, if we deliver an imagery exercise with a client, we do so as a step in the assessment, formulation, intervention, evaluation, and communication process. How we do what we do is the central focus of this book.

CBT in sport and the processes in this book are outlined to do good work, informed by best practice, and set an example of accountability for others; however, as Andersen (2005) remarked, '... there are so many ways to be a poor sport psychologist ... there are so many errors you can make ... all sport psychologists aren't the same. There are some more competent than others' (p. 15). Our focus is on giving the practitioner a text which enables them to develop their competency and apply it within the field.

2 CBT Training, Supervision, and Delivery

The training needs of novice practitioners

What we presented in the last chapter lays a foundation on which we can understand the philosophical underpinnings of cognitive behaviour therapy (CBT) within the overall professional development of a practitioner. But before we begin that discussion for the context of sport and performance psychology, we need to understand the training and supervision needs of trainees preparing to deliver CBT to clients. Sound, efficacious training in applied sport psychology begins with an outline of what trainees should learn (i.e., learning outcomes) followed by learning experiences to meet these learning outcomes.

Such learning experiences encompass any event (e.g., course, programme) or experience in which learning occurs (e.g., supervised traineeships). Within the training and development means available, we highlight the scale of options for training programmes in sport and exercise psychology, such as practical experience, modelling good practice, role plays, peer learning, supervision, and reflective practice. Hutter et al. (2015) reported 19 common learning objectives trainee sport psychologists wanted to learn from supervision. The authors divided the topics into two chief categories: know-how and professional development. The know-how grouping referred to practical, pragmatic skills and its lower order themes included 'intake', 'treatment plan', and 'execution' while the 'professional development' grouping referred to issues, challenges, and dilemmas that practitioners face and need to learn how to manage. The lower-order themes included 'reflections', 'working principles', and 'coping with dilemmas'. Generalising from these findings, one can picture how effective supervision depends on the preceding (and ongoing) appropriate learning outcomes gained through varied learning experiences.

Research exploring effectual learning experiences gathered pace over the past 15 years highlighting activities such as practical experience, peer and training staff interaction, role-plays and live expert demonstrations (e.g., teachers or supervisors). With these foundations and Hutter et al.'s (2015) know-how and professional development as dominant categories to meet trainees' needs in supervision, we need to match learning experiences to learning outcomes. In the following sections, we shall explore effective learning experiences and supervision before proceeding with the philosophical underpinnings of CBT and its place in sport and performance.

DOI: 10.4324/9781003274513-3

Assumptions in CBT client-therapist relationship

Person-centred and psychodynamic psychotherapies place the relationship at the heart of their enterprise, underscoring warmth, genuineness, and empathy to deliver necessary and sufficient conditions for worthy therapeutic outcomes. This trust in relationship factors seems so obvious we might forget their centrality in CBT. This book offers practical, specific, and clinically useful knowledge with skills and tips from leading researchers and practitioners in their fields who seek evidence, rigour, and balance. For example, though we might accept a person-centred perspective that emphasises genuineness, positive regard, empathy, and unconditional acceptance as characteristics of a therapist to promote change and growth, we are also keen to explore the evidence for the association among these factors and therapy outcomes.

For effective practice using CBT, we need to accept that a good relationship between a client and practitioner forms the bedrock from which all therapeutic work unfolds. From this bedrock assumption, we can register people as the sole proprietors of change. Therefore, there are certain active ingredients to facilitate this change tied to this assumption as well working alliance/therapeutic relationship is one such active ingredient. The working alliance refers to the task-focused, deep trusting relationship between the client and practitioner whereas the therapeutic relationship is the richer personal bond of trust between the two. The practitioner must recognise that it is important to have the client believe and buy into the practitioner's ability to help and secure a safe space before nurturing a mutual relationship and working on the tasks of therapy. The therapeutic alliance harbours the following three features: goals, tasks, and bonds. This is a *mutual* agreement on goals, undertaking tasks, and developing bonds between the client and the practitioner. Yet, for this relationship to germinate, we must briefly consider what each member brings to the relationship. Some elements are as follows:

- Relationships between the client and practitioner should be based on mutual respect
- Present circumstances and personal history of the client should be acknowledged
- The quality and strength are determined by an agreement on goals and tasks for the benefit of the client
- The relationship <u>must</u> be non-judgemental, safe, characterised by trust and transparency
- The therapeutic relationship has both client factors and practitioner factors (be aware of your own biases, desires, needs, pressures)

A question often researched is whether a good therapeutic alliance = outcome or therapeutic alliance leading to a good outcome. There is a mix of client factors, psychologist factors, and contextual factors in therapeutic meetings. All of them combine to deliver good outcomes. The client problems are disentangled through the foundation of a good relationship that progresses through phases to form, grow, and sustain it. We briefly explore each segment of the whole.

- Forming a good relationship with a client predicts better outcomes and keeps clients in therapy (Martin et al., 2000). This proof being so, it hinges on shaping a client's expectations of therapy, igniting their intention and motivation for change, and kindling hope. If we imagine our therapeutic journey resembles climbing a hill, not too steep but somewhat testing. As we begin our ascent, we need at least one safe foothold and perhaps a dependable stone to grasp. When an athlete contacts a practitioner, the prepared practitioner presents a foothold and a dependable stone to grasp by outlining what we expect of the client and practitioner and the possible therapeutic outcomes. We can take heart from the Latin proverb: *Initium est dimidium facti* (the beginning is one half of the deed). As we gaze up to the summit of the hill, we might feel the journey is beyond us and our intention and motivation for change wanes; however, the opening session with a client, for example, stages a refuge to amplify an emotional bond and meaningful connection. Although the client needs to institute hope in themselves, the practitioner ought to see or stimulate hope in the client and together they can tackle hope early in the developing alliance.

- Once the client and practitioner achieve hope, growing a good relationship depends on trust, openness, and commitment. The client needs to trust the practitioner, be open to the process of therapy, and commit to working with the practitioner; but the practitioner needs to focus on issues of these relationships, such as countertransference – a therapist's conscious and unconscious reactions to a client.
- Finally, sustaining a relationship depends on satisfaction with the relationship, a positive, fruitful working alliance, the ability and safety for clients to share their feelings and a change in how they see themselves and others. For long periods (6+ months), it also depends on how the relationship can evolve as the client evolves.

Supervising and being supervised in CBT

Ethical, practical, and engaging supervision offers the supervisee and the supervisor resources for personal and professional change and growth throughout the supervision lifespan. Research has shown that supportive supervision includes:

- Consistent and planned meetings
- Clear professional development goals and evaluating actions that work towards them
- Close, attentive, controlled challenge in supervisory relationships
- Encouraging self-refection
- Adjustment of supervision to developmental needs and levels of supervisee
- Clear feedback at different stages
- Promotion of reflective action and reflexivity
- Understanding and development of a professional philosophy of an applied psychologist.

To summarise, good supervision, rests on the structures of time, attention, feedback, and reflection, which involve the supervisee and the supervisor in equal measure. For instance, an effective supervisory relationship means that the supervisee feels supported and can trust their supervisor with sufficient time available to the supervisee. Supervisors can distinguish what is required in supervision and modules to prepare the supervisee for service delivery. Although the supervisor can offer direct feedback about what to do or not do, supervisees need sufficient experiences in class that model and guide them to learn about assessment, formulation, intervention and evaluation so that modelling or guidance (e.g., Socratic method) in supervision offers independence and choice for one's practice.

The process of reflection might include journaling, reflecting upon feedback from one's supervisor, or completing self-assessments. Cropley et al. (2007) described how reflective practice could advance service-delivery competence by building rapport, adapting interventions to specific clients' characteristics, opening an athlete-centred approach, better listening, and being perceptive while engaging with the client. On its own, however, reflective practice is challenging and does not substitute for supervision, but is an *add-on*. Finally, one's stage of development as a practitioner matters because novice supervisees are often anxious, and dependent, with limited knowledge, so their needs are clear – they need more meetings to increase knowledge and support to regulate their anxieties. When we realise our memory is an unreliable narrator – a literary term to describe a person telling a story but who is not telling the story precisely – we comprehend that our stories in supervision might benefit from audio or video evidence because what we remember might not reflect what happened in a session. What we mean here is that we can stimulate self-reflection by supervisees watching themselves in videos with interpersonal process recall exercises (reviewing their sessions with a supervisor). The supervisee can reflect on their experiences, decisions, and reveal blind spots. Good supervisory relationships mean defining boundaries, developing trust and safe environments, encouraging self-disclosure, identifying transference and countertransference, and considering multicultural issues.

Getting started with good supervision

Getting starting with supervision needs an acknowledgement of the differences between best practices and minimally acceptable practices. This is especially important for early career practitioners because we must protect client welfare while meeting the professional development needs of a trainee. The best practices guidelines (Borders et al., 2014) offer direction on starting supervision, setting goals, giving feedback, conducting supervision, the supervisory relationship, diversity and advocacy considerations, ethical considerations, documentation, evaluation, supervision format, the supervisor, supervisor preparation (supervisor training and supervision). Rigorous supervision in CBT in sport and performance contexts needs to include the following:

- Thorough intricacies of CBT theory and practice
- Larger context of sport, and sport-specific issues
- Context of service delivery
- Performance v/s mental health focus of work
- Developmental needs of trainees

One part of good supervision is stitching evidence to experience and experience to evidence. But when we can combine the best research with expert consensus and theory, we have a formidable trident for supervisors, supervisees, and clients. Like Socrates, if we believe that questioning and confrontation bring us to universal truths, then the process of questioning and confrontation can be transformational. In short, we partition through analysis and unite through synthesis. Supervising CBT practice in sport and performance contexts depends on supervisees laying solid practical foundations, such as cultivating a therapeutic alliance, erecting structured sessions, engaging in skills training, and undertaking self-monitoring. We shall briefly address these three parts before illustrating effective supervisory support for a trainee stepping out on a therapeutic journey.

1 A therapeutic alliance involves a working relationship between a psychologist and a client with three following interdependent components: goals, tasks, and bonds. (1) Goals mean whether the psychologist and client agree on the goals of the treatment. (2) Next, tasks refer to agreement on how to achieve those goals. (3) Bonds encompass the affective bonds between the psychologist and client.
2 Erecting erecting structured sessions matters because they allow the psychologist and client to plan how they will spend their time together in a session. They can even review it to include modifications for the next session. A typical session structure begins with a mood rating. Next, we have a bridge (a review of the previous session summary), then an action plan (homework) review, before setting and completing an agenda. Finally, we spend the bulk of the session working on the agenda. At the end of the session, we summarise what happened, seek feedback about the session and make a new action plan (homework).
3 Skills training is the principal aim of therapy, so clients become their own therapists. To reach this juncture, however, we need steps one and two above to be in place. Skills training, like most good learning experiences, comprises five steps: (1) introducing the skill, (2) demonstrating and practising the skill, (3) feeding back on the skill, (4) capitalising on new learning, and (5) practising in real-world settings. This is particularly effective since people learn well through experiential methods (i.e., learning through doing).

One effective model to use is Kolb's (1984) four phases of experiential learning: concrete experience, reflective observation, abstract conceptualisation, and active experimentation. Here's a simple description of the four phases of experiential learning that can be applied to CBT practice:

1 **Concrete experience**, we explain how the skill works and how it will address the problem at hand, followed by a sensible demonstration. One simple example is a thought record sheet that shows the connection between a thought and a distressing emotional response or problematic behaviour (see Chapter 6).
2 **Reflective observation** presents the client with time and space to check how the client is doing, their view on the skill, and any issues that arose for them. Positive, reinforcing, and constructive feedback helps clients through this phase of the experience so that this skill can be used as homework, for instance.
3 **Abstract conceptualisation** phase presents a critical point in the learning process because clients can consolidate their learning from the skill practice. Two critical components are necessary here: competence and schema. Learning experiences present opportunities to fathom small wins which have the potential to alter one's schema or way of understanding themselves from the past. For instance, if a client used a breathing technique to reduce distress and felt its benefits, then the client can see how they have some control over how they are feeling rather than believing a faulty belief about themselves such as *'I can't help how I feel'*.
4 **Active experimentation** means practising the skills in the world outside, away from the therapy room. In sport settings, clients often intend to use the skill they are learning in a crisis (e.g., in the changing room before a critical cup game) rather

> than practising the skills in progressively more stressful circumstances. This phase of the experiential learning process ought to include overlearning. *Overlearning* is a Behavioural Principle, which means practice or learning characterised by continuing beyond the point at which one already knows the skill well. Overlearning boosts memory by enhancing the encoding of information. This phase of learning raises two questions: how to practise and when to practise. In sport settings, we can practise skills at home, in and around, training and competition. Depending on the skill being learned, for example, emotional regulation, we need sufficient practice in low-demand situations before progressing to high-demand situations.

This must be conducted through self-monitoring, that is, to teach people how to be aware of themselves to notice and label their thoughts and feelings. With any self-monitoring target, we examine frequency, intensity, and duration and the context in which the thought, feeling, or behaviour occurs. A client might wish to catch automatic thoughts automatic thoughts – but may confuse the thoughts with a situation or an emotion. Through dialogue with a client, we can listen and label. The psychologist can label thoughts as thoughts, emotions as emotions, and behaviours as behaviours which help the client recognise and gain awareness of their experiences. When we cultivate the soil with self-awareness and self-monitoring, other skills propagate quickly. Many athletes seek the support of a psychologist because of emotional stumbling blocks with differences in their awareness, tolerance, and beliefs about emotion. We might expect an athlete to label basic emotions (i.e., fear, anger, sadness, disgust, happiness, and surprise); however, we can temper this expectation because such emotions might be outside the awareness of the client. As with thoughts and emotions, clients are also self-monitoring behaviours to increase or decrease, but often clients are not aware of the target behaviour when they are doing it. The client might recognise the consequences of their behaviour and then notice the events preceding it. The client might track what happens before treatment begins. Although retrospective recall is helpful, it has its limits and the client might miss or mistake specifics, such as the context and the co-occurring mood and thoughts.

Good supervision begins with an assessment of the supervisee's knowledge and understanding of CBT and its processes. This is the practitioner's self-monitoring. Without this footing, it is difficult to learn and reflect on the experience of delivering CBT to a client. Some key touchpoints in an effective supervisory process comprises initiating supervision, setting goals, giving feedback, conducting supervision, the supervisory relationship, diversity and advocacy considerations, ethical considerations, documentation, evaluation, supervision format, the supervisor, supervisor preparation (supervisor training and supervision), we attend here to the initial needs of the supervisee especially setting goals, giving feedback, conducting supervision.

Setting goals

Supervision must set clear goals and *then* work towards them. This process is one of navigation through the core competencies of the trainee which includes relationship building, cultural competencies, and professionalism while acknowledging and addressing traditional competencies (e.g., counselling performance skills, cognitive counselling skills and case conceptualisation, diagnosis and treatment planning, self-awareness, and professional behaviours). Finding where one lies on this map of competencies solidifies the needs and learning priorities of the supervisee, the supervisee's developmental level, and the setting within which the supervisee trains (e.g., academic course) and practises (professional football club). The supervisor assesses the supervisee's skills along with the supervisee's goals and prioritises those skills and issues throughout supervision.

Giving feedback

Regular and ongoing feedback is a hallmark of dependable support in a supervisory relationship. This feedback, however, ought to be delivered in manageable chunks that challenge and support the supervisee, considering the supervisee's experience, developmental level and client case load. Feedback, in whatever form, ought to be processed with the supervisee. For example, after directly observing a session with a client (e.g., live, audio, video recording) with the supervisee's self-reflection and analysis of the session, the supervisor can offer direct feedback as necessary relating to behaviours to change. Constructive feedback is specific, concrete, and descriptive and offers a precise understanding to the supervisee of the issue at hand.

Conducting supervision

The frequency and modality of supervision ought to be negotiated between the supervisee and supervisor considering needs, developmental status, and recommendations for professional standards. Some taught university programmes will combine weekly supervision with triadic and group supervision. Supervisees thrive in a safe, supportive, and structured supervision setting, so establishing structured, purposeful, and goal-oriented supervision benefits both parties. Though the bulk of most supervision sessions addresses professional learning, personal learning deserves attention too. A good supervisor recognises the well-being of the client and the client's immediate needs owing to the caseload and environmental challenges of working in sport and performance settings. At the outset of a supervisory relationship with a new supervisee in training, counselling skills, case formulation, self-awareness and professional behaviours might dominate supervision. With accruing practice, this balance might shift towards any of these elements, but also paying more attention to the supervisee's development and current goals. Some alternate forms are:

- **Group supervision**, for instance, offers supervisees an opportunity to learn from the experiences of their peers and complements their individual and triadic supervision. Effective group supervision depends on sound supervision, so that there are structure and goals, especially rules for all members of the group. The supervisor supports the group, includes all members and addresses dominant members to encourage participation by all. As the group matures, the group manages itself, its autonomy and leadership.
- **Triadic supervision** comprises a supervisor and two supervisees. The supervisor ought to explain and show how triadic supervision complements individual and group supervision. In triadic supervision, we address the needs of each supervisee in each session, encouraging constructive and balanced peer feedback. One challenge in all supervision settings is understanding, accepting and working with the feedback offered. Sensitive issues require time and understanding from

all parties. Feedback from one's peers, when unregulated, often triggers resentment and frustration. The supervisor can help peers to frame feedback that recognises achievement (i.e., what went well?), changes (i.e., what we could do differently next time?) and learning (i.e., what did you learn from reviewing your peer's session with a client?)

Professional philosophy and its underpinnings

There are theoretical and philosophical roots of cognitive-behaviour therapy in empiricism, pragmatism, functionalism, and early behaviourism. The work we do as practitioners arises from our training, supervision, and practice, but what lies behind these processes? According to Poczwardowski et al. (2004), 'Professional philosophy refers to the consultant's beliefs and values concerning the nature of reality (sport reality in particular), the place of sport in human life, the basic nature of a human being, the nature of human behaviour change, and also the consultant's beliefs and values concerning his or her potential role in, and the theoretical and practical means of, influencing their clients toward mutually set intervention goals' (p. 449). They also presented a hierarchical structure of professional philosophy discussed and implied in the sport psychology literature with components arranged from the most stable and internal to the most dynamic and external:

- Personal core beliefs and values,
- Theoretical paradigm concerning behaviour change,
- Models of practice and the consultant's role,
- Intervention goals,
- Intervention techniques and methods

These components continually influence each other and ultimately one's professional philosophy shapes the practitioner's approach to the process of service delivery, which contains assessment, formulation, intervention, and evaluation. In short, this philosophy of practice guides and directs the process of service delivery.

Corlett (1996) presented the philosophy-practice connection to indicate the direction of travel of two approaches to sport psychology service delivery: a sophist approach (i.e., 'technique driven and concerned solely with specific skills', p. 84) and a Socratic approach (i.e., 'rigorous personal examination and improved knowledge of self', p. 84). We see evidence of each approach in the sport psychology literature, though perhaps the leaning towards a Socratic approach is clearer in the literature 25 years hence. We see this development in the literature through reflective practice and the developing practitioner. The anxiousness one might expect in the beginning of the journey of becoming a practitioner resonates with those in counselling, for example. This anxiousness, doubt about one's abilities and dependence on one's supervisor subsides and a more client-centred, self-aware practitioner emerges with greater cognisance of the needs of their clients, which promises better relationships with clients.

The challenges of sport often demand an immediate solution to a pressing issue rather than a philosophical discussion about a method of intervention. With this challenge in mind, focusing on the applied sport psychology canon (i.e., relaxation, self-talk, goal setting, imagery, and concentration) makes sense from a practical perspective because one can appreciate why applied solutions (e.g., relaxation exercise) suit these pressing demands in a sport and exercise context. Pragmatism, with origins in the work of Peirce (1984) and James (1907), is a philosophy of knowledge construction that focuses on practical solutions to applied research questions and the consequences of inquiry. Pragmatism represents an attempt to offer practical solutions to contemporary problems experienced by people and society. Pragmatists prioritise the problems under investigation and the specific research questions over the underlying philosophical assumptions of the method.

Basic competencies and principles

Beck's original work was called 'cognitive therapy' before it integrated 'behavioural' techniques and principles into what is now known as 'cognitive-behavioural' therapy. Beck's work established the original model of CBT describing a theory of how people develop emotional difficulties, how they heal distress, and how these may be further prevented. Although CBT was built for treating depression, it has been validated globally as a highly effective psychological support modality to prevent mental illness and promote mental health. In sport psychology, for example, it is used to reduce distress and increase cognitive awareness of performance. The core principles are outlined below.

Cognitive Principle

As we highlighted earlier (Chapter 1), CBT is rooted in the understanding that our cognitions (i.e., our thoughts, beliefs, interpretations, and mental images) provide the *meaning* we assign to events, which lead to emotional reactions and behaviour. For example, a gymnast whose cognitions centre around her not being the *'perfect body shape'* is likely to face emotional distress from body image, leading to changes in eating and exercise behaviour.

Although this appears to be rather obvious once stated, the common-sense perspective would place any events directly leading to emotions. In ordinary situations, if we ask individuals to recount what led to their emotional state, they are likely to describe a situation. For example, footballer A shouting *'I am fed up, I cannot understand where I stand with the manager, he gives nothing away'*, footballer B says *'yeah, he plays it close to his chest, but yeah, I'm chill'* in response to the same manager's behaviour. If, however, we go by the assumption that events lead to emotions, the event would lead to the same emotions in everyone, all the time. Every footballer would be similarly fed up if their manager is not satisfied. But this simple explanation does not work because people react differently to similar events. The manager gives no indication whether a player is in his good books, but Footballer A is *'fed up'* whereas Footballer B is *'chill'*.

Even terrible and obviously distressing events such as major injury, loss of funding, and suffering bereavement do not produce the same emotional response in everyone. Some cope reasonably well, others are crushed, and most go through both in phases. Hence, it is not merely an event which sparks an emotion, but rather there is a 'cognition' or a thinking interpretation of the event. When two people react differently to an event, it is because their cognitions allow them to *see* it differently (see Figure 2.1). When the same person reacts differently to an event, it is because they infer it differently. Footballer A was probably having an emotional reaction because he was interpreting his manager's behaviour as a reflection of his skills whereas footballer B was not.

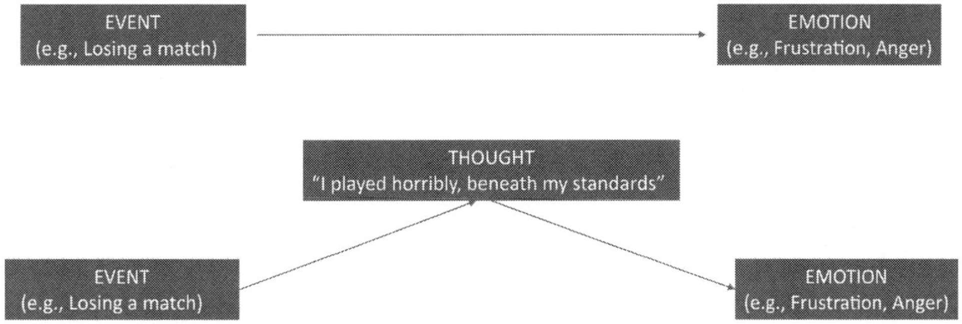

Figure 2.1 The Cognitive/Event Model (cf. Beck, 2020)

Therefore, we clearly see how two different individuals react differently to the same event, which is because each person has their own thoughts and beliefs about the event (i.e., an idiosyncratic meaning). Suppose you are a young tennis player who is practising the serve after a growth spurt. This has reduced your usual consistency. There are several thoughts that can come up from this situation. Specific thoughts cause different interpretations. These different interpretations lead to different possible emotional responses.

- *'I can't even get it over the net. What is going on? This is how I have been serving for the past year? I have not done anything!'* (Triggering anger)
- *'My contact point and follow-through is not how it's supposed to be. I should probably talk to my coach if this keeps happening'* (leading to calmness and emotional safety)
- *'My serve is not working. Gosh, I have a tournament on Wednesday. What will I do?'* (Leading to anxiety)

These examples illustrate the Cognitive Principles by displaying how different emotions arise from different cognitions. There is an association between certain kinds of thoughts and certain emotional states giving us a pattern. For example, thoughts which put events out of our control and focus on outcomes alone generally cause anxiety. What does this Cognitive Principle look like when we are getting started with CBT? When a client comes in, we try to understand (A) What are the thoughts of our client? (B) How are these thoughts causing emotions? (C) What is the pattern of these thoughts and emotions?

Behavioural Principle

Remember how we considered cognitive therapy assimilating behaviourist theory to become CBT? The Behaviour Principle in CBT outlines a focus on *what we do/how we act,* (i.e., our behaviour). CBT holds that our behaviour is a manifestation of our thoughts and emotions. Therefore, it is a crucial factor in maintaining – or in modifying psychological states. Our thoughts appraise the influence of events and lead to particular emotions, which lead to 'emotion-driven behaviours' (Barlow et al., 2011). We outline some common examples in Table 2.1.

In sport, what we do in skill execution and sport performance is the event, leading to certain thoughts. With the young tennis player above, the thought arises from

Table 2.1 Thought and emotion-driven behaviour

Thought Appraisal	*Emotion*	*Emotion-Driven Behaviour*
Loss (of person, goals, needs, desired, passion, sport, etc)	Sadness,	Search (to recover/undo loss), mourn, grieve, confusion
Threat (to sport, goals, person, relationships, etc)	Anxiety, fear, feeling out of control	'F-F-F Response' (Fight-Flight-Freeze)
Violation (of self, sport, goals, needs, principles, beliefs, etc)	Anger, rage	Lash out, attack
Development (of skills, goals, relationships, etc)	Delight, happiness	Self-praise, Increase drive,
Happiness (from success, recovery, goal achievement, etc)	Contentment	Continued behavioural engagement with task

the performance failure of executing a serve > emotion-driven behaviour, which with anger may pathways in throwing racquets, smashing the ball harder and other behavioural cues. On the other hand, if the player were anxious, they are likely to avoid the situation causing the emotional effect to worsen. If the tennis player had the more logical thought appraisal leading to calmness and emotional safety, they are inclined to engage in a structured help-seeking behaviour without negative emotional upheaval.

In the first, second, and third thought appraisal-emotion-behaviour pathways, the tennis player's behaviour (throwing racquets/avoiding situation) will have a significant effect on whether those thoughts and emotions of anger/anxiety persisted. Whereas, if the tennis player engaged in the fourth or fifth thought appraisal-emotions-behaviour pathway, their coach would support them, and help them correct their technique leading to rectifying the situation. In the future, if similar tennis-related difficulties occur, the player will be less inclined to think negatively. This reflects the 'Conditioned Learning' component of the Behaviour Principle (i.e., the process by which behaviours and the influence of behaviours evoke thought-emotion responses). They become 'evidence' supporting or refuting whether thoughts and emotions arising from events are valid. Therefore, in CBT, behaviours have a substantial influence on thought and emotion. What does this Cognitive Principle look like when we are getting started with CBT? (A) After understanding the thought-appraisal and emotions, we try to uncover behaviour patterns, (B) We can review how these behaviour patterns cause conditioned learning, and (C) We try to modify unhelpful behaviour patterns because changing what individuals do is a powerful way of changing how they think.

Continuum Principle

The Continuum Principle in CBT reinforces the idea that mental health difficulties arise from extreme versions of normal processes (see Figure 2.2). They align pathological states inexplicably different from normal states and processes. To use an analogy, the car is having difficulty running because the engine is misfiring, not because the entire machinery has been replaced with paper mâché. Psychological difficulties are at one end, mental health and optimal functioning are at another. Psychological difficulties can happen to anyone and are not a bizarre oddity.

Viewing mental health concerns from this lens allows an understanding that they are not from another dimension, but merely misfiring versions of normal patterns in

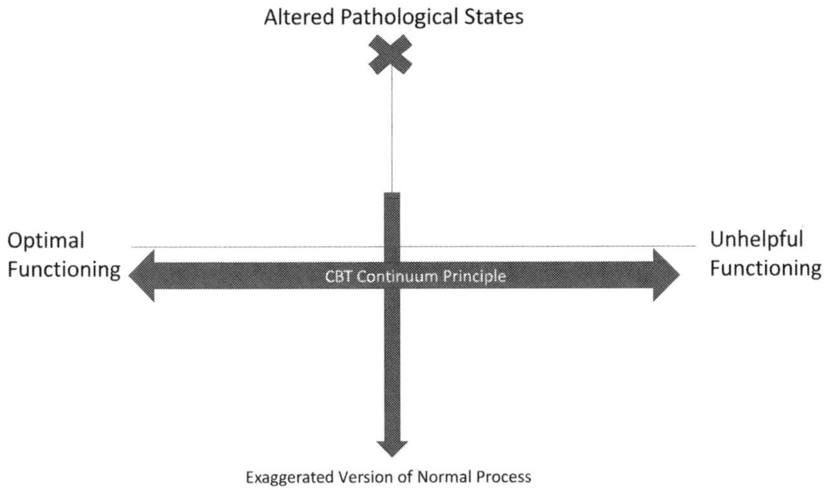

Figure 2.2 CBT Continuum Principle

an exaggerated (usually negative) manner. For example, a rugby player may be fixated on having a high percentage of catches. Their normal high standards force them to push themselves harder in training to be the best they can be, which translates into flawless catching in competition. The difficulty may arise during a natural performance drop, causing a mistake or two, resulting in dropped catches; however, the thoughts hammering on the high standards now are unhelpful and cause emotional difficulties from perfectionism. What does this Continuum Principle look like when we are getting started with CBT? We can explain it to clients which allows normalisation, and we can guide interventions because misfiring patterns can be altered so they work helpfully again.

Immediacy/Present/Here-Now Principle

CBT is markedly different from the earlier form of psychotherapy called 'psychoanalytic/psychodynamic' approach. Traditional psychodynamic theory postulated that looking at the symptoms of a problem (perfectionism) was insufficient. Successful treatment in psychodynamic therapy was focused on uncovering developmental processes, hidden conflicts, and unconscious relations that were the root cause of the problem.

Those of the Behaviourist approach were of the view that the symptoms were the sole target of treatment, and one could target perfectionism by looking at behavioural processes that maintained it. CBT has inherited this, adding a cognitive flavour to it in the years of its development. The Immediacy Principle of CBT outlines that the focus of therapy is on the here-and-now for most of the time. We work with clients on what is happening in the present, looking at cognitions, emotions and behavioural concerns that are maintaining the problem, rather than things which may have led to its development. For example, CBT work with perfectionism would involve thoughts causing it and behaviours reinforcing it. Not that CBT scorns things from the past. Rather, CBT looks at the conditioned learning (see 'Behaviour Principle' above) experiences in the past, such as a highly critical parent who had high standards, causing the athlete to strive to be 'perfect'. But that is not the focus. What does this Immediacy Principle look like when we are getting started with CBT? (A) We look at the thoughts-emotions-behaviour that are occurring in the present, and (B) We seek overt behaviours and slightly less obvious cognitions with the client to see how the problem is being maintained in the present.

Proof Principle

One characteristic which made CBT unique and prompted a change in the way psychotherapies were viewed is the Proof Principle. CBT outlines we should always evaluate our theories about what are the client's difficulties, what is causing them, what is maintaining them, and treatment/intervention plans rigorously using scientific proof. The focus is on evidence, rather than only clinical anecdotes that the client shares, which allows us to be evidence-informed practitioners, track our client's progress and modify interventions when needed. We know this as *'collaborative empiricism'* where the therapist and the client engage in a collaborative and systematic process to establish priority difficulties, and goals in treatment and test the efficacy of treatment and revise them if necessary (Kuyken et al., 2008). Keep in mind that there are various types of scientific evidence and applying CBT with clients can use a variety of them, which we shall outline in Chapter 6.

The Proof Principle is valuable for several reasons when we are applying CBT as practitioners, they are outlined in the '3E' rule-of-thumb below,

- **Evidence-Informed Science,** so that as practitioners, we can curate interventions founded on established theories and literature in line with best practice guidelines. CBT continued to develop, finding its feet in new fields. This book is an example of that. For example, when working with perfectionism, we would look at integrating sport psychology literature on tenets of perfectionism, its influence on individuals and integrate that science to be the evidence informing CBT intervention with the client.
- **Economics** matters in CBT. CBT is cost-effective and time-limited to ensure the limited mental health resources are maximised. This is even more so in sport psychology, where licensed practitioners are limited.
- **Ethical,** so that we can showcase our practice and its efficacy transparently, indicating that the individuals receiving it and paying for the service are benefitting. The 'proof' we gather during CBT reinforced efficacy of your practice -by extension reinforces the legitimacy and effectiveness of sport psychology in the sport world.

What does this Proof Principle look like when we are getting started with CBT? (A) We are conscious of backing up our hypothesis about what is the difficulty and what is working for the client with scientific evidence, (B) This scientific method allows us to be accountable and be evidence-informed, (C) We can also feed the proof back to the clients, which acts as a tangible intervention prompting change.

Evolution Principle

The evolution tenet of CBT is related to the Proof Principle and is a valuable part of 'Formulation', to which we have dedicated an entire chapter (Chapter 5). CBT is based on an *ever-evolving* conceptualisation of the client's difficulties based on assessments, new information or reflective breakthroughs (i.e., 'insight') that occur in sessions. This constant evolution aids the unique conceptualisation of the difficulty of the client in that moment of time (i.e., Immediacy Principle) and the factors maintaining it. Usually, we start off with (A) Identifying the problem areas and difficulties the client is facing (anxiety from not serving properly), (B) We isolate factors causing this perception and maintaining it (rivals serve better therefore I am incompetent and will lose), (C) We identify developmental events that may have contributed to this way of cognition (parents always gushing about how their sibling is a master server).

CBT practice adheres to the Evolution Principle when we are engaging the client to self-reflect and discover A-B-C. It rarely happens in one session. Think of it as an onion, where we collaboratively work to peel the layers of the problems, checking the 'proof' to support our understanding and then working to alter it. The Evolution Principle in CBT allows both the client and the therapist to take it one step at a time. For example, after identifying the problem area of the anxiety from not serving properly, the first step would be to introduce an anxiety management relaxation intervention to ensure the behaviour does not influence cognition and emotion even further (i.e., Behaviour Principle). After doing so, we move onto the next step.

What does this Evolution Principle look like when we are getting started with CBT? (A) We do not start with the pressure that we need to know *everything*. We start with the obvious and then evolve as we go along, (B) It releases pressure on the clients as well. Incremental changes are easier to make and last longer than dramatic major changes.

Interpersonal Principle

CBT is a form of psychotherapy. It involves working with people from different levels of engagement with a diverse array of individual differences. Although CBT offers a more or less standard way of going about things, we have to keep idiosyncrasies and uniqueness in mind. This highlights the Interpersonal Principle of CBT where the therapist strives to demonstrate all the basic ingredients necessary in a therapy session (see Katz & Hemmings, 2009; for applying counselling skills in sport psychology). These are called 'therapeutic micro-skills' which are fundamental to building helping relationships by strengthening communication, building an alliance, and engaging with individuals meaningfully. The Interpersonal Principle in CBT is crucial to establishing a strong therapeutic alliance which has a direct effect on the efficacy. We recommend that sport psychology practitioners should encourage clients to view CBT work as 'teamwork' where both of you actively participate to decide what to work on, how often to meet and how to maximise benefit between sessions. We have dedicated Chapter 4 to explore and demonstrate this in depth.

Since few practitioners have an exposure to counselling/psychotherapy training, we have outlined some of the fundamental therapeutic micro-skills relevant to the Interpersonal Principle in CBT work. These are outlined in the Table 2.2, which is a handy guide for a quick refresher.

What does this Interpersonal Principle look like when we are getting started with CBT? (A) We employ these micro-skills in CBT sessions to build a therapeutic alliance, (B) We ensure the client understands the helping nature of therapy and actively participates in it.

Table 2.2 Fundamental therapeutic micro-skills

Micro-Skill	*Description*	*Examples in Session*
Empathy	Empathy is the process of continued engagement by the therapist to recognise and relate to the clients' emotions and thoughts. It is crucial to make the client feel they are understood.	Letting the client dominate the session and 'being' there empathetically. There are different types of empathy which we have outlined in 'Types of Empathy' learning sheet.
Authenticity	Therapist authenticity is indicated by the present, real and responsive actions of the therapist which are congruent to the context and knowledge of complex dynamics of the relationship. Authenticity enhances trust and relational depth.	Representing your philosophy of work and techniques (such as CBT) professionally being honest and reliable in your responses to the client, and responding congruently to your ethics and worldviews
Positive Regard	This is the complete and total acceptance of your client for who they are, irrespective of their background, differences, and what they say while placing no conditions on acceptance.	Not attempting to change their differences or diversity, not dismissing behaviours or thoughts you feel are 'bad', not judging the client for what they think, feel or do, not attaching any conditional worth to who they are or what they do
Attending Behaviours	They demonstrate you are interested in the client's experience and value them. They are used to encourage clients to talk and share.	Facial expressions appropriate to context; Attentive body language (eye-contact, leaning forward slightly, encouraging gestures such as nodding)
Reflective Questioning	It is crucial in understanding and bringing out the underlying feelings to add on to the emotional dimension to facilitate self-awareness in clients.	Socratic Questions (we will cover it in Chapter 7) 'What-when-who-where-why-how' questions
Paraphrasing	It is a process by which the therapist states what the client has verbalised in a clear and condensed form without altering the meaning of what the client said. It helps facilitate mutual understanding and engage clients in reflection.	*Recall* what the client said and its meaning. *Restate* it in a condensed and clear form. *Recheck* that you captured the client's meaning with them. *Repair* to change and repeat if you missed their meaning.

Reflective Exercise

- Think about your applied practice. Pick situations which prompted emotional reactions in you (positive or negative). Try to place the cognitive model to make sense of what happened in that situation.
- Go through the table of thought appraisals-emotion-laden behaviour and try to reflect on three such events where you have engaged in that (e.g., when your favourite team won the championships or when you dropped your phone in a bowl of soup).

- Think about the last time you had a slightly rocky time with your mental health. Reflect upon what caused it along the lines of the Immediacy Principle. Do you trace back to the past to explore the difficulty?
- Reflect upon the process and outcomes of (A) working with a client with whom you struggled to have an alliance with v/s (B) a client you automatically seemed to form an alliance with.
- Reflect on your applied practice. When was the last time you had ‘proof’ or ‘evidence’ of your work? How often was it requested? What did this ‘proof’ or ‘evidence’ look like? (It can be more than one form of proof or evidence).

Section II

Getting Started with CBT

3 CBT in the Field

Getting Started

In this chapter, we start with the two major publications by Aaron Beck and his colleagues, *Cognitive Therapy and Emotional Disorders* (1979) and *Cognitive Therapy of Depression* (1979) but integrate the subsequent developments that have led to cognitive behaviour therapy (CBT) that it is today. So, which elements comprise the building blocks that form the foundation of CBT? We begin with the basic principles universal in all CBT. Much like the skills of mobility and vision are shared by all sports, these principles may not be the sole property of CBT but are shared with other psychological approaches; however, the specific perspective provided by the combination of these foundational principles allows any practitioner to get started with CBT in the field. We start with orienting the client and the practitioner to the four-factor model.

The four-factor model

When we are upset or undergoing any overwhelming emotional experience, it is difficult to understand exactly what is making us upset. We default to blaming the situation. Imagine a basketball player named Stefan who is a star performer in high school basketball. He is 18 and lives with his parents. He has applied to various colleges but has received only conditional offers because his academic scores were lacking. Stefan was in his room all day, upset, doom scrolling and throwing things because he regrets that he should have done better in his exams. When he meets with the practitioner, Stefan echoes the sentiment and notes that he is feeling extremely sad, disappointed in himself, and wondering 'what's the point even'. Of course, he notes that if he had got even one acceptance offer, he would feel differently. Stefan's reaction is like a confusing pile of thoughts, beliefs, emotions, and behaviours that have been crammed into an overloaded moving van. Because of the excess weight, the van had broken down. The four-factor model allows the client and practitioner to unpack, sort, and clear out some of the clutter.

The four-factor model is a map and a structure (see Figure 3.1). When clients have a structure, it is easier for them to be aware of, and understand, their own reactions. They are less overwhelmed by the situations and find it easier to isolate specific things which are influencing them. Let us look at how the unpacking process works with Stefan with the four-factor model.

STEFAN: *I have not got a solid offer. I am such a failure, I could not even get admission to college, this was all for nothing. I feel sick to my stomach, I don't want to play basketball... in fact I haven't been to training in a couple of days... coach thinks I'm out of town on a college interview, what a lie...I feel angry, I should have studied and got my grades up, I am disappointed in myself.*

DOI: 10.4324/9781003274513-5

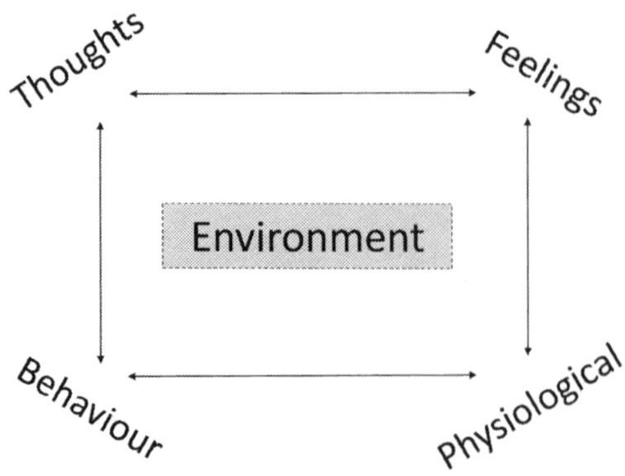

Figure 3.1 The Four-Factor Model

That is the complicated, cluttered, loaded moving van which has led to difficulties. Let us sort out the specific thoughts, emotions/feelings, physical reactions, and behaviours from that monologue.

- **Stefan's Thoughts:** I am a failure, everything is doomed.
- **Stefan's Feelings:** Anger, anxious-feelings, sadness, guilt.
- **Stefan's Physiological/Physical Reactions:** Sick to the stomach.
- **Stefan's Behaviours:** Avoidance of coach and basketball training.

After the practitioner has understood the experience and difficulties of the client, the practitioner frames them in terms of the four-factor model. This model helps understand the thought-feeling-behaviour link maintaining distress in the link. In Stefan's case, the cognitions of failure and doom lead to emotions of anger, sadness, and guilt, which triggers an avoidance behaviour in him. Once the practitioner has an understanding, a key component of CBT is educating the client on the four-factor model, so that the individual can also share that insight and demystify the confusion that often accompanies distress.

Orienting the client to the four-factor model

You can orient the individual you are working with to the four-factor model. For example, if the client is briefed on, and understands the thought-feeling link, it helps facilitate their understanding of confusing thoughts, emotions, and behaviours. For example, with Stefan, it may be helpful for him to know how thoughts of his, *'I am such a failure'*, lead to negative emotions, causing avoidance behaviour which is causing more negative cognitions. When Stefan can understand the link, it helps simplify his understanding of his own reactions.

There is no standard rule of the 'best time' or 'ideal moment' to introduce the four-factor model. The practitioner can take two broad approaches to teach the model to the client:

(A) **A reflective stance**, where the therapist asks questions to allow the client to bring up his own experience and connect it to various elements of the model. An example with Stefan would be, 'What thoughts are going through your mind right now after not receiving any offers yet?'. Stefan may reply, 'I am worried that I will never get an offer, and I am a failure, and this has all been for nothing'. The practitioner can ask the client if those thoughts are leading to specific emotions, 'When you have those worrying thoughts you will not get an offer, what emotions come up?'. Socratic questions (see Chapter 7) are a helpful technique to apply when using the reflective stance to orient the client on the four-factor model. The description of the model is provided in parallel to these reflective questions.

(B) **A didactic stance**, where the therapist is more directive in teaching the model to the client. Often, an example is used. With Stefan, 'Do you think our feelings are linked to the way we think Stefan?'. Stefan may be unsure. The practitioner continues, 'Allow me to explain. Let's say that there are two professional basketball players just finishing up their rookie season. Both players only played for the first team for three or four matches after senior members of the squad got injured. They both had similar performance stats in those three to four matches. They both do not know whether they will get professional contracts. Now it's the same situation for both of them, uncertainty, but one of them keeps thinking they were not good enough, while the other keeps thinking that they got an unexpected opportunity and gave it their best shot. The first player is feeling more stressed than the second one. It is not the situation that makes each individual feel how they do, but how they interpret the situation, which influences how they feel'. The practitioner can then go to the client's experience to help them map their own experience onto the model.

Remember that the reflective and didactic stance is not oppositional. Both can be (and usually are) used simultaneously. In both cases, value and emphasise the client's experience to tailor the model to the situation the client is facing (Blackburn & Davidson, 1995). During this orientation, the practitioner asks questions and answers queries that the client may have. Often a client may understand the model, but not yet reflectively realise how their own experience fits within it. A major error to avoid is to 'prescribe' the model to the client and have an 'assumption' that understanding leads to agreement and insight. Remember, the client might not be aware of how the model applies to every area of their lives.

This orientation of the four-factor model is not a one-time event while working with CBT. It is not a one-off. Rather, we return to it frequently with the individual taking greater ownership and responsibility for making thought-feeling-behaviour links. For many individuals, this represents a minor/major success in CBT work as they have greater awareness and responsibility for their emotional reactions to situations. They also perceive it as controllable, rather than being at the mercy of changing situations.

Reflective Exercise

- Think about your applied practice. Pick a client that you have previously worked with. Try to frame the client's distress/situation in the four-factor model. Was it any different to what you had done with the client?
- Think about your applied practice. Pick a client that you are working with now. Try to frame the client's distress/situation in the four-factor model. If there is any missing information, think about how you may reflect with your client to fill the gaps.
- Think about both these cases and the mapping onto the four-factor model.

Levels of cognition

When we discuss 'cognition' we realise it is not a singular concept. Cognitions comprise thoughts, perceptions, images, and also our beliefs. CBT distinguishes between different types or 'levels' of cognition. It is helpful to view these as categories. We follow on from Key Point 2 (see Chapter 1) and go into greater detail.

Level 1: Automatic thoughts

Automatic thoughts (ATs) are the first category of cognitions used to describe a stream of thoughts that we can notice if we focus our attention on them. They are positive, negative, or neutral. For example, after getting put on the reserves list for a league game, an athlete may think it's just for squad rotation (neutral), think they need the rest (positive) or may have thoughts about the threat of permanent deselection (negative). Negative automatic thoughts (NATs) were first described by Aaron Beck in his work with depressed clients and are fundamental to most forms of psychological distress. NATs contain negative appraisals (i.e., a negative interpretation of any situation). When NATs occur, we only infer negative meanings from what happens within us or around us.

NATs are a common experience for any individual at any point in time. For example, think about a time when you were fed up, annoyed, sad, and angry, and remember the situation. You should be able to pick out some NATs you experienced. For example, you may have had thoughts about others being unfair, or even viewed yourself as a failure. ATs, especially NATs, influence us from moment to moment and are a key part of CBT work in sessions. Some considerations for NATs while working with clients include:

1. They are automatic and happen without effort, but it usually takes focusing to notice them. They are brief, frequent, and habitual if they become a part of our mental environment.
2. Individuals can notice NATs with CBT work. Most individuals are already aware of them or can notice them after monitoring situations where they arise.
3. NATs are specific reactions to specific situations or events. For example, the NATs for executing a poor javelin throw may be completely different to the NATs after one gets a sprain in their shoulder; however, for chronic problems (such as highly critical self-dialogue, low self-esteem, body image issues), they follow patterns.
4. NATs often feel like they are true, particularly when powerful emotions are at play so individuals do not question them, which allows them to persist and have a greater effect. For example, in Stefan's case above, the NATs of 'I am a failure' was prominent after things did not go his way and he was experiencing powerful negative emotions. To Stefan, that NAT was a statement of fact. A crucial step in CBT work is to help individuals pause and question the validity of their NATs.
5. NATs are easily accessible in therapy, and so are tackled early on. Challenging and questioning NATs also allows changes in emotional states and a resultant change in behaviour, which offers evidence to the client that their difficulty can be changed and is not a permanent state.

Level 2: Underlying assumptions

Underlying assumptions (UAs) are the intermediate level of cognition. UAs are the causes underlying the ATs. We hold UAs for ourselves and about everything in the world. Maladaptive UAs lead to and maintain our NATs. Often called 'rules for living', UAs are shortcuts to reasoning and patterns of behaviour which are guiding us on what to do in different situations. UAs sometimes, but not always, take the form of '*If …must, then …should*' statements and can be both adaptive and maladaptive. For example, Fiona, a long-distance runner, competes at 5000 m and 10000 m events. Fiona has a UA: *'I have to succeed at all events I do'*. This UA will indeed adaptively motivate Fiona to try harder and do more; however, it is also maladaptive because it is impossible to consistently deliver on that for various factors. Therefore, it is more of a maladaptive UA than an adaptive one.

So, what makes a UA a maladaptive one? UAs are often considered as being dysfunctional if they are rigid, inflexible, and lead to counterproductive thoughts-feelings-behaviours. With Fiona, the rigidity of *'I have to succeed at all events I do'* is detrimental, because it will probably spawn many NATs when performance is below acceptable standards at any point in time which will probably lead to unrealistic self-expectations and negative self-appraisals. Eventually, it often leads to burnout and mental health concerns. UAs become dysfunctional when the rigidity and overgeneralisation become too inflexible for them to cope with the inevitable complications, confusions, and setbacks of life. In this sense, UAs are like an umbrella which is sturdy against a headwind and therefore helpful, but becomes maladaptive (unhelpful), if they cannot cope with crosswinds.

How does UA play a role in our distress? UAs are a rulebook about how to live life. But, when we have UAs framed as conditional statements, it makes every situation 'if… then', or 'should/must … or'. Any violation of the UA, or even any friction against them, causes distress. For example, Fiona has an average heat in the 10000 m, below her expected times, but still comfortably qualifies for the finals. This violates her rigid UA of 'succeeding at everything I do' which brings thinking patterns of 'if I cannot achieve my personal best times in the 5000m heats, then I will not be good enough'. This leads to numerous NATs of self-criticism, and feeling of failure, which leads to emotional difficulties, all of which puts her in a disadvantageous place before the 5000 m heats.

How do UAs develop? Unlike ATs, UAs are not obvious and may not be easily verbalised. They are the backstage prompts, which lead to the ATs and often must be inferred and reflected upon from the patterns of common ATs. UAs are developed from developmental experiences such as repeated criticism, or performance standards imposed at a young age. Often, UAs are culturally reinforced. For example, if the sporting culture an individual has been in has always approved of success as winning outcomes, it may become a part of the UA of an individual.

Level 3: Core beliefs

Core beliefs are fundamentals of the individual's psyche. They represent a person's fundamental building blocks in how they view themselves, others, the world, and the future. Fennell (1997) also called core beliefs the 'bottom line' because they represent the person and their way of being. They are called 'core' beliefs because they are beliefs and ideas that one holds strongly and deeply. They are likely to be developed during childhood and early in adult life through landmark life experiences. They form the deepest layer of cognitions. For example, Fiona may have a core belief around the lines of *'I am competent only if I win'*, which drives her UAs and NATs.

Core beliefs are not always negative. In sport, powerful positive core beliefs often form the foundation of long-term sporting success. For example, let us take Akash, a cricketer who was raised in a nuclear family where his father was a cricket coach, and his mother was a college professor. Being raised in a household where both parents highlighted the importance of learning eventually moulds Akash's core beliefs. A major core belief is, *'Learning constantly from success and failure is important'*. This then guides his UAs, *'I must learn from losing this final'*, which influences his ATs, 'I feel horrible for not winning, but I can learn from this'. As with all cognitions, interpreting our cognitive core beliefs determines its influence on emotions and on behaviour.

Negative core beliefs often cause emotional difficulties. For example, after missing a learning opportunity where traffic caused him to be late to a training session, Akash appraises his core belief negatively. He thinks, *'I cannot trust people'* (core belief about others), because he thinks the transport deliberately made him miss the training session, causing emotions of frustration, anger, and sadness. Working with core beliefs represents deep CBT work because they are inaccessible to conscious awareness most of the time. During sessions, the practitioner helps the client infer characteristic thoughts and behaviours which represent core beliefs (see Chapter 7). Once we infer this, core beliefs often manifest as general and absolute statements such as 'I am not worthy', 'Others cannot be trusted', 'The world is a highly threatening and competitive place'. Being the foundation of who we are, core beliefs are pretty stable and rarely vary across situations. They are fundamental truths that apply in all situations. For example, Akash's core belief in always wanting to learn will be seen in a school examination, when he learns how to cook and when he is learning how to perfect his cover drive. Individuals favour behaving according to the core beliefs they hold. Let us look at some case examples of how core beliefs influence emotions and behaviours:

- **Case (A):** Maria believes she is unlovable, and that other people cannot be trusted. Therefore, she favours being passive with her coach, to always seek reassurance that they will not abandon her or hang her out to dry and to become insecure when she cannot reach her coach. She has a similar pattern with her partner. In the past, partners have gotten fed up with jealousy and insecurity and finish the relationship, therefore reinforcing her core belief. Since Maria operates according to the core belief that she is unlovable and untrustworthy, she behaves in ways that make it difficult to be with her. Maria is not aware of how her core beliefs are causing insecurity and problems. Instead, each time someone leaves her or moves on (even if they do not leave because of Maria), Maria views it as further evidence that she is unlovable, that people are untrustworthy, and that she is not good enough.
- **Case (B):** Daniel, an under-18 football player, believes he should not draw attention to himself because one of his core beliefs is that 'other people are aggressive' and 'I am not important'. Growing up in a difficult and often neglectful household has reinforced this notion. He is quiet in social situations and is reluctant to be assertive. This is becoming a drawback in his game because he is expected to be vocal and assertive as a centre-back to marshal the defence. His avoidant, non-assertive

behaviour means that he cannot control the back line, and others run amok, which feeds the core belief that *'I am not important'* and *'others are aggressive'.* Daniel often believes that others are likely to respond aggressively to him, and therefore acts diffidently in his defensive line despite the manager expressively telling him not to do so. Recently, when he captained a match, he stuttered in the team huddle, and was not eloquent, which caused the attention of his teammates to wander, again reinforcing the belief that 'I am not important'.

Working with Daniel and Maria, the practitioner would invite them to examine core beliefs. It may seem to them that everything in their lives is conspiring to make the negative core beliefs magically come true. In reality, it is likely that the core belief is leading them to take a prejudiced and tainted view of events. *'I am not important'* or *'others cannot be trusted'* eventually distorts and manipulates how Daniel and Maria are processing information. They are only letting the negative bits of events in and then confirming them. Positive information, or any information that contradicts negative core beliefs, is ignored/rejected/avoided. Core beliefs *reject* information that *contradicts* them and *collect/search* information that *supports* their validity (this can be problematic if it is overly negative or overly positive). To use an analogy, this is like someone with a peanut allergy deliberately picking desserts with peanuts in them and ignoring peanut-free options.

Overpowering and rigid core beliefs can lead individuals to distort positive to negative and negative to positive to make it seem like beliefs are true and valid. For example, an individual with the core belief, 'the world will always support me', may be over-optimistic and lose realistic appraisal ability because it is unlikely that every factor in the world will support them. This will eventually lead to a rude awakening when someone in the world does not support them.

Core belief sectors: The triad

Core beliefs fall into three main camps/sectors.

1 **Beliefs about yourself**, (i.e., 'Self' – core beliefs about the self), you can trace their origins to influential early experiences. These may be positive or negative. For example, if an athlete has consistently performed well in tournaments but ends up losing in finals, they may develop a core belief that 'I am not good enough to win'.
2 **Beliefs about people around**, (i.e., 'Other' – core beliefs about others) develop because of key interactions with other individuals or involving other individuals such as parents, teammates, coaches, rivals, and others. Influential incidents with others may have been things done to the individual or witnessing others behave or act in a certain way. For example, if an individual's coach is extremely curt, emotionally unpredictable, and even funny when they wanted to be, they are likely to develop a core belief that 'others are unpredictable'.
3 **Beliefs about the world**, (for example, 'World' – core beliefs about the experience and characteristics of the environment in which an individual lives) have a profound influence on developing core beliefs about the world. For example, if an athlete has been in an environment focusing on body shape and body size (e.g., gymnastics), then they are likely to develop a core belief that 'the world will value me if my body is thin'.

Downward arrow technique for cognition

We have so far discussed the levels of cognitions from the most easily accessible level (i.e., ATs), to the deeper level (i.e., UAs) and then onto the foundational core beliefs (outlined in Figure 3.2). This is the downward arrow technique we use in CBT practice where we facilitate individuals from the easily accessible level to the deepest level. Think of it like swimming on the surface of a pool (i.e., ATs), submerging a few metres underneath (i.e., UAs), to diving straight down and exploring the floor of the swimming pool (core beliefs). This downward arrow facilitates the client's awareness, as individuals are much more aware of ATs, than of their core beliefs. ATs facilitate understanding of UAs, which guide the individual to uncover their core beliefs; however, the makeup of the person (let us think of the person as a tree), starts from their foundational core beliefs (the roots), then to the UAs (the trunk & branches), and then finally the ATs (leaves and branches) (see Figure 3.2).

What is the 'downward arrow technique'? This technique involves identifying a situation that is distressing or uplifting for the individual. We then progressively guide the individual through their levels of cognition (We discuss this process in greater depth and explained it with a worked case example in Section II).

Reflective Exercise

- Let us reflect upon a situation which was of some importance to you. This may be positive or negative. Can you identify the ATs you experienced in that situation?
- Reflecting upon the same situation, can you guess the UAs that may have guided your reactions and ATs in that situation?
- Reflecting upon the same situation, can you ponder the core beliefs that hold which may have led to you holding those UAs? How did the core beliefs influence your end behaviour?

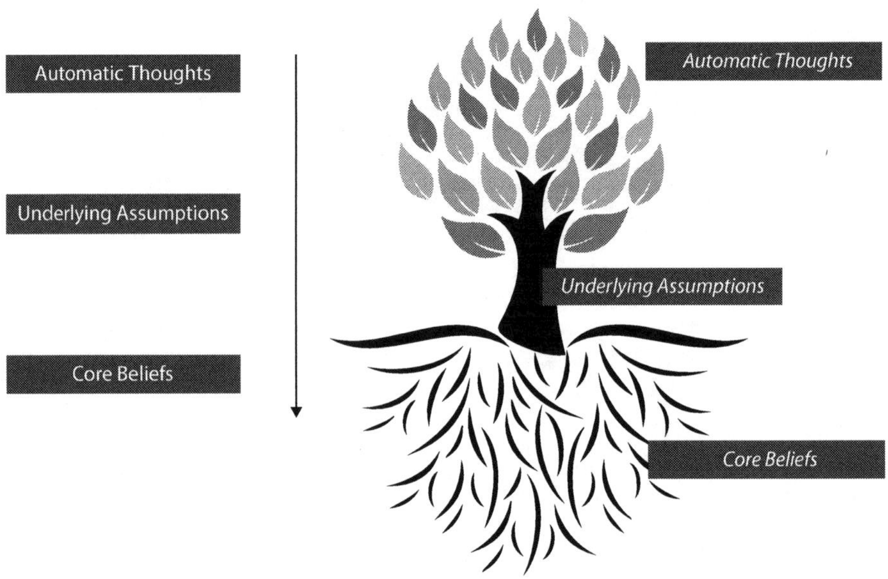

Figure 3.2 Levels of Cognition – Tree Downward Arrow

- Think about your applied practice. Pick a client that you are working with now. Use the downward arrow to frame the client's levels of cognition from ATs (negative or positive) all the way to their core beliefs. Did this provide you with more information about the client's way of viewing the world than you had before?

Getting trapped: Cognitive distortions

Imagine that the individual is going along in their life, and in doing so, they encounter a situation. As we have highlighted above, this will prompt a (1) thought; (2) feeling; (3) physiological reaction (if any); and (4) action. We have also seen how these thoughts initially arrive as ATs which are fuelled through some UAs and are rooted in the core beliefs of individuals. When there is friction between the core belief of the individual and the reality they are in, there is psychological distress. Now, an individual who has no training in psychology could just say 'just snap out of it' or 'think differently' (we have often encountered individuals in the sporting domain who do). But, we must stop to wonder, why are people not snapping out of it?

One reason is that individuals (all individuals) have some forms of cognitive thinking traps; formally known as cognitive distortions (i.e., how our cognitive system distorts/changes our interpretation of reality). Usually, these distortions or traps lead us to engage in inaccurate thoughts that trigger and maintain negative thinking patterns. Sometimes they are irrational, at other times they are just wrong. As we know from CBT (see Chapters 1 and 2), it is our *interpretation* of events which causes a reaction in cognition and behaviour. These thinking traps skew and distort the interpretation of the situation itself. Remember that cognitive distortions occur automatically – we do not intend to think inaccurately; it is a by-product of the ultrafast processing of events and situations by our brain.

How do these thinking traps operate?

Most of the time, these thinking traps remain quiet. They activate when there is an important event or at least an event that our cognitive system says is important and causes us to have some feelings associated with it as well. For example, if you are studying this book during your professional training, you are less likely to feel pressured to take all the information onboard. In comparison, you would feel a lot of pressure if a client was coming in three hours, and you were scanning this book to find an answer to something. It is likely that some negative cognitions and thinking traps would activate in the 'pressured' scenario. We all experience some inaccuracy or inconsistency in our cognitions and the way we think about the world; however, during pressure situations and in ones where extreme thought patterns are operating (extremely positive/extremely negative), we find a *systematic error bias* in the cognition. For example, when a highly rated player joins the club we support, we often think that everything will be perfect (extremely positive, systematic error bias). If correspondingly a highly rated manager leaves the club, we feel that most things will be bad (extreme negative, systematic error bias). In both situations, the reality would be somewhere in the middle.

When individuals are in situations/are responding to events that are ambiguous and uncertain, our minds automatically work to fill that gap – this prompts the activation of thinking traps. In its rush to answer or reveal something, the cognitive system uses

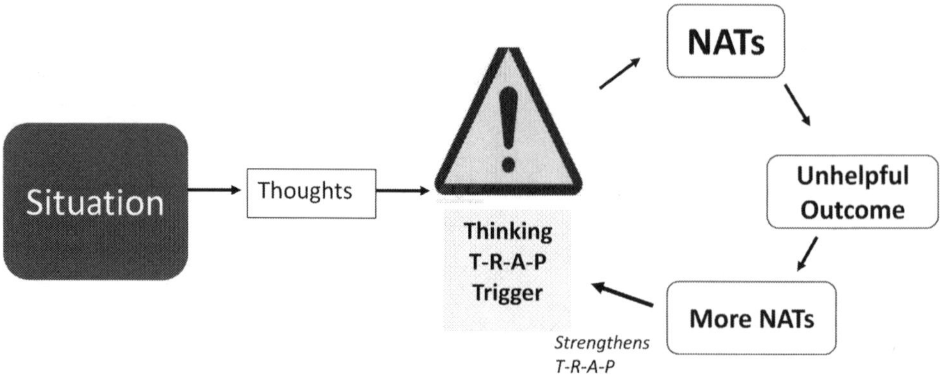

Figure 3.3 Thinking Traps Process

these faulty information processing systems, which are thinking traps. If you look at Figure 3.3, you see that the first appearance of the thinking trap causing faulty thinking to increase in occurrence. This has a knock-on effect on the feelings and eventual behaviour that the individual undertakes, which then reinforces the thinking traps and activates more frequently in those situations. Eventually, the event/the particular influence of the event on the core belief roots in the thinking trap. For example, every time a tennis player loses a point, the thinking trap of 'all-or-nothing' (See Table 3.1) gets activated and creates a negative spiral in thinking. Eventually, this has a knock-on association with every time they lose a point, diminishing their confidence in being a competent tennis player and a competent person. Because of the continued presence of this faulty thinking system, there is often an effect on the core belief too, with newer negative core beliefs about the self – *'I will never be good enough'* that negatively influences one's self-esteem.

Where do these thinking traps come from? These thinking traps start small and eventually, through consistent presence, grow larger and prominently feature in the individual's cognitive system, constantly distorting the way they process the world around them. Or they may be a by-product of deeply rooted negative core beliefs that the individual has developed because of their early experiences. For example, in Annette's case, she grew up in a high-performance, success-achieving household with both parents in successful careers. Although her parents were supportive, they were also critical, with a great emphasis on achievement, both academic and sporting. Her older brother Tim has an exceptional academic record and has found success as a finance professional while being a youth orchestra pianist so she has had a core belief of *'I must be good to be worthy'* and *'Others expect me to be good at things'*. Therefore, when she finds success in tennis, this core belief is satisfied; however, at that level, when mistakes occur, this core belief brings high levels of friction with the protective assumption, *'as long as I achieve I am ok'*. This core belief brings thinking traps when faced with pressure and failure.

To get a case-based understanding, let us look at the case of Mo. Mo is on a lucrative contract and thinks about the expectations he has placed upon him. His core belief always pushes him to do well and work hard to give back to the fans; however,

Table 3.1 Commonly seen thinking traps and how they are seen in the applied world

Thinking Trap	*Description*	*Assumption*	*Example*
All-or-Nothing/Black-or-White/Dichotomous Thinking	This trap causes individuals to look at any event in terms of absolute extremes. There is only black and only white. Only good or only bad. Only all going for it or nothing going for it. An absolute success or an absolute failure with *no middle ground*. In sport, this is common during mistakes and when individuals fall short of expectations, viewing themselves as total failures.	Everything is either good or bad and must be classified as such. High levels of rigidity.	Player loses a match, thinks nothing about that match was good and therefore, nothing will be good moving forward in the context of that situation
Personalisation	Personalisation happens when the individual tends to relate external events to themselves, especially when there is *no basis for that connection*. This is particularly tricky to identify in sport, because performance factors are mostly linked to individuals. For example, a player loses because they played sub-optimal, and hence must be seen carefully. A helpful way to distinguish between a normal performance analysis and personalisation is if the individual attributes *all elements of the event to themselves*. For example, if the individuals completely discounts their opponents performance in their assessment and all other factors beyond themselves.	I am the only person responsible for all that goes on in my life and sport. There are no external operations that are happening.	Player only thinks that they are to blame for their team losing a cup final, and that the opponent team and have no role in that outcome.
Temporal Causality	Temporal causality-based trap occurs when the individual makes a judgement on an event with the only evidence sourced from another instance or another time. This is often seen when the individuals draw upon experiences to interpret current or future events.	It has happened before; it will happen again. It has been this way in the past. It will be this way now and again.	A golfer thinks he will be horrible at St Andrew's Open in 2023, because 2022, which has challenging conditions and gust was a poor outing for him. He also discounts that in 2022, he was recovering from a hip injury, and uses the previous example event as the justification.

(Continued)

Table 3.1 Commonly seen thinking traps and how they are seen in the applied world *(Continued)*

Thinking Trap	*Description*	*Assumption*	*Example*
Should-musts	This form of thinking trap is formed up of ironclad rules about how one should or must be, do, act as and react in events. This is often associated with high standards of self (often unrealistic standards). When the expectations fall short of reality, and perfection is not achieved, this triggers frustration, anxiety, self-directed anger and disappointment. These should and must 'rules' are initially formed to motivate us, but paradoxically become overbearing and too rigid to be adaptable across situations. They are often accompanied by shame and guilt and activate all-or-nothing thinking traps as well.	I should be in a certain manner I must be doing a certain thing I should be succeeding at this I must be thinking a certain way or else.	A tennis player thinks 'I should be making that shot' which causes guilt and self-directed anger when a mistake occurs. This causes them to overcommit and pressure, increasing the likelihood of a mistake. This then causes a discrepancy with the expectation, reinforcing the trap.
Hindsight bias	Hindsight bias trap is the tendency to perceive that an event could have been foreseen and predicted when it could not have been. One common consequence of this trap is a thought pattern of self-blame despite little evidence to support it. This form of trap is seen most often after a major loss or failure which has a major tangible negative effect. The need to explain or find answer to a bad outcome often fuels this trap.	All events (bad) are foreseeable and predictable. Now that I think of it, I could have predicted the outcome.	A player who is recovering from an injury says 'I should not have pushed that hard that match, we were already winning, if I had taken it easy, then this would not happened'. In and of itself this statement is absolutely fine. But when there is a hyper fixation around it, then it becomes an issue leading to a maintenance cycle.
Labelling	Labelling refers to the process wherein an individual attaches a label to themselves or someone else or even a behaviour. This trap attaches a label to a single event or mistake, that is highly self-critical and leads onto all-or-nothing thinking traps as well.	I can describe myself with that label My action justifies that label. That label describes me and often means I cannot change it.	A bowler who makes a mistake yells out, 'you stupid prick' referring to themselves and follows it up with 'can't land one to save your life'. This label reinforces the negative self-talk and thought cycle causing lower self-efficacy making it likely for the mistake to happen again.

(Continued)

Table 3.1 Commonly seen thinking traps and how they are seen in the applied world *(Continued)*

Thinking Trap	*Description*	*Assumption*	*Example*
Overgeneralisation	This thinking trap makes the individual draws a broad and general conclusion about their ability, performance, self-worth, and competence according to a single incident. The trap leads to the individual concluding that a single negative event is actually a part of a series of unending negative events.	If it happened once and is true, it can apply to any case which is even remotely similar.	A cricket batsman has just gotten out for single-digit scores for three games in a row because of a combination of mistakes and bad luck. They conclude that they have 'lost their form' and things are not working out for them.
Filtering	Filtering refers to the process where the trap forces the individual to only focus on negative or positive aspects of a situation, leading to thinking of the whole situation as only negative or only positive.	The only events that matters are completely successes and failures There is only one dimension to this event.	An athletics middle-distance runner only focuses on the 2nd place and their bad start off the line. They filter out that they ran their personal best of the year to only focus on the negative events.
Fortune Telling	Through the fortune-telling thinking trap, the individual arbitrarily declares that the future will turn out a certain way based on a selection of facts. Usually, this involves a prediction that bad things will happen, although it has little evidence to support it	I can predict the future The future can be predicted based on what happened in the past.	The tennis player thinks that because their serve was broken in the first set, they are fortune telling that it will be broken again in the next set. This causes safety behaviours and effort disengagement.
Emotional Reasoning	Emotional reasoning is a common thinking trap where emotions are used as the primary source of evidence for the truth. This makes the individual engage in reasoning based on the emotion they are feeling in the current moment.	Decisions are always okay to make regardless of the emotional state I am in##	The athlete feels fear and therefore 'knows' that they will play bad and lose.
Control Fallacy	Control fallacy thinking trap often operates because there is an illusion that the world will operate on the individual's terms. The individual can control and needs to control elements of reality that are out of their control. This is often common in sports which have umpiring/referee-based decisions made in then.	Things need to work out in my favour. Life should be fair.	The footballer feels that the opposition player should have been given a red card. By focusing too much on that, they engage in a thought cycle that causes them to lose focus on the match leading to another player scoring a winner against the team.

(Continued)

Table 3.1 Commonly seen thinking traps and how they are seen in the applied world *(Continued)*

Thinking Trap	*Description*	*Assumption*	*Example*
Magnification + Minimisation	A magnification or minimisation thinking trap inflates or deflates a situation that the individual encounters out of rational or acceptable proportion. This then leads to a corresponding effect on the actions of the individual and their corresponding behaviour patterns. This trap reduces long-term thinking/big-picture thinking by magnifying small, often inconsequential details. Or it minimises the effect of certain events for some outcome in the future that is not fully supported.	Things/events are better or worse than they appear.	An athlete needs his pre-match 'ritual' to be perfect, and magnifies when a little detail (e.g., forgot to pack wristband) is missing. This takes away focus from the thought processes required to prepare for the match.
Catastrophising	The catastrophising trap involves imagining and believing that the worst possible thing is going to happen and a cognitive predictive that you won't be able to cope when it does. It is a worst-case scenario imagination cycle that usually never happens, or does not come to fruition the way the thinking trap imagines it to be. Catastrophising often presents itself as a chain, with one worst-case scenario feeding into another until it snowballs to a doomsday scenario. This is commonly seen during medium/long-term injuries and when athletes have a highly externalised locus of self.	The worst will always happen to me. The world will not be a good place for me.	An athlete makes a mistake in training right in front of the coach. This initiates the trap causing a thought pattern such as 'Oh my god, coach saw me mess up' >> 'I will not be rated' >> 'I wont be picked in the next game' >> 'I will lost my place in the team and be sold off' >> 'my career is over'.

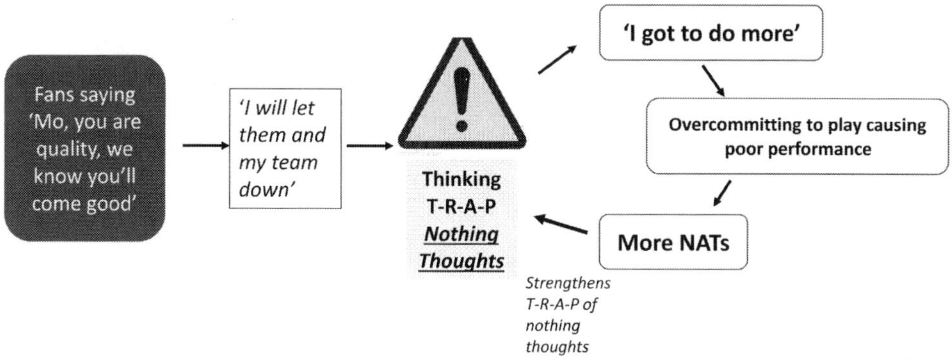

Figure 3.4 Thinking Trap – Case of Mo

adjusting to a new team and playing style means that he has not automatically found the great form that he was expecting. During this time, he sees a Twitter post outlining how he was a 'waste of money' which got 32k retweets and comments. This situation acts as a trigger for negative thoughts, emotions and behaviours. In the middle of this process, when he saw the initial post and stayed on Twitter there was a thinking trap that was operational in Mo- he only takes onboard the negative comments by the fans and skips right over the positive supporting comments, including the man of the match performance he had in his third game (see Figure 3.4)

This cognitive distortion, known as filtering (see Table 3.1), acts as a trap in his cognitive system. This makes Mo's thought pattern continue with filtering only the negative feedback, which makes him have powerful negative feelings and an adverse physiological reaction that he calls 'nerves'. This causes him to try harder, but not in the focused manner that made him so successful, reducing his performance. This makes the filtering trap activate again, causing more negative thoughts that are self-accusatory, leading to a full-blown cycle. The process is accelerated because each thinking trap has an assumption that fuels the inaccurate trap. These may arrive from core beliefs, or find themselves in reaction to the situation itself (see Table 3.1)

Now that we have understood how thinking traps operate, we need to know what they are. In the future chapters of Measurement (Chapter 6) and Intervention (Chapter 7), we will consider how to work with and design interventions for thinking traps. The following table below is a quick access manual to learn and if needed 'refresh' on what thinking traps are and how they may manifest, which helps in the process of formulation (Chapter 5).

The table below highlights all the thinking traps that we usually encounter in applied practice. You can use it as a quick referral during formulation and for continuous professional development. Once you have used this framework within your practice, you become more familiar with understanding them and discriminating between thinking traps as well; however, care needs to be taken because it is during this learning process, we think that every thought our client has is a thinking trap and must be rectified. Remember that some of them are natural by-products of the individual's cognitive system and may not be harmful. We discuss these traps and distortions in greater detail in Chapters 5–8 and their implementation in CBT practice. In the interim, three major points to keep in mind during applied practice are outlined below:

1 **Find the *primary threat*:** We all have thinking traps. So will our clients. The client automatically recognises these traps most of the time, and they keep them under control; however, some thinking traps are worse than others and are the primary threat to the rational cognitive interpretation of events leading to distress.
2 **Presence, pattern, and prevalence:** Thinking traps are only classified as thinking traps if they are present in the cognitive system ('does the individual experience them?'), if they have a pattern ('are they coming up in similar situations/similar cognitive events?') and if they are prevalent ('are they repetitive and prominently present'). This 3-P system is a helpful rule of thumb when distinguishing between what might be an errant cognition, which we all experience, and a thinking trap which is causing a maintenance cycle (see Chapter 5).
3 **Concrete examples:** Clients are usually not aware of thinking traps until psychoeducation outlines them, and the practitioner takes them through a process of reflection. Even then, it 'makes sense' to some clients, but they do not gain insight. Thinking traps stay beneath total conscious awareness. Use Socratic questioning and reflection to source concrete examples. This is useful to the practitioner and the client.

Reflective Exercise

- Think of a challenging situation that you have encountered recently. Can you sit down, pause, reflect and trace it with the four-factor model?
- Do you think you have patterns in your cognitions? For example, have you faced similar situations and had similar responses to them in your life? Could you list a few down and investigate that pattern?
- Reflect on how you process events which bring up some stress and other distressing emotions. What thinking traps might be operational there?

Case vignettes

Mo – A professional football player

Mo, a 26-year-old professional football player, came to the United Kingdom following some time in Europe at one lower division club in France and a first-division team in the Netherlands. Mo grew up in Northern Africa and enjoyed playing football with friends and family. A family friend, Rio, who coached football took Mo for one-to-one training when he shone among his peers at 14 years of age. Mo played football every day for more than six hours with formal training at his local club, one-to-one training sessions with Rio, and playing with his friends on the streets. Football dominated Mo's life and football became a route out of his constrained life in Africa.

Mo's time in France and the Netherlands presented several challenges. He first moved to France as a 17-year-old and spent four years developing physically, technically, and tactically between the youth squads and the first team. Each season Mo improved and at 21, he moved up the football ladder to a club in the Netherlands and grew in confidence and stature within the club. Any psychological, social, and emotional development grew from natural processes rather than any structured support within the clubs.

When Mo met me, he did so online. During our initial meeting, Mo explained he had never worked with a sport psychologist before in a one-to-one space. At his previous club, there was a sport psychologist working with the coaching staff, but no direct contact with the players. He never felt he needed support, but intrigue got the better of him because it seemed normal to work with a practitioner here in the United Kingdom. He did not want his opponents to gain an advantage over him. And his agent felt he needed support to explore all the changes in his life happening rapidly now. His agent, Mark, enjoyed 18 years playing at the top level and the practitioner at his club during the late 1990s helped him to excel in the last ten years of his career. Owing to his time working in other European countries, understanding, and acclimatising to new cultures and societies, he wished to develop good relations with his team and backroom staff.

Mo disclosed he felt uncertain about his ability to play in the best football league in the world. His exceptional performances in the previous season in the Champions League brought him a coveted transfer to the best club in world football. Several clubs were interested in signing him and the transfer fees kept rising. Eventually, he signed a deal worth £ 400000-a-week, excluding bonuses. At his previous club, he felt like 'the chosen one'. The manager and players expected him to save them when things were going awry on the pitch. The fans expected him to rescue them from impossible situations. But at his new club, everyone is a superstar. The media attention, paparazzi, and fans appear to be everywhere all the time. From being so certain of himself and his ability, he now felt a little less sure. The season started well, but Mo described it as 'lukewarm, but not hot' and he understood that the tempo of a season would bring times when he felt unbeatable and times when he felt beatable.

Annette – A junior Wimbledon champion

Annette, a 16-year-old tennis player, won Junior Wimbledon when she was 15 years old. Since this victory, her life changed in several ways. First, her schooling changed to private tutoring. Second, she spent more time away from home and home comforts. Her parents were highly involved in all aspects of her life now, especially in her tennis. Annette is the youngest of two children. Her older brother, Tim, graduated with a double first from Oxford and is currently working in the financial sector in London. Tim excelled in music and education, winning prizes for his achievement every year. Annette's parents both graduated in medicine from Oxford and although they had an interest in sport, it was a passing interest. Her parents especially valued educational success.

Annette did well at school but struggled with the constant comparison with Tim. Annette got used to being emotionally neglected. She tried her best to be perfect and be no trouble to her parents, who held stressful jobs in medicine. She had an overwhelming need to make others happy around her. Her grandmother, Sue, looked after Annette from a young age and they held a strong bond. Sue loved being physically active and enjoyed playing golf and tennis. The moment Annette raised a racket on a tennis court when she was 8 years old, she felt like she belonged. Tennis became her safe space, her thing to excel in, and her time with her grandmother. Her parents paid little attention to her or her achievements in tennis until she played at junior Wimbledon and won. Tim was living his own life in London and Annette's success brought fame, recognition, and adulation across the globe to her parents.

Her parents could not resist the draw from television companies, radio stations, podcasts to tell the story of their amazing family and wonder child – Annette. Annette just loved tennis, but she was so uncertain about becoming a professional tennis player. All she wanted was to play tennis. But now, she was where she wanted to be for so long, at the heart of her parents' worlds.

The presence of agents, sponsorship deals, media outlets, and requests for radio and television appearances bore no interest for Annette. She felt complete on the tennis court. Her mum, more than her dad, acted as if Annette were a basket to fill and empty as the requests flowed. Her mum took a sabbatical from work to travel with her daughter across the world. One week, they were in Dubai and the next in New York. Annette's image – tall, blonde, tanned, slim, athletic, and dimpled smile made her the darling of Wimbledon. The media and people simply could not get enough of her.

Annette felt torn. She wished to please her mum and dad, but it was her grandmother Sue who made it all possible. Her gran was on Breakfast TV at their local tennis club the morning after her success, at Junior Wimbledon. When asked if she would like Annette to turn professional, she said, 'Annette is wise beyond her years. Whatever Annette would like to do is always fine by me'. Her grandmother's unconditional love and support knew no bounds. Annette felt, 'It's my gran who should be with me – she's, my strength'.

It was Annette's brother, Tim, who contacted me to support Annette. Though Tim was seven years older than Annette, he looked out for her always. Tim explained, 'She will need help now more than ever. She's a gentle soul and I'm not sure she will cope if she turns professional. She tells me the truth about things – well, me and her gran, Sue. I know how mum and dad can be. They just can't help themselves. I survived because of Jim, our grandad, Sue's husband. He, like Sue, always had a way of making the impossible sound possible and giving you the sense of inner strength and confidence to deal with things. It was almost like he taught you how to love doing something for its own sake and that's the gift I got from Jim and Annette got from Sue'.

4 The Therapeutic Relationship and the First Session

At the start of a therapeutic relationship and the 'first session' there are two central truths. The practitioner does not know the client, and the client does not know the practitioner. Forming a relationship is the first step in delivering effective cognitive behaviour therapy (CBT) support. The evidence-based CBT process will be of little use if there is no established rapport and collaboration between the client and the practitioner. Reading the literature on applied sport psychology, you might consider that problem-focused goals are the primary mechanism for good outcomes; however, the process starts with focusing on the therapeutic relationship, with warmth, genuineness, and empathy. Good outcomes depend on building rapport and a collaborative partnership for CBT (Moorey & Lavender, 2019).

In this chapter, we aim to deepen your understanding of the therapeutic relationship in your work with clients and show how this therapeutic relationship runs throughout the time of your work with your clients. Keeping with the central themes of this book, we will guide you towards specific, practical, and clinically useful knowledge with skills and techniques embedded as we go. We can attend to the therapeutic relationship without being routed away from problems and goals and vice versa.

Structure of a CBT session

A standard CBT session includes the following things:

1. Agenda setting
2. Setting or reviewing client training tasks
3. Introducing new learning and skills
4. Applying new ideas to client issues
5. Developing training tasks for the following week
6. Feedback from the client about the session (Greenberger & Padesky, 1995).

This structure across the therapy hour represents one step in the CBT journey (see Figure 4.1). Initial sessions identify and conceptualise presenting issues and strengths. Next, CBT plans form the middle therapy sessions addressing automatic thoughts, underlying assumptions, and behaviours, maintaining client difficulties, teaching clients new skills, applying those skills and beliefs to life circumstances with gradual exposure. Finally, the latter sessions consider how the client might use newly gained skills and beliefs to lessen relapse and gain resilience (Kuyken et al., 2009). This chapter focuses on key elements of early sessions.

DOI: 10.4324/9781003274513-6

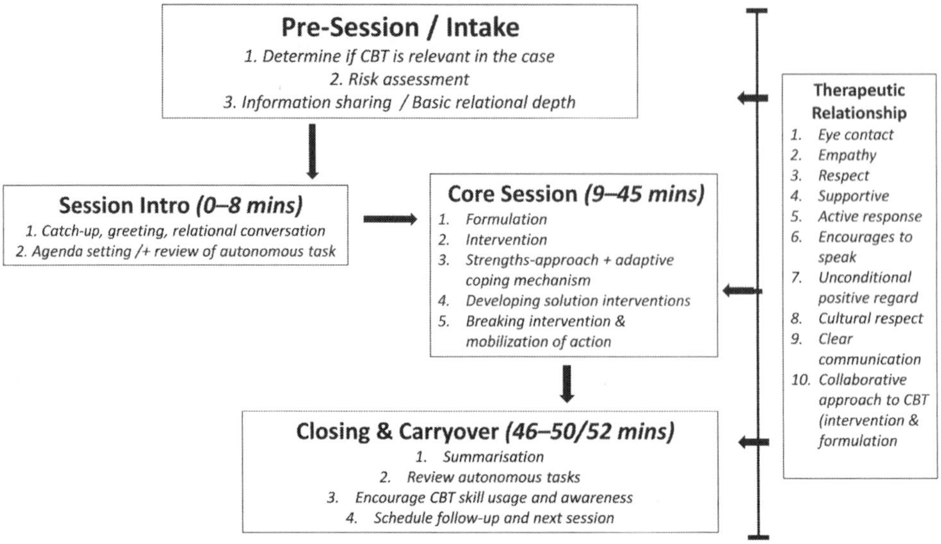

Figure 4.1 Structure of a CBT Session

What does a treatment/therapy session look like?

Athletes do not jump out of bed and into high-intensity sport, and similarly practitioners should take care not to plunge into core CBT to help the client as quickly as possible. The start of any 1-on-1 work with individuals must be focused on (1) ethical debriefing (confidentiality and practitioner competency), (2) building a relationship (see 'Interpersonal Principle', Chapter 2), and (3) getting to know the individual (as an athlete and as a person).

These are crucial steps because CBT work is underpinned by the interpersonal therapeutic relationship between the practitioner and the individual. Without this, long-lasting change becomes difficult, if not impossible. Imagine that you are an athlete, and you went to a sport psychology practitioner because of a performance block, which began after you started having marital troubles. How would you feel if the practitioner had no interest in your non-sport life? Or in your values, principles, and the way you live your life. What if the practitioner just started solving your problems, and you did not feel heard?

We must remember that *'There is an overlap between sport and non-sport. Sport influences personal life and personal life influences sport, in a good and bad way'*. For the sake of simplicity, let us say that you have done all the absolute basics. What next? In this following section, we will demonstrate key points and concepts showing what these might actually 'look like' in practice. We will start by considering how you might approach an early session and identify a target list with a client.

Application Time: Case of Annette

Annette seeks a practitioner's support because she is unsure whether she wants to change to professional status. She has two major concerns: (A) She feels that because her mother has been with her since the Junior Wimbledon, she is still treated as a teen and forced to play and (B) her recent performance slump which maybe because she is worried about so many other things, including a big row with her mother, where her coach took her mother's side. This has caused a communication gap, and distrust with her coach which makes going to coaching feel like a grind. Annette realises this is causing a strain on her 'mental peace' and negatively influencing her game.

Let us look at the following dialogue to do the fundamentals, the 'warm-up' before plunging in:

PRACTITIONER: So, Annette, now that you have been briefed about the how the sport psychology support goes, why don't you tell me a little about yourself?

ANNETTE: Well, I'm a tennis player, as I told you when we talked on the phone. I have been playing tennis for ... well because as long as I can remember really, because I was about 8 years old ... and then, I have always loved the game, really, even when I was a kid I would go for tennis not football or rugby like the other kids.

PRACTITIONER: That's lovely to hear!

ANNETTE: Ha ha yeah! Well, it's been going great. When I was 15, I won Junior Wimbledon, as you may know [looks nervously] I think it was 2019, I've won a few, lost a few too (chuckles), but it's been great. I have been privileged to have a great team around me, but recently it's been a bit of a difficult period ....

PRACTITIONER: Is that why you sought the support?

ANNETTE: Umm. Yeah, ... I mean, am I supposed to tell you that now? I don't know how this goes, never done this before.

PRACTITIONER (SMILED): There is no compulsion, we can take it at your pace and slowly get into it.

ANNETTE: Right, no that's cool, so I have been having some rough times with my mum and coach recently, and like I am in between decisions and it's confusing and it's affecting my game badly. Training has become a pain ....

[this 'warm-up' allows Annette to feel comfortable that the sessions are for her, and at her own pace. This also builds trust and rapport with the practitioner to build the foundation of their working relationship. This is the 'Interpersonal Principle' of CBT at work.]

Annette clearly has a lot to discuss. This is when it is helpful to draw up a 'Target List' to help structure and guide the CBT session. Individuals tend to have multiple issues and difficulties. Making a Target List provides the client with a path or trajectory to follow and simplifies the process to ensure the outcomes of the CBT process are met.

Application Time: Case of Annette

PRACTITIONER: Annette, if we were to make a 'Target List' of why you sought the support, say something like a top five reasons. Would that be okay?

ANNETTE: Yeah, I think so. (*thinks for a while*). Well, number 1 would be my game, it's been struggling lately, I have been struggling, and I feel lost, number 2 would be my relationships with my coach and mum ... and what decision I need to make, because tennis for the first time has become a drag, but I think that is number 3.

PRACTITIONER: And do you think numbers 1, 2, and 3 are related?

ANNETTE: Oh yeah, definitely, but that would be the order of priority.

[this 'Target List' allows Annette to sort out the priority she assigns to the difficulties she requires support with. The practitioner asking if there is a link between them highlights the 'Continuum Principle' which outlines how difficulties arise from extreme combinations of multiple events in our daily lives, rather than in isolation]

PRACTITIONER: What's it like for you when your game does not go well?

ANNETTE: Well ... it sucks (*sigh*). It really does. I feel like (*slumps her shoulders to show an example*), and just so sad and a bit annoyed too.

PRACTITIONER: Annoyed at?

ANNETTE: Myself mostly, but also at my coach, for the way we have been stuck .... I mean, it's like I am mad at myself for not sorting it out with my mum and coach.

PRACTITIONER: How does that reaction usually go?

ANNETTE: Umm ... good question. So, let's say I made a mistake on a point and I sort of know it's a mistake that has been happening for a while now, especially now that I am playing in different conditions ... but I then think my coach almost refuses to work on that, skirting on other things like what my mum thinks needs to be done to make me a tournament player. What else can I do? I get irritated, tense, then the rest of the game goes to bad ....

PRACTITIONER: It seems that it is hard for you to know what else you could do, especially because what you wanted to do is not happening?

ANNETTE: That's right.

PRACTITIONER: What's that like for you?

ANNETTE: It makes me feel like I am not good enough no matter, and that I have no choice. It's like I am fifteen all over again, but I am not.

In the above session dialogue excerpt, the practitioner focuses on expanding the experiences associated with the client's Target List. As seen above, Annette's thoughts, feelings, physical reactions and behaviours are all displayed, but it is really difficult to know how best to continue. There are also some things that the practitioner does not know (i.e., everything related to the coach's behaviour), and therefore cannot make inferences about.

Let us see what happens if we continue on in that session and orient the client to the four-factor model as a structure to understand how Annette's thoughts are influencing his feelings, physical reactions and behaviours.

Application Time: Case of Annette

PRACTITIONER: Let us try to input a little structure or framework to understand your reactions. Let me give you an example of how that works. You see in humans, when we encounter situations or events, we react with certain thoughts. Our thoughts (i.e., thinking) influence how we feel. An example would be if someone goes to work, thinks they are good at their job, and then feels satisfied and content. Would you agree with that?

ANNETTE: Umm ... yeah I think so.

PRACTITIONER: Can you give me an example from your own life on how your thoughts influence your feeling?

ANNETTE: Well yeah, if I make miss an easy shot, my thinking usually goes 'Get your head out of your arse', and then I feel angry with myself and not calm.

PRACTITIONER: Thank you for sharing that. Does this emotion then have a physical reaction? In your body?

ANNETTE: Yeah, I sometimes get sweaty and have to change my racquet, or I sort of get the urge to flex my muscles like the hulk.

PRACTITIONER: Hmm, I understand that, and then does all of that, the thoughts-feelings-physical reactions influence your behaviour and performance as a tennis player?

ANNETTE: Well, not always, but I think that's an issue, isn't it? Sometimes I go off the cliff, sometimes I maintain stability. But in tennis, you have to be consistent and stable, and this doesn't let me be that.

In the section above, the practitioner has facilitated Annette to trace her cognitive-emotion-behaviour reactions to a particular situation that she placed on the 'Target List'. This is also an example of orienting the client to the cognitive model. This was a glimpse into what the principles and theories of CBT may 'look like' in a session. The following sections will go into greater detail on the working alliance, considerations when working with young people, and then will end with a consideration of agenda setting.

Reflective Exercise

- Let us reflect upon situations/major events in your life that you think have influenced you in the past year. These may be positive or negative. Can you try to process them and list them on a 'Target List'?
- Thinking about a client you worked with in the past (if you have not started applied practice, think of a case you discussed in class or read in an academic paper). Try to make a 'Target List' for the case. Reflect on how you can increase collaborative interaction during this process with a client.
- Critically reflect on some challenges you may face if (A) You alone make the Target List for the client; and (B) The client is left without guidance and support while making the target list.

Contract or working alliance as a 'joint project'

Helping an athlete using CBT requires us to acknowledge their needs, manage them sensitively, and work in partnership with them to meet their goals. To establish, build, and maintain such a partnership depends on values such as respect, curiosity, understanding, empathy, and warmth, among others all of which contribute to a strong therapeutic relationship. Empathy, congruence, and unconditional positive regard are the foundational characteristics a therapist should embody to promote growth and change. CBT practitioners should accept these characteristics allowing them to form the basis of the therapeutic relationship.

In CBT, the primary goal is to change cognitions and behaviour using empathy, congruence, and unconditional positive regard to facilitate that change. Clients with better outcomes rate their clinicians more positively on core therapist behaviours (Norcross

& Lambert, 2011). One methodological criticism, however, concerns when researchers collected the data. Researchers typically collect data after the relationship, so it's possible that a client with good outcomes judged the therapist as more warm, empathic, and genuine. These therapist qualities encourage the client to engage in the tasks of therapy and enhance the working alliance. In CBT, we refer to the therapeutic alliance as collaborative empiricism and we explore this in more detail now.

Building a collaborative relationship

When two people work together, it seems sensible and self-evident that they build a partnership to achieve their goals. We call this partnership a working alliance or a therapeutic alliance. The therapeutic alliance comprises three areas: (1) the goals; (2) the tasks of therapy and, critically, (3) the emotional bond between the client and therapist. Thinking about the process of therapy and what it involves, such as identifying goals and tasks, undertaking experiments, and completing homework assignments, nothing can truly begin without the client engaging and attempting these tasks. The practitioner and the client each hold responsibility within this working alliance. To start off, there needs to be an arranged schedule, then once attending sessions regularly, the practitioner and client identify and work towards specific goals. In each session, they collaborate on setting an agenda and working through that agenda within the session. They also collaborate on designing behavioural experiments and autonomous tasks.

The goals set ought to be clear and operational. For example, 'raise my confidence so I can fulfil my role on the team'. With CBT, the primary aim is to resolve problems. Within this problem-solving process, the client learns strategies to manage their condition/presenting issue(s) and learns how to prevent relapse. All the above happens *within* the collaborative relationship. This affective bond allows the client to feel understood, respected, accepted, willing, and able to trust their practitioner and to enter a therapeutic relationship. In the relational contract, the client presents experiences openly and honestly, and engages in the problem-solving approach. The practitioner, in return, creates a safe space, a trusting environment, while attending, observing, and listening compassionately to understand and validate the client's experience.

One of the most robust factors associated with successful therapy is the correlation between the therapeutic alliance and outcome (Horvath & Symonds, 1991; Horvath et al., 2011). Not only does the client's rating of the alliance best predict the outcome but also these alliance-outcome associations relate more to the practitioner's ability, than the client's, to establish an alliance. The working alliance comprises (a) agreement on tasks and goals, and (b) the relational bond. The broad research within CBT suggests that the alliance is complex; however, what we do know is that agreeing on tasks and goals sets up a sound working alliance (Horvath & Symonds, 1991). Some clients might require greater focus on the emotional elements of this relationship to take care of the affective bond, something which can be trained using supervisory processes (see Moorey & Lavender, 2019).

Collaborative empiricism

In CBT, collaboration means *active*, shared work between the client and practitioner. Together, they solve problems by comparing old ways of thinking and acting with new. The clients lay their beliefs on the metaphorical workbench. This raw data (thoughts and behaviours) allows the practitioner and client to see what is going on and then get to work. Although the practitioner offers structure and expertise, the practitioner and client work together on the problem. They collaborate at all stages, for example to develop a case formulation, structure sessions, plan self-monitoring, and design experiments and between session tasks.

The empirical approach we draw on in CBT means the client's beliefs are formulated as hypotheses and so are the practitioner's ideas. Then the client tests those predictions, working with the practitioner to explore different options and courses of action. For example, a client who wishes to exercise and begin a physically active lifestyle but remains sedentary might consider two alternative hypotheses:

1 It is possible to overcome sedentary behaviour by understanding the cognitive and behavioural processes maintaining it, and then changing those thoughts and behaviour.
2 Becoming more active could generate more motivation to be active.

The client might tackle the issue by comparing two plans: (a) continue as usual (e.g., avoiding, delaying) and await motivation to come or (b) gradually becoming more active by doing simple activities to overcome avoidance. Here, a 50:50 ratio of contribution to collaborative empiricism might slide towards a 70:30 ratio, with the practitioner offering more energy and direction when the client feels stuck. Then, with an understanding of the process of CBT, the client can assume more responsibility and accountability for setting the agenda, creating and undertaking homework tasks, and so on.

In the example above, we might assume the therapeutic alliance runs smoothly. However, breakdowns or ruptures happen occasionally and fall into two broad categories: confrontation and withdrawal (see Safran & Muran, 2000; Safran et al.,2011):

- **Confrontation ruptures** represent disagreements over the tasks and goals of therapy and the relationship. For instance, a client and practitioner might disagree about the goals of therapy or the tasks undertaken to meet these goals. The client might attack the practitioner's competence or personality. Confrontation ruptures are where the client expresses dissatisfaction with progress or with the approach being taken.
- **Withdrawal ruptures** are often more indirect or subtle. They might consist of changing topic, intellectualising, or avoiding the first person to escape discussing the feared topic (e.g., loss of form) and failure to conduct behavioural experiments or to engage with homework tasks. Clients here may have difficulty expressing their concerns or may not even fully be aware of them. Likewise, practitioners may know something is not right but have difficulty articulating that. There can also be concern from clients that they will cause offence if they outline their dissatisfaction.

Ruptures, whether confrontation or withdrawal, offer a chance to work with a client to manage the alliance issue and return to an effective collaboration. We need to explore the problem, check we have not caused the problem, and choose a way forward to repair the rupture (Moorey & Lavender, 2019).

Transference and countertransference

Transference refers to transferring feelings from significant attachment figures from our past to someone in the present. The client gains insight and new ways to think, feel, and act by recognising and exploring these patterns because the client repeats them in the therapy relationship. In this way, our past relationships with others enter the therapy room. This commonly happens with similar presentations across clients. For example, the more a relationship with a client resembles one from the past, the more likely we will react as if they are the same. These habitual ways of thinking and acting are difficult to overcome; however, the practitioner can address them by externalising the issue presented, working with the client to solve the issue, and being open. The practitioner, in these ways, encourages the client to relate on an adult-adult level when working with adults and reduce the misunderstandings by the client of the practitioner's motivations, intentions, and thoughts about the client. One example of a source of transference might emerge from the collaborative and problem-focused relationship, which might appear controlling for a client whose caregivers were exceedingly strict. Another example might be 'autonomous training' which reminds a client of rigid training schedule during a burnout episode.

Countertransference happens when the practitioner relates to the client from their own maladaptive beliefs or the client's maladaptive interpersonal schemas, rather than a rational, healthy perspective. A practitioner's cognitive, emotional, and behavioural reactions to a client might be conscious or unconscious. An example of an unconscious countertransference might be anger towards a client for behaving irresponsibly; yet, we might not link this anger to our implicit, procedural rules for behaving such as you should be self-reliant and not expect others to do your job for you (Moorey & Lavender, 2019). We can manage transference and countertransference by noticing negative emotions like disappointment, anger, and frustration for the client and overly positive reactions such as idealisation, praise, or attempts to divert the therapy onto the therapist.

Working with young people

Normally, models and techniques developed for working with adults are changed when applied to children. These changes need to account for the cognitive, social, emotional, developmental, and verbal needs of the child/adolescent. Like working with adults, the individual presentation drives the focus on cognitive and behavioural aspects of the CBT process. Many young people receive support from a practitioner because their psychological difficulties generate a problem for the surrounding system (e.g., sport, school, home). Then the coach, parent, or teacher, for example, seeks support on behalf of the young person. The young person, however, might not see a need for any intervention or might not wish to seek help from a professional. Under these circumstances, a positive therapeutic alliance is even more crucial. This establishes and develops engagement and better outcomes for children and adolescents. See Shirk et al. (2011) for more reading on this. Regardless of the presenting issue(s), a strong therapeutic alliance from a genuine, warm, and empathic practitioner drives the process with the client to begin, engage, and follow through with the CBT intervention. At least three issues appear prominent when working with child and adolescent athletes: motivation, communication, and adapting sessions to suit their needs. It is almost *crucial* to remember that children and adolescents in sport fit within several networks and systems (e.g., family, friends, school, sport). Family system holds prominence due to the child's engagement in therapy often depending on parents or caregivers scheduling, prioritising, and transporting the child when sessions are face-to-face. This influence should also be accounted for within the formulation (see Chapter 5).

Motivation for support with young people

Few child or adolescent athletes attend sessions with a practitioner of their own volition. For this reason, we, as practitioners, need to understand their motives, or lack thereof, for attending our clinic. A young athlete presenting with anxiety or distress might believe we can do little to address their issue. The young athlete might have developed several safety behaviours and be unwilling to quit or, perhaps, feel unable to cope without them.

Occasionally, whether because of limited motivation, a reluctance to respond, or an uncertainty about how to respond to open-ended questions, children and adolescents need some time for themselves in the session. During a pause, we, as practitioners, can reflect on how the young client feels and work with this struggle rather than against it. The client and the practitioner need to work within the boundaries and expectations set out at the beginning of treatment. We might need to return to the foundations of good practice to promote motivation through partnership by creating a warm and accepting atmosphere, attending, observing, and listening actively and collaborate with the young client on the goals and tasks. We need to watch out for traps we fall into, such as (1) assuming responsibility and control, (2) telling the young client what to do, (3) placing behaviour change before empathy, and (4) reinforcing the external demands for change. Some major actions to consider are as follows:

- Sensible adjustments around concrete and abstract concepts as by translating complex, abstract concepts into simple and understandable examples, we show the client how we are working with them.
- Be a *Practical Practitioner* – adjust therapy materials and concepts which might involve a creative approach to motivate and engage the client, such as music, social media, imagery, metaphors, movies, and games.
- The pace, structure, and language within a session ought to match and move with the child's ability. For example, complex language such as 'whereas', 'conscientious', and general psychologist speak should be avoided
- Asking the young client for feedback at the end of the session helps because it allows the practitioner to adjust and move with the client's needs.

Leaning towards the goals of therapy and maintaining structure helps the client and practitioner, because while some activities might appear loose or less therapeutic, they keep each person on track. Many cognitive activities like monitoring, exploration, analysis, and reflection influence the experience and value gained by undertaking therapy. Many child and adolescent athletes combine sport with school, family, and other social and practice activities. These networks form part of our deliberations when working with young clients because systemic issues sometimes support interventions; sometimes they work against them. For example, schoolteachers might emphasise progress over perfection, which matches the work of the practitioner, but a sport coach might eschew such activities in sports training (see Chapter 6 for sources).

Of all these families of systems, parents or caregivers play a critical role in bringing the child to therapy, supporting homework tasks, and believing in psychological support. Because of these critical roles, the practitioner also develops a relationship with the parent or caregiver. Some parents or caregivers feel responsible for the child's difficulties or might minimise the child's difficulties, so careful formulation and engagement through co-working are required. Walking this path means the practitioner educates the parent about the treatment and the transfer of skills learned in therapy into real-life settings. Throughout the helping process, the practitioner helps the child or adolescent athlete to become their own practitioner. The supporting and encouraging role to help the client remain autonomous and active in therapy and prompts the client to continue in this role when therapy finishes. Knowing that therapy contains a beginning, middle, and end means that the young client grasps that when therapy ends, they feel self-sufficient to continue helping themselves.

How many sessions?

One question that most athletes ask before beginning work with a practitioner is how many sessions they *need to have* with the practitioner. This is a sensible question and while we suggest a course of CBT usually takes 6 to 15 one-hour sessions, we temper this guidance because there are no specific rules about the length of each session or the number of sessions. The work between a practitioner and an athlete depends on several factors (e.g., presenting issue, time, finance) but there is one key point, that the practitioner works with the athlete to reach a satisfactory outcome. Sometimes, sessions may last much longer than 60 minutes. For example, the course of treatment might mean working with a golfer on a golf course during a practice round or with a tennis player on a training weekend or even being away with an entire squad for a training camp and world cup. The complexity of the problem is a guide to the time spent in treatment. Sessions are usually weekly to begin with and then become more spaced out as treatment progresses and finishes with a couple of follow-up sessions at the end of a formal treatment plan. We shall explore the range of issues that influence the number of sessions with an athlete in this book. Maybe an athlete can only afford five sessions, so the practitioner will need to align and adjust to this condition wisely by focusing on the manageable and trackable intervention targets. On other occasions, there might be no limits with time or finance, so the work can continue flexibly.

What is the typical course of events?

The first two or three sessions usually involve assessing the presenting issue or problem(s) and working towards a shared formulation. Because CBT is usually a new concept to the athlete, you will educate and explain the active role an athlete plays in treatment and the details of CBT. The athlete is a collaborator in the treatment process, which is often a surprise to the athlete because they might not hold such a schema for treatment in their minds. This active participation on target problems will be in sessions 2 to 12, and the last sessions focus on how the athlete moves forward independently following treatment. Kennerley et al. (2016) explained that the course of treatment typically includes the following features consistently:

1. Setting the agenda
2. Self-monitoring
3. Dealing with setbacks
4. Updating the formulation

In the remainder of this chapter, we go into depth about setting the agenda, because it occurs from the get-go. In other chapters, we will outline self-monitoring (Chapters 6–7), dealing with setbacks (Chapters 8–10) and updating formulation (Chapter 5). Though these are separated here, they often operate in parallel in applied practice.

Setting the agenda

A key feature of CBT is setting a mutually agreed agenda at the beginning of each session. This process is necessary because we often limit the time together each week and the total number of sessions – that is, the practitioner and athlete need to use their time wisely. An agenda is sensible and helpful for at least three reasons: (A) You and the athlete can prioritise issues to be addressed in the session, (B) an agenda helps you and the athlete to focus on the relevant issues, and (C) an athlete recognises their active participation in the therapeutic process and contributes to the focus on their needs. Setting the agenda is presented in the first session or two and followed through each session thereafter. Athletes like to know *what* they are doing and *why* they are doing what they are doing. It makes sense then to explain the value of setting the agenda and how it makes up to the treatment process.

Setting the scene

Our work together is to help you get what you need in the best way possible from this treatment plan. We each play an active role, so we usually find it helpful to check-in at the beginning of each session to judge what we will cover in the session. For example, starting with something like, *'I have some ideas, but this is for you, so I am sure you have things that happened that you want to discuss'*. Lots of athletes find it helpful to think about what they would like to cover in the session before they arrive. We can then take a few minutes at the start of the session to work out our agenda. Then we can check in, *'How does that process sound to you?'*

Athletes become used to setting the agenda, and it sets up what follows in the session. When the athlete has shared their items to include, you can share yours afterwards so that the athlete has time and space to put forward issues that are important to them without feeling your items to include are the most critical. Without these five minutes at the beginning of the session, you might find that the session meanders or a sense of being lost. You normally review these topics in setting the agenda:

- **The events of the previous week:** This review is brief; however, it can be difficult for clients to raise a major agenda item without going into detail. You can guide the client by explaining that we will explore the item after setting the agenda, but you can summarise briefly so that the athlete feels heard, and the item is on the agenda. You can emphasise that at this stage, the overall outline is sufficient.
- **The last session:** A review of the last session helps you and the athlete capture the main points and any issues that arose. Some athletes like to take notes from the session or occasionally the athlete records a session of their own volition or as part of a homework exercise. In the intervening week, the athlete can become more involved in the change process by reflecting on experiences in the session or raising pertinent points while setting the agenda. Sometimes an athlete cannot remember anything of the last session, and that point ought to be tackled as a problem and how to be more engaged in the therapeutic process addressed.
- **Current mood:** Sometimes athletes record mood or another psychological constructs as part of the entire intervention process using a psychometric inventory.

At other times, we might ask: has the athlete's mood changed because of the last session? We can use an informal scale, for example, 'How would you say your mood has been over the past week from 0 to 10, where 0 is as low as it could be, and 10 is as good as it could be?'

- **Autonomous Tasks:** These are tasks that the athlete has been working on in their own time and space. You can refer to it as 'tasks for the week' or 'assignment'. This usually coincides with other major topics on the agenda too. Remember that setting homework or 'tasks for the week' takes time and you might need ten minutes to set it up at the end of the session.
- **Session topics:** The principal topics might include internal or external problems. Some internal problems might be low mood or worry, while external problems might be issues with teammates or the team manager. The items for your agenda (e.g., covering a CBT skill, such as learning to identify negative automatic thoughts [NATs]) often coincide with the problems being raised by the athlete.
- **Feedback:** This is a critical element of the therapeutic process to understand how the athlete experienced the session – what went well and what could be improved. This process might challenge at first because the athlete might be unwilling to share feedback that might upset you, so you need to put the athlete at ease and explain that this feedback helps to improve your work together.

If you are using an hour session format, you see that the following agenda-setting, agreeing on homework at the end and getting feedback usually leaves approximately 40 minutes for the agenda items of the day. This time limit means you might only cover two topics on the agenda, and together you will need to judge which topics to prioritise. From the practitioner's perspective, you might consider urgent problems (e.g., change of contract for an athlete, imminent competition), levels of distress, and potential for change or risk to the athlete or others.

Part of the CBT process is for the client to learn the processes of the work in each session and gradually to review tasks before moving towards highly distressing and complex problems. This gradual movement each week is sensible because the athlete often needs to develop skills to handle highly distressing and complex problems. There is a balance here because we are also focusing on dealing with what is important to the athlete. You might find it best to explain your actions and intentions with the athlete so each person is clear and can agree on the process.

Working on an agenda keeps us on track in a session; however, we need to acknowledge that we do not set the agenda in stone. Sessions can quickly run away from you because one item on the agenda took longer than expected or the athlete pivoted to another issue to express feelings about a difficult situation. We can always communicate to the athlete where we are in the session and ask what the athlete would like to do. This focus on the task at hand helps both parties to judge what is the next best step – to continue to focus on the issue or place it on the agenda for the next session.

5 Assessment and Formulation

Assessment and formulation form two steps of the helping process between a practitioner and a client. Assessment in applied sport psychology introduces the first step in supporting a client through service delivery. It allows us to understand what the make-up of the client is, their needs, wants, and strengths alongside the best ways to support the client (i.e., the process of formulation is at the heart of what we do as practitioners). Though the terms 'assessment', 'measurement' and 'evaluation' are used interchangeably, they represent different parts of the service delivery process and have nuanced meanings. Assessment represents the primary function of generating a formulation. Assessment is an active and flexible process to generate and test hypotheses (Kennerley et al., 2016). By definition, Cone (1995) suggested assessment is 'obtaining a snapshot-like view of a person at a moment in time in order to determine the person's status with respect to a cumulative knowledge or skill' (p. 201) or *what does the client bring to the table?* Measurement; however, is 'the dynamic act of charting changes in dimensional qualities of all or a portion of that repertoire over time' (p. 201) or *what is the exact nature of what the client presents? And how much of it in what form?* Finally, evaluation is the process of analysis, integration, and interpretation of the data collected from assessment or measurement. Or *how can we see the change, or if there is any change present?*

The practitioner *always* begins with assessment. With it, we see a multitude of challenges before us because of the many sources of information we can gather about a client. We discuss specific techniques of measurement in Chapter 6. Through the process of assessment, the practitioner gathers information to get sufficient information to create a formulation. In short, we try to gather a comprehensive understanding of the client and any potential problem they are facing in-depth before moving forwards. In a sport setting, an athlete might reveal some simple maintaining patterns. For example, Mo might say, *'when I have not played up to my usual standard on match day, I feel more anxious about what others are thinking of me and I feel even more miserable about my other performances'*. We add to this information, gain more detail perhaps about the origin and trigger for the issue, and formulate the maintaining cycle(s). During the cognitive behaviour (CBT) process, we continuously gather more information which 'updates' the formulation – sometimes minor changes, sometimes major reformulation of the problem. Now that we understand what formulation is, let us look at how to go about making effective formulations.

DOI: 10.4324/9781003274513-7

Formulation: A step-by-step guide

Dealing with now

The maintenance processes in CBT means we spend most time figuring out the details of current experiences (e.g., what are the cognitions/emotions involved in it). This level of detailed questioning at interview and gathering other sources of information, such as observational data, helps us to describe the problem at hand (see Chapter 6, 'Measurement'). In CBT terms, for example, we are examining the level of patterns of cognitions, behaviours, and emotions to understand what the client is presenting. Presenting problems are partitioned initially into cognitions, emotions (or affect), behaviours, physiological changes or bodily symptoms, and the environment. Let us explore each one.

- Cognitions represent words or images. We might ask the client, 'When you are feeling anxious …' or 'What's going on when you are feeling low' or 'In your last competition, what was going through your mind as you entered the last corner …?' to generate some detail about what they are thinking when they experience the problem. In sport, many images come to mind because the client can remember them, or they watch a recording on television.
- Emotions represent the client's emotional experience. Some clients struggle to recognise and distinguish between cognitions and emotions and among emotions because they are aware of a few feelings only. We usually describe our emotions in one word, 'annoyed' or 'happy'
- Behaviour represents what the client does (and can be seen). Some questions we might ask range from 'What has your problem stopped you from doing?' (e.g., avoidance) or 'What do you do now that you did not do previously?' (e.g., safety-seeking behaviours).
- Physiological changes or bodily symptoms represent symptoms of autonomic arousal (e.g., anxiety to a loss of appetite).
- Environment represents physical, social, and organisational influences on presenting problems. These might be the reactions of coaches, the stresses of a young family, financial commitments or organisational dynamics.

These five dimensions help us work through the most recent experience of problem symptoms. The granular process to capture thoughts, feelings, behaviours, and bodily sensations paints a picture the client and the applied practitioner can follow (see Figure 5.1).

Triggers and modifiers: What and where are they?

Problems or those maintaining difficulties do not arise out of nowhere. They always have associated triggers (i.e., factors that start a thought, emotion, or behaviour). Triggers can be associated with both positive and negative consequences. For example, the player feels elation after successfully accomplishing a task and feels inadequate after failing at it. The trigger in this case is engaging in and the outcome of the task. Aside from triggers, there are also modifiers (i.e., contextual factors that change the severity of the problem when it occurs).

Both triggers or modifiers may be situational, interpersonal, cognitive, affective, behavioural, or physiological. The practitioner should systematically work with the client to cover and recognise how each part plays a different role in the different situations which

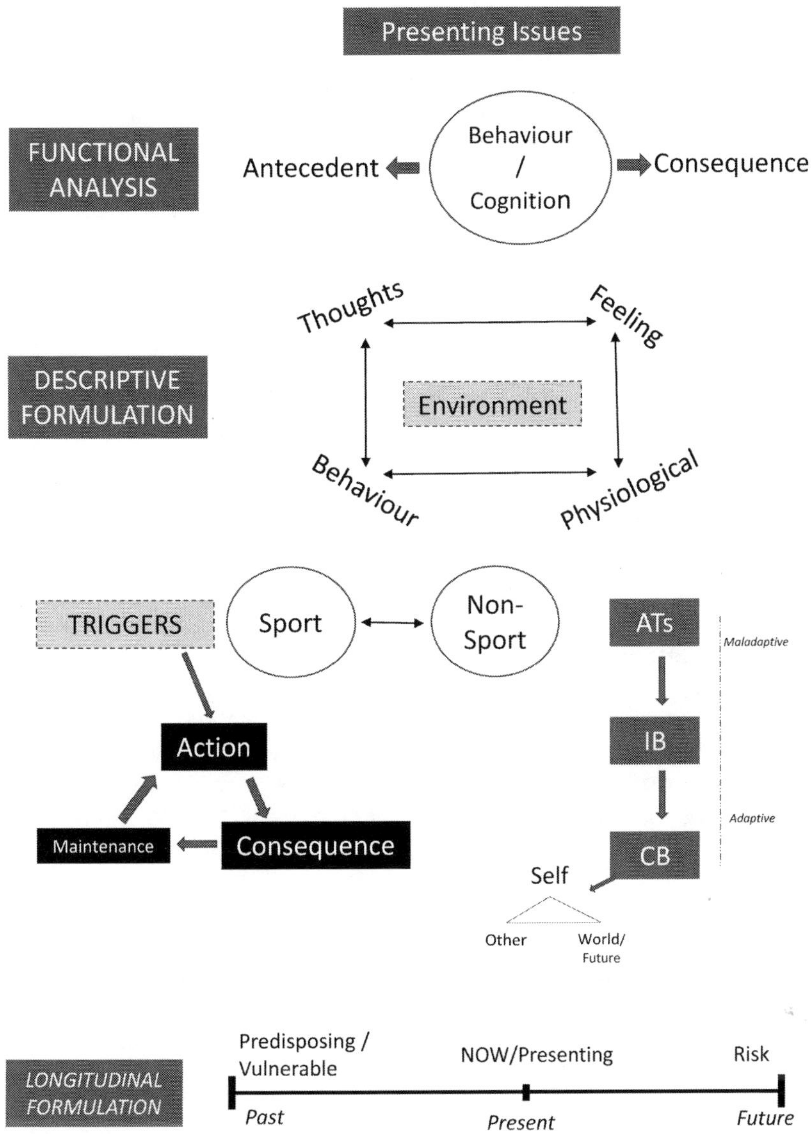

FORMULATION SUMMATION

- Client presents ________ causing ______ consequence through ______ Antecedent
- Their major triggers are __________ / ___________/ ____________
- Causing ___________ action & ____________ Maintenance
- This is fueled by __________Ats that are maldaptive / adaptive (tick appropriate)
- Which comes from __________/ _________/ ____________ Core Belief

Figure 5.1 CBT Formulation Model

create different specific reactions. The client may be required to have self-monitoring and awareness exercises to access the exact details of the experience in a situation and by doing so understand the nature of their triggers (see Chapter 6 for measurement indices and Chapter 7 for potential interventions). The practitioner can also be in the contexts which may prompt a trigger itself, such as at training or competition, to gain a third person perspective of the experience that the athlete has. For example, observing Annette at training, the practitioner witnesses the fear of negative evaluation during a skills test at a training session when her mother is present, but a much more relaxed response when she is alone with her coach. A formulation could be the thought of how her mother perceives Annette is upsetting triggering beliefs about her (lack of) worth or (un)lovability leading to an overall effect on self-esteem. Care needs to be taken to understand the *repeated patterns of similar occurrences to formulate something as being a clear trigger or modifier.* For example, if Annette's upsetting reaction is present every time she performs less than optimally in her mother's presence, compared to a different reaction when her mother is not present, then that gives us the *pattern* to formulate it as a trigger.

Examining patterns and traces

The traces of these problems in the client's life are worth examining because the client will probably have changed because of the problem. Those around them (e.g., team-mates, coaches, family) might well have noticed and responded to the problem as well, causing modifiers to be added to the maintenance cycle. Also consider that the athletes will have tested numerous ways of coping. Some may have been successful, although others might bring more problems with them. Occasionally, athletes cope with medication or other substances that might bring serious consequences. Athletes can also have referred to 'experts' or internet sources or well-meaning advice, which brings adjustments in behaviour that often maintain and sometimes exacerbates the primary trigger or modifier. For example, a coach tells an athlete to 'pump up'. The individual has an unstable self-esteem and has anxious feelings. Before an important game, he 'pumps up' but had thoughts about fear of failing, which combined with the high arousal of 'pumping up' leading to a full-blown anxiety attack.

Often in psychotherapy and CBT in non-sport settings, a helpful suggestion is to aid the client in removing themselves from the situation, causing the trigger or modifier. In sport, however, such threatening situations are often found and are usually unavoidable (e.g., playing in front of a hostile crowd who to put it pleasantly 'despises' the away team, making individuals feel judged). Often these triggers start in such high-pressure situations but then get generalised into other situations. It is normal for an athlete to feel stress playing a big match. But it is an issue if that stress continues and is compounded before every match, leading to pre-competitive anxiety. The practitioner needs to understand the 'origin story' of the trigger and then the examples of multiple situations where it turns into a pattern of repeated occurrence of the trigger (see Figure 5.1).

Maintenance factors: Things that keep the problem going

Maintenance patterns are psychological processes that keep a problem going, often in vicious cycles. In these cycles, the original cognition, behaviour, affect or physiological response prompts effects that work back to the original symptom to continue or exacerbate the cycle (see Chapter 3). Maintenance factors keep the problem going.

For example, if we look at the case of fire, it needs heat, fuel, and oxygen to keep the fire burning. Therefore, the maintenance factors of fire are heat, fuel, and oxygen. Among humans, the maintenance factors can persist across the spectrum of cognitions (thoughts that keep the cycle going), emotions (that trigger and repeat the intensity of the cycle), and behaviours which have a direct effect on the outcome of something which feeds into the maintenance cycle.

Mostly, CBT assessments, formulations, and treatment plans focus on current maintenance processes – what's keeping the problem going? One challenge here might be that what started the problem originally differs from what keeps the problem going now. What matters now to the client and practitioner is understanding the evidence of *current* psychological processes. We do, however, gain from the history or development of a problem because it interests clients and also, they wish to avoid repeating the cause. Sometimes part of a problem stems from the past (e.g., childhood trauma) and needs therapy to focus on it. The past is present – experiences from one's past act in the present. Overall, however, while past events hold implications, the primary focus is on the present. Some common maintenance factors seen in sport are illustrated below:

- **Safety behaviours** are ways in which the client protects herself from a perceived threat. In some sports, for example, athletes grip tightly on their racquets or golf clubs to guide the skilled movement and avoid committing a mistake after they initially feel a little anxiety or fear. Although such actions seem sensible and understandable, the unintended consequences can take effect. On some occasions, the golfer steers the ball down the fairway so the safety behaviour worked; however, the beliefs about the threat have not decreased. On other occasions, such attempts to control the motor pattern to drive the golf ball down the fairway mean the opposite occurs and the ball lands in thick rough or out of bounds. This brings unstable performances.
- **Ironic processes** are instances when asserting conscious attempts to suppress a negative automatic thought (NAT) makes them more likely to surface and guide actions. This manifests itself via self-instructions to not perform a certain action that the athlete wants to avoid under pressure, leading to the higher chances of that very action happening. For example, if Annette's thinking process includes NATs which tell her 'don't miss the first serve', she will focus on avoidance of missing the box, and therefore take focus away from hitting a serve down the line. In higher pressure conditions, this takes away focus from task execution, and increases chances of error. This error increases Annette's self-critical NATs, causing more errors and therefore becoming a maintenance cycle.
- **Ruminative cognitions** refer to the ways of responding to pressure and stress that is predominantly focused on repetitively and passively focusing on the symptoms of stress ('oh no, I feel heavy') and the consequences the stress may have ('I am stressed therefore I will not play well'). This type of cognition is often settled in the past or focused on the future. By taking the focus away from the present, the client gets trapped in a negative maintenance cycle loop that often features thinking traps (see Chapter 7).
- **Relationships and environment** factors that the individual has in their life influence the way they interact with difficulty and success. They may also cause distress. For example, Annette's relationship with her mother is laden with conditions of performance and her mother pressuring her to do better. We often see such

pressures from the coach or parents as a major maintenance factor in anxiety and self-image presentations. Mo's environment is elite, where there are high expectations of him, which magnifies the high standards and expectations that he sets for himself as well. When engaging in formulation, the relationships and environment that the individual has around them need to be placed under a magnifying glass and explored thoroughly. This gives insight into problem cycles and on strengths such as strong support networks that the individual may have.

- **Low self-awareness** refers to the individual having a low sense of how his thoughts and actions operate across multiple different situations. This can often become a maintenance factor because the individual is not aware of how they are contributing to keeping the maintenance cycle going. For example, Mo knows he is under 'pressure' to perform and regularly keeps checking the newspapers and the supporter clubs Instagram to gauge how he is being perceived. Focusing on other's opinions is increasing his stress levels, but he is unaware and keeps doing it. This adds to the stress that he is experiencing and he has to engage in other coping strategies. Low self-awareness can also be present as a 'self-blindness', where the individual athlete thinks that all the things wrong with the situation are outside their control and engages in a highly externalised thinking style or with developing athletes who have simply not been taught to pause and reflect.
- **Emotional volatility**. Sport settings that once presented engagement, enjoyment, and mastery often seem to transform into its opposite and the positive feelings and pleasure of achievement fade. Without this positive feedback from being purposeful, working with teammates, and enjoying the achievement process, the athlete's mood drops. This drop in mood continues the cycle of negative thoughts, reduced activity, and fewer positive rewards, and so one's mood falls again and the cycle continues. Most sports involve competitive elements where we compete directly or indirectly against opponents, often under the gaze of coaches, teammates, fans, and so on. In such settings, it's common to experience an increased heart rate, dry mouth, muscular tension, and butterflies in your tummy. These are examples of the signs of autonomic arousal and are often interpreted as some immediate threat and fall into the unhelpful category. These thoughts generate more anxiety and more symptoms, which sets off the alarm of imminent threat and the maintenance cycle continues. This creates *misinterpretation* where the normal stress is inflated into something bigger leading to *hypervigilance* or excessive scanning, which means we become more aware of bodily symptoms and interpret them as confirming our fears. Often what happens here is that these stimuli gather relevance and we experience them even more. Our worry about being overly anxious means we scan and check for symptoms and those symptoms, when noticed or produced, mean we worry about being overly anxious. This is a major occurrence in presentations such as pre-competitive anxiety, fear of failure, injury recovery, and performance slumps.
- **Externalisation**. Most sport, especially interactive sport (e.g., rugby, football, tennis, cricket) feature the actions of the opponent within the training and competition. Mo needs to know which defensive line they will be up against and Annette needs to know how big of a serve and forehand her opponent will have. These situations mean the athlete needs to anticipate and expect certain behaviours from others. They also have to plan for it, over a behaviour they have little control. This often creates an externalisation cycle where the individual focuses too much on

the external elements they are about to face and worries that they will not perform well in the match (e.g., pass accurately, make the tackle) which leads to anxiety which disrupts these elements of performance (e.g., passing, tackling) which strengthens our unhelpful beliefs about performance and we have constructed an unhelpful pattern for ourselves (Readers are referred to Bennett-Levy et al., 2004).

- **Escapism**. Escape or avoidance is another form of safety-seeking behaviour and its subtleties are worth noting because, while an athlete might be anxious about performing competitively, she might not avoid the situation but struggle to perform to her potential or assert herself in the game. In some team sports, the anxious athlete might keep himself busy tackling players on the ball to avoid receiving the ball in open play. He subtly avoids rather than obviously avoids. In tennis, Annette might be 'pushing' the ball over the net rather than striking it hard. Escapist behaviours often are important and obvious indicators of actions that reduce performance and therefore keep the maintenance cycle going; however, the practitioner needs to take care in formulating 'sport appropriate' escapist or safety behaviours, which requires (a) a knowledge of the sport; (b) checking in with the athlete if the interpretation is correct; and (c) speaking with other observers, such as coaches.
- **Perfectionism** is often seen because of the standards of performance in sport, especially at elite level, demand excellence, or so it would seem. Some maintain rather than reduce the rigid rules that athletes hold and the high standards expected means athletes cannot attain these lofty heights all the time and so the sense of disappointment and worthlessness, prompting athletes to push the attainment bar even higher. The short-termism in sport means winning now and getting the reward matters and the negative longer-term consequences are dismissed. We see the consequences of these short-term and long-term consequences in sport with athletes' eating disorders, aggressive behaviour, escape and avoidance, seeking reassurance and so forth (Kennerley et al., 2016). A problem behaviour like aggression is rewarded in the short-term because of the positive feelings and perhaps recognition from a coach or teammates; however, the longer-term consequences might be uncontrolled aggression within or outside sport, leading to a loss of relationships or legal issues.

Action-consequences effect

So, these are some examples of cognitions, emotions, and/or actions that keep the maintenance cycle turning on. But what is the process behind this cycle working on? The maintenance cycle continues on due to what we call the action-consequences effect. This operates when the individual's actions are less than the optimal standard required for success in their sporting domain because of the prevailing maintenance cycle. This lower standard creates consequences (usually negative) which then strengthens the maintenance cycle that generates the continuation of the lower-standard actions, leading to more negative consequences, and so on. This happens everywhere, but is exposed most easily in the world of sport where the scoring sheet or the stopwatch rarely lies. For example, the cricket fast bowler is worried about the injury rehab leading to ruminative thoughts, causing a maintenance cycle. They slow down their run-up and force impact on crease landing by 5%, that is, action (safety behaviour). This causes them to lose their biomechanical rhythm causing some errors which the batter capitalises on (i.e., consequence) leading them to have more ruminative thoughts and also blame their injury (externalisation) for their poor performance. This continues and reduces confidence in the long run. Psychoeducation for the client on this action-consequences effect is extremely helpful, because it promotes self-awareness and aids intervention. Now that we know how to spot maintenance cycles, we now move onto the skill of formulation, one of the fundamental skills that the psychologist must be good at.

Formulation

A formulation, or a case conceptualisation, is a framework for treatment or intervention. This framework is a portrait to help us understand and explain a client's problems and their entire worldview. An organic, developing formulation helps you to plan for an efficient and effective treatment (see Kuyken et al., 2009). From the moment you meet your clients, you construct the conceptualisation and refine it at each contact thereafter. We need this cognitive formulation for the client's diagnosis(es), the typical cognitions, behavioural strategies, and maintaining factors (see Beck, 2020). This formulation needs to match your client. Some key features in the process of formulation while supporting a client are (see Figure 5.1):

- Collecting data, summarising what you heard, checking out hypotheses with the client and changing the conceptualisation as necessary.
- Some details remain hidden in the first few sessions that transpire later. With new information comes the challenge of confirming, disconfirming, or modifying your hypotheses.
- We are judging whether the new information is new or part of a pattern. This noting helps us to distinguish patterns of data as we go.
- Our conceptualisation, when shared, offers the client an opportunity to judge whether it sounds right.
- Any discrepancies can be addressed together, leading to a more accurate conceptualisation and treatment, and the sharing is therapeutic (see Johnstone, 2013).

Formulation: Making it and a model

A good CBT intervention process depends on a sound process of formulation. The more time we spend on a formulation, the more likely we are to deliver efficient and effective therapy for the client. One issue arising in the short-term and pressing nature of sport is time. Clients often wish for problems to be addressed quickly and jump right into the treatment process. One or two sessions devoted to assessment seem reasonable. Because of the time-sensitive nature of some client engagements, a thorough formulation of the presenting issue can also be conducted for 30 minutes in the first session, with initial interventions. But in such cases, the formulation must run in the session's background and the future sessions.

Some practitioners wish to have a longer initial assessment rather than splitting assessment over two sessions. The time between the two assessment sessions gives space to make sense of the information and devise a temporary formulation. This temporary formulation after the first session offers an opportunity to spot gaps in the first assessment session and an opportunity to fill in the gaps with questions in the second session. Towards the end of the second session, you can develop a formulation with the client; however, there are various factors to consider. For example, some problems present complex knots or developing a therapeutic relationship takes more time. In sport settings, a period of observation in training or competition helps clarify issues raised within the initial assessment. As a general rule of thumb, the longer the 'issue' has persisted, the longer and more detailed the formulation process should be.

Sketching a formulation

Formulation is often sketched and visually represented on a whiteboard or a flip chart. These tools allow the client to participate in the formulation process. Many clients take photographs of their formulations away with them on their mobile phones. There are several templates to follow, and most practitioners wish to create their own to match their style. With CBT being an art and science, we witness this blend most in formulation (or case conceptualisation (see Figure 5.1)). Formulation is a therapy skill – one we develop with practice. We can work with each client to:

1 Describe presenting issues,
2 Understand these issues in cognitive-behavioural terms, and
3 Find helpful ways to ease distress and build resilience. Kuyken et al. (2009) emphasised linking theory and research with the individual's life experience using (a) collaborative empiricism, (b) levels of conceptualisation evolving from descriptive to explanatory, and (c) combining client strengths.

If we are to ease distress and build resilience, we can achieve these goals using our formulation. From a top-down perspective, a good CBT practitioner uses cognitive theories to plan and navigate therapy because these theories offer an evidence base to describe clients' presenting issues and allow one to generate and test hypotheses about triggers, maintenance, predisposing, and protective factors. Likewise, CBT theory grew from sound clinical experience and widespread research. From a bottom-up perspective, a formulation ought to be reliable, valid, affect the process and outcome of therapy and be suitable and worthwhile to clients, practitioners, and supervisors.

There are three levels to sketching/having a model of formulation, each with its own characteristic features that must be appropriately chosen according to the needs of the client, timeline of CBT engagement, and the nature of the 'issue' at hand. These types are differentiated by what their central point of focus is. All three levels may be combined. At times, they will not all be covered fully, with a formulation explaining the client problems sufficiently at one level, instead of all three. We have outlined them separately in Table 5.1.

In summary, we can explore client content at a situation-specific, cross-sectional, or longitudinal level. A descriptive conceptualisation shows the links among thoughts, feelings, and behaviours and an explanatory conceptualisation searches for patterns in these links across situations and presenting issues and the relative weight of each component (e.g., a trigger or maintenance factor).

The goal of the three levels of formulation is to (a) synthesise and summarise the client experience; and (b) link it to relevant and contemporary evidence that allows us to explain it. This allows the practitioner to *meaningfully interpret* and integrate the client experiences. Putting all these together, we showcase a CBT Formulation model for sport that has integrated features of classical CBT, evidence trends from sport psychology, designed and tested through the reflective practice of the authors (Figure 5.1).

Table 5.1 Types of formulation

Level	*Formulation Type*	*Description*	*For Use in*
1	Descriptive Formulation	Formulation begins at the descriptive level (i.e., describing the individual and their issues in cognitive and behaviour terms and placing them explanatorily within the CBT 4-factor model).	• Initiation of formulation • To generate basic client awareness • Confirm that the 'client' issues are being appropriately gauged by the practitioner
2	Cross-sectional Formulation	Formulation at this level builds upon the descriptive level to dive deeper into the triggers and maintenance cycle that the individual is dealing with. This stage often uses theories and evidence from literature to 'frame' the client's difficulties with empirical basis and allows formulation to become evidence based.	• Gain a thorough idea of triggers and maintenance cycle • Debrief the client as to 'why' something is happening • Understand patterns and link to wider evidence base to guide intervention
3	Longitudinal Formulation	This level follows on after the cross-sectional level, and tries to uncover a historical explanation of (a) when the maintenance cycle started; (b) were there any predisposing vulnerabilities that played a role in developing the issue? (c) understand the client's life before that point as well, to understand strengths and vulnerabilities.	• For complex and chronic issues that have been present for 6+ months • In multi-presentations (e.g., pre-competitive anxiety and low self-worth)

The following sections will take you through every single section of the model, and highlight how it looks like in applied practice through the case of Annette. We recommend that once you finish reading, you can apply your formulation skills and this model to formulate the case of Mo for your own learning and development.

How does a formulation begin?

A formulation begins by describing presenting issues in cognitive and behavioural terms (see Figure 5.1). This starts with a functional analysis and then, during the early phase of assessment, a practitioner helps the client to describe the presenting issue(s) in thoughts, feelings, and behaviours. What you will notice here is the client and practitioner labour together using *collaborative empiricism* – the component integrating client experience, research, and CBT theory. Though the practitioner might bring theories and research to describe and explain the client's issues, it serves little purpose without the client's experience, observations, and feedback. Though we write much

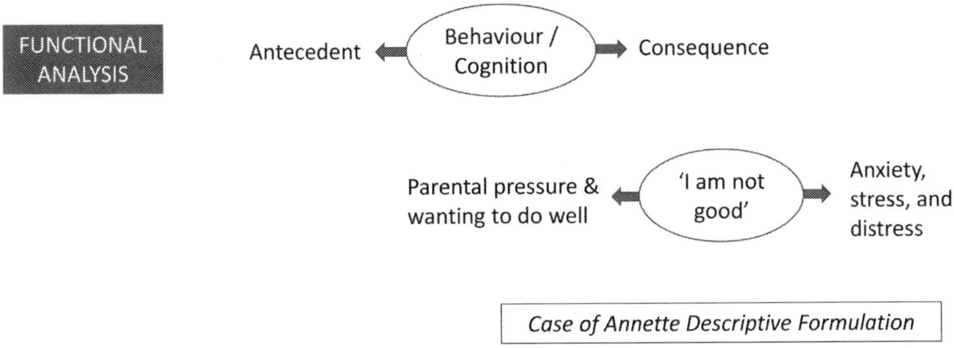

Figure 5.2 Model Level One Formulation

about problems and issues brought by the client, without due attention we forget the client's strengths to forge a change in their recovery. These three levels of conceptualisation, collaborative empiricism, and client strengths coalesce as primary principles in formulation. In practical terms, we can create a descriptive conceptualisation for a client using the five-part model (Padesky & Mooney, 1990a). The five-part model comprises thoughts, feelings, physical reactions, and behaviours within an environment (i.e., situation or setting). These two levels the (1) Functional analysis (see Figure 5.2) and (2) Descriptive formulation are fundamental processes and need to be completed before the formulation process moves any further. Sometimes this might be quick and 'obvious'. Whereas, in more complex cases, this will be less so, and will require more time. The figure below shows the completed functional analysis and descriptive formulation of Annette.

As you can see, Annette's anxiety is both behavioural (e.g., safety behaviour) and cognitive ('what will others think of me?), which comes from the antecedent of high parental pressure and has the consequence of consistent distress on and off the tennis court. This brings certain thought, emotion, physiological and behavioural outputs, that is captured within the 4-factor model and sourced from Annette through Socratic dialogue, open-ended questions, and confirmed through observations (see Chapter 6 for measures). This was then followed up with collaborative empiricism where the practitioner, shared his thoughts that Annette continually served the needs of others before herself:

PRACTITIONER: If you look at those thoughts we recorded … I think you believe so strongly that other's needs ought to be met before your own that you dismiss your needs entirely.

ANNETTE: Yes, that's hit the nail on the head. Aw my god – that's it!

Linking Annette's perceptions, thoughts, emotions and behaviour through interpreting her past and present experiences alongside her strengths and vulnerabilities, values, personal attributes, biology and genetics (see Beck, 2020). Annette's coach too suggested that 'what's strong is what's wrong' and what she meant was that a player's strength was such a positive that no one could see what might be the weakness within it. Mostly, however, helping clients to log their positive attributes and skills lightens a heavy load and these strengths and resources become a counterweight through challenging times towards better functioning, elevated mood and resilience (see Kuyken et al., 2009).

Going deeper: Cross-sectional formulation

Next, using CBT theory, the client, together with the practitioner, explains how or what triggers and maintains the presenting issue(s). Then, the client and practitioner consider those factors predisposing the client to, and protecting the client from, presenting concerns. Remember, it is not the situation that governs what people feel and do, but how those people *read* a situation (see Chapters 1 and 2). CBT is grounded in the cognitive model. The cognitive model hypothesises that people's emotions, behaviours and physiology are influenced by their perception of events, whether internal (e.g., distressing physical symptoms) or external (e.g., losing a competition). Runners on the start line of a 1500-metre Olympic final lean forward awaiting the starter's pistol to fire but harbour different emotional and behavioural responses to the same situation owing to the train of thoughts chugging through their minds. We might assume how the athletes think, feel and behave; however, it seems sensible and most respectful to allow them to tell us.

Play the detective: Finding triggers and the maintenance cycle

Practitioners focus on the cross section of a client's life to gather information about presenting issues. In short, what situations trigger and maintain the client's current presenting issues? In this phase, we use CBT models to explain what triggers and maintains clients' presenting issues. For example, we could use a disorder-specific CBT model, a functional analysis (Hayes & Follette, 1992) or situation-thought-emotion-behaviour sequences (Padesky & Greenberger, 1995).

At this stage of cross-sectional formulation, once the practitioner and the client know the four-factors and how their interplay is operational, it is time to play the role of a detective. The client is not the suspect in this scenario. Rather, both of you are detectives, looking at the clues in the formulation and client experience so far – you both are asking and reflecting on what the triggers could be. The triggers for automatic thoughts can be internal or external emerging from a memory, image, behaviour, physiology, discrete event, or stream of thoughts.

As illustrated in the model, the triggers can be found within sport and outside of it as well. We often make the mistake of compartmentalising sport and non-sport areas of the athlete's life as if they were a neat wardrobe arrangement – the reality is far more complex. An athlete might have a lower performance because of sleep issues, which is what they come in to see the practitioner for; however, the practitioner uncovers through formulation that the sleep disturbance is being caused by the twin factors of being a father to a young infant, and having marital problems at the same time. In such cases, merely a relaxation intervention will do little. Rather, the primary issue of marital problems and his response to them needs to be uncovered. Like good detectives, trust is key to this process, because the client must also feel safe enough to divulge these intimate details. Like good detectives, we must have an *open mind* and consider all options.

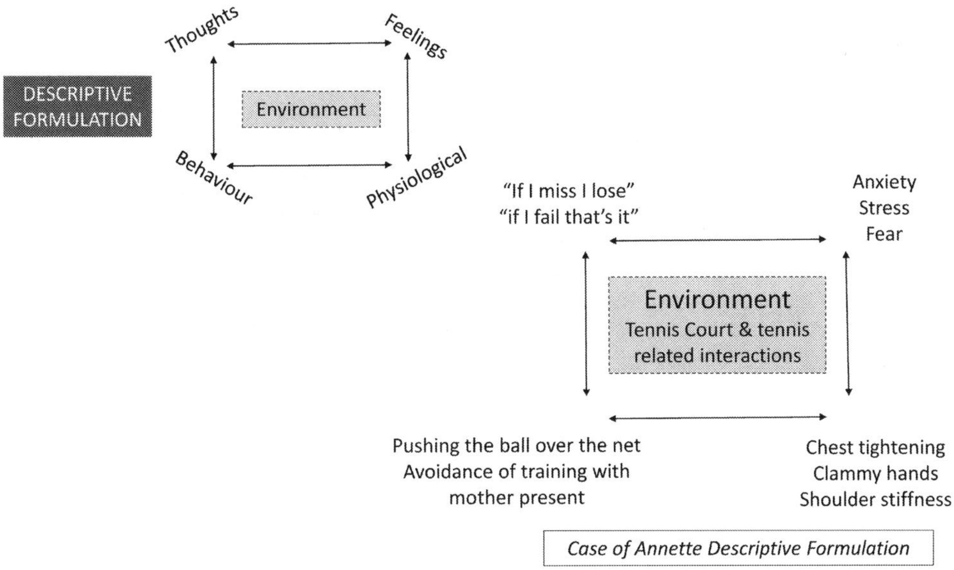

Figure 5.3 Model Level Two Formulation

In a thought-record sheet, for example, Annette sees how thoughts influence emotions and behaviours. A perceived criticism from a mother triggers a thought of *'I'm not good enough'* and a feeling of embarrassment and shame, which Annette manages by avoiding the risky shot, causing the perceived criticism (safety behaviour). Through the process of CBT, clues to the maintenance cycle unfold. A maintenance cycle shows how emotional, physical, and behavioural reactions to situational triggers maintain client difficulties. The client can see why their problems are not getting better. Witnessing these maintenance cycles also means spotting the point or points at which the client might choose to intervene and alter their circumstances. Looking at such a cycle on paper, for instance, the client can see how other cognitive or behavioural strategies might address the problem.

In Annette's case, we see that there are three main triggers which are causing the maintenance cycle. Pressure of winning and expectations (sport), pressure of delivering as a professional for contractual and sponsorship issues (sport-personal) and her inherent high performing pressure from her mother causing her self-worth to be determined by outcome (personal). Visually presenting this and checking it with the client is important at this stage (see Figure 5.3). It is also crucial to take it at the client's pace. Remember that while these are just triggers to the practitioner, they are difficult situations and instances for the clients, some of which they may not be prepared to work with immediately (especially if in initial sessions).

The body of cognition

One theme arising in our work with athletes is where do cognitions live within our mind? There is often an adventurous search for the mill or foundry, producing these automatic thoughts to install new gear for better function. Athletes are curious to gauge why two athletes can interpret the same situation so contrastingly and even more perplexing is how can one athlete construe an identical situation so distinctively one time from another? The answer lies with enduring cognitive phenomena: beliefs.

One set of thoughts about a situation is quick and evaluative. We call these cognitions – automatic thoughts. These automatic thoughts bound suddenly rather than following a deliberate or reasoned thought process, but the emotion or behaviour that follows grabs more of your attention. Most of our thoughts walk on by in the passageways of our mind without us questioning them; we accept them without analysis and believe them to be true; however, we can identify automatic thoughts by noticing the changes in our affect, behaviour, and/or physiology. An athlete might ask himself, *'What was going through my mind when …'.*

> *I felt agitated/I feel like quitting and walking in off the court/I feel short of breath and racing thoughts on the first game*

Once we help clients identify their automatic thoughts, we can help them to estimate the legitimacy of their thinking. Take the automatic thought, *'I'll never be ready for this match'.* If we were to check this thought with reality and experience, the client might find, *'It's fine. I've felt like this before, and I've turned up in fine fettle for the start'.* This thought exchange, though simple, holds ample store for what follows because correcting how we were interpreting a situation often sparks an adaptive mood and functional behavioural responses and/or physiological arousal. In the cognitive wheelhouse, challenging dysfunctional thoughts with sober reflection generates a functional change in emotions, behaviour, and physiological reaction. In this way, the process of formulation also allows an immediate transition to small interventions and cognitive challengers that act as a prelude to more widespread interventions.

Once we have identified the automatic thoughts (see Figure 5.3), we can start tracing their roots. Intermediate beliefs lie between core beliefs at the bottom and automatic thoughts on top. Core beliefs influence the development of this intermediate class of beliefs, which comprises attitudes, rules, and assumptions.

- **Attitude**: 'It's not good when shots are off line '
- **Rule**: 'I must hit the ball straight down my service line'
- **Assumption**: 'If I hit my shots off line, I'll lose the match'

These beliefs alter her view of a situation which colours how Annette thinks, feels, and behaves. But from where do such core beliefs and intermediate beliefs stem? Learning to make sense of the world is a process unfolding from early childhood to organise experiences and function harmoniously. The vagaries of our genetic predisposition, interactions with others and the world mean we develop specific understandings: our beliefs, which vary in accuracy and functionality. Some of these beliefs will be functional and others will be dysfunctional, which we note on the model on one side after understanding the automatic thoughts, intermediate beliefs and core beliefs. In Annette's case, the automatic thoughts act as major triggers which led to her intermediate beliefs (maladaptive ones) operating in a certain manner (see Figure 5.3).

Core beliefs hold the ideas about ourselves, others, and the world we inhabit beginning in childhood. Our base or core beliefs are so deep and elemental we scarcely articulate them, if ever. Their ideas are absolute truths about how things are (see Chapters 1–3).

The stream of realistic positive beliefs flows underneath our conscious operation in this world. Negative beliefs; however, activate partially or fully under vulnerabilities or stressors. Like a stream filling with rainfall from a torrential downpour, the water level rises and currents race, tearing at its banks with menace. Core beliefs can be traced through the intermediate beliefs if

(a) They have been present for a significant amount of time in the individual's life
(b) They implicitly or explicitly guide their behaviours and cognitions
(c) They are stable over multiple situations

These core beliefs may be adaptive or maladaptive. The individual experiences massive friction when their core beliefs (adaptive or maladaptive) are not aligned with the reality they are experiencing. These core beliefs are based on the 'self' (e.g., *'I am worthy'*) or other (*'people will help me'*) or the world/future *('the future will be good if I stick to my processes'*). Let us look at adaptive and maladaptive core beliefs in detail, while focusing on Annette's case.

Adaptive core beliefs

Our adaptive beliefs are flexible, helpful, and reality-based about ourselves, our future, others, and the world. The person we recognise in the mirror is effective, likeable and worthwhile. Our views about other people are precise and nuanced. We decide between those who are benign and those potentially harmful. The world is a mix of predictable and unpredictable. We see the future with challenges but with an ability to cope alone or with the guidance of others. Our core beliefs may comprise: love, effectiveness, and worth (Beck, 2020). An athlete might hold effective core beliefs like 'I'm competent, useful'; lovable core beliefs like *'I'm good enough to be loved by others'* and worthy core beliefs like 'I am worthwhile and acceptable'.

It becomes an issue, however, when these powerfully held positive beliefs such as *'I will be a champion'* or *'working hard will guarantee sporting success'* encounter a major setback about our effectiveness, an interpersonal problem, or action related to their belief compass. This causes massive friction between the guiding core belief and the reality. For example, if one holds the adaptive core belief that *'working hard will guarantee sporting success'* and does not find medium term sporting success because of many factors, it is likely to cause distress through friction. Most people bounce back to their reality-based core beliefs after a period; yet, there are athletes and coaches with no, or underdeveloped, positive, and adaptive beliefs growing up who need help to develop and strengthen adaptive beliefs. This is pervasive in sport because of its nature, we often find overly positive beliefs, those who see themselves, others, the world, and/or the future in an unrealistically positive light. Media and representations of sport also add to this attitude through 'rags to riches story' and through the exposure via social media which might be unhelpful as well.

We can see this in Annette's rise to stardom as well, which has led to certain beliefs that are adaptive, such as *'I can actually compete at this level'*; however, pressure from her mother and occasional poor performances (which are normal for all athletes) triggers a reaction. In the case of Annette, we can see that she has a strong adaptive core belief about tennis, that is centred of her 'self' in relation to where she finds her relationship with tennis to be.

Table 5.2 Common dysfunctional core beliefs in sport performers

Helpless Core Beliefs	*Unlovable Core Beliefs*	*Worthless Core Beliefs*
Incompetent	Unlikeable	Immoral
Useless	Undesirable	Worthless
Powerless	Defective	Unacceptable
Weak	Unimportant	Dangerous
Needy	Unattractive	Toxic
Ineffective	Boring	Evil

Maladaptive core beliefs

Some people hold strong, negative core beliefs. When these beliefs developed, they may not have been realistic and/or helpful, but under strain and turmoil, such beliefs are extreme, unrealistic and highly maladaptive. These negative core beliefs fall into three categories: helpless, unlovable, and worthless (See Table 5.2). When one holds helpless core beliefs, they believe they are ineffective in getting things done, cannot protect themselves, and do not measure up to others. With unlovable core beliefs, one's personal qualities prevent one from getting or maintaining love and intimacy from others. Finally, worthless core beliefs mean one believes on is to be an immoral sinner or dangerous to others (Beck, 2020). Here are some core belief examples from sport performers.

The lives of athletes mean that for some, they hold a negative core belief in one category, or perhaps negative core beliefs in all categories. Some experiences can be painful losses but an athlete might see positives in the future like the Brazil and Paris Saint-Germain football player, Neymar, who reflected after losing the Champions League Final to Bayern Munich: *'It's really tough to lose a Champions League Final ... I suffered, I cried, I wanted this title for France, but unfortunately, we didn't do it. We'll do all we can this season to get back there and win this first title'.* (Burt, 2021). It is often-disheartening that we handle maladaptive dysfunctional core beliefs more often than adaptive ones. It is typical for adaptive beliefs to be outnumbered by dysfunctional ones in the body of cognition. Let us critically analyse how this operates in Annette's case.

Application Time: Case of Annette

Annette developed her game for 24 months after turning professional and sensed she couldn't automatically prosper in the professional game. She clenched to the core belief 'I'm incompetent' which was reinforced by her reaction to parental pressure and it operated at pace during practice and tournaments. When this core belief is active, Annette interprets situations through the lens of this belief, even though rationally, it may be invalid. Annette focuses selectively on the information that confirms her core belief, deftly discounting and dismissing contrary information. She did not recognise that her trouble in the game could be because of a lack of concentration or focusing on external opinions during games rather than a lack of competence. She overlooked how she secured professional status because of her mastery of the skills of the game. Her incompetence belief, when activated, meant she inferred the situations in a highly negative, self-critical manner. Despite her skills practice at the tennis court and games, she maintained her belief notwithstanding its inaccuracy and dysfunction. Annette is not trying to be any less, it happens automatically. This took her away from the present to the future where Annette foresaw a future lost and everything she loved being wrenched away. Somehow the fun and excitement she once knew faded unceremoniously from the game.

When Annette played well, the positive data did not fit into her schema 'Yes, I played well, but the opponent and conditions were easy'. This positive data from playing well could not fit the schema, but with this interpretation the data fit into the schema and strengthen the negative core belief. Other positive data goes unnoticed. For instance, Annette acknowledged some good net approach shots and baseline play; however, if these actions fell below a self-set standard, she would interpret her comparative failure as supporting her dysfunctional core belief. These elements of performance disappear and slip through the net of the schema, and over time Annette's core belief of incompetence strengthened like a vice.

From the practitioner's viewpoint, athletes can unlearn dysfunctional beliefs and develop more reality-based and functional beliefs and strengthen these through treatment. Helping an athlete to feel better and behave more adaptively works by helping them to identify and strengthen their positive adaptive beliefs and modify their inaccurate beliefs. From this space, athletes constructively interpret current and future situations or problems. According to Beck (2020), we can work directly and indirectly on positive beliefs from the outset of treatment; however, we usually work indirectly on negative core beliefs before addressing them directly. We tread carefully identifying negative core beliefs because they can trigger strong negative affect and lead to clients feeling unsafe. We focus on specific interventions for reappraisal in Chapter 7.

Understanding time and life: Longitudinal formulation

Presenting issues often have a developmental history. These predisposing factors describe any component, making one person more likely to respond specifically to a life circumstance or event. Although a range of factors might predispose people to problems, their strengths and positive experiences (e.g., good enough parenting) also act as protective factors. We identify and include these predisposing and protective factors into the conceptualisation process.

When conducting a longitudinal formulation, it is helpful to understand time and lifespan better. The client at this point in the present time has arrived from somewhere. When conducting longitudinal formulations, the practitioner needs to understand the characteristic features of this temporal location of the past. This may be a different environment (club, sport, culture, family, etc) or developmental stage and certainly will be from specific life experiences that count as milestones. It is up to the practitioner to exercise judgement on how far back the longitudinal formulation needs to go. It is typically advisable to explore in time by jumping back in seasonal/Olympic cycles (depending on sport and age range). For example, a line of questioning could be,

Application Time: Case of Annette

PRACTITIONER: Tell me about your U14 days. Did this happen back then as well?
ANNETTE: Umm … yeah, to be honest … well, not always.
PRACTITIONER: What do you mean by that?
ANNETTE: Umm … like I remember I stayed with my gran for a month in September every year and played a couple of tournaments, at that time, I did not feel any pressure or you know … anxiety … but other than that yeah.
PRACTITIONER: What about before that?
ANNETTE: Yeah … it's sort of always been there in the back of my mind, you know?
PRACTITIONER: Of course.
ANNETTE: It got worse … as I started to do well, and then really bad when mum quit to be full time with me … and like … woah why do that? Tennis is difficult … and it suddenly …. (*chokes*)
PRACTITIONER: It's okay … did it suddenly become too real? (*softly*)
ANNETTE: Yeah … waaay (*stretching and emoting*) too fast.

The past ≫ present ≫ future (see Figure 5.4). If unchecked, a predisposing factor becomes a maintenance factor in the present and a continuous risk factor in the future, causing continued distress throughout a lifespan (i.e., what is known in common parlance as an 'unresolved issue'). Remember that longitudinal formulations peek into the past to understand the present. But also, to forecast the future. This allows intervention planning to be more comprehensive. In Annette's case, the past has a critical moment where the effect of her mother's decision to join her on the tour full time hyper-professionalised tennis for her. This is manifesting in pressure and a self-critical thought pattern in the present. This may lead to a compounded mental health problem and attachment issues later, if interventions are not undertaken.

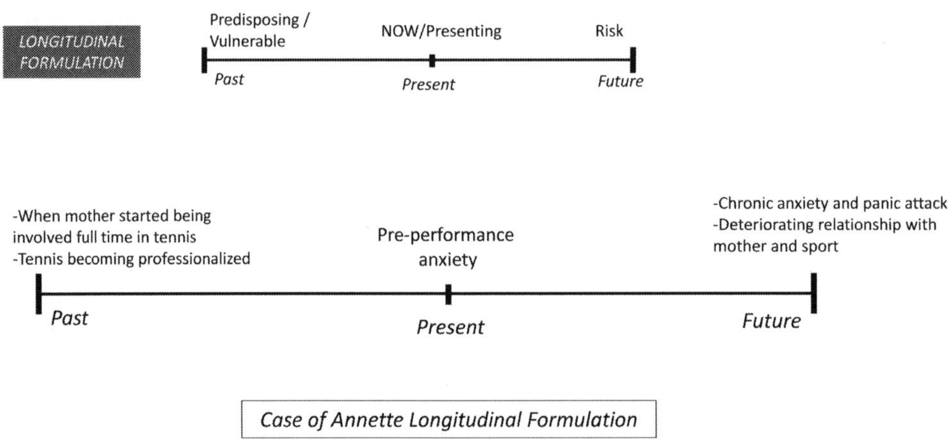

Figure 5.4 Longitudinal Formulation

Working together

Developing a sound formulation depends on the client and practitioner working together. This *co-creation* might begin with a practitioner leading the process in the early phases of therapy and the client gradually takes the initiative. Together, the client and practitioner edit the formulation to account for the client's experience in therapy and outside therapy. Formulating and testing hypotheses, and gathering data bring a predictive strength, too. Though the roles differ between the client (e.g., bringing historical information, current observations) and the practitioner (e.g., empirical research, psychological models, experience), the union of all the information helps the process.

Working together on a formulation ought to stack support in favour of the client. Building on one's resources means using one's strengths to manage one's areas of difficulty. Because a central feature of formulation is building resilience within the client, together we help the client intercede adversity. Resilience means drawing on one's strengths to adapt psychologically to challenges to maintain well-being. Working with a practitioner resembles learning at the training ground for the athlete where the athlete learns how to tackle problems better. This emphasis cultivates growth and development rather than immediate mastery. Mastery follows therapy through practising these cognitive and behavioural coping skills (Beck, 1979). This last part stands to reason for athletes familiar with growth and development in their sport because they usually acknowledge helping themselves in their own time. In our experience, many athletes, given the opportunity, hold far more capacities than incapacities. To illustrate, when we ask clients how they coped with adversities previously, they present several examples of adaptive coping skills. These personal and social resources might be overlooked while scoping the problem (See Figure 5.5).

Doing formulation: Process actions

Below we have outlined a few process actions that characterise a good formulation process. They also double up as skills required to be a practitioner who can formulate well.

1 **Understand the data**: Though assessment means gathering data, and we cannot move far without it, how we assess influences how we engage the client, how the client feels about the process and their openness to engage in active collaboration throughout.

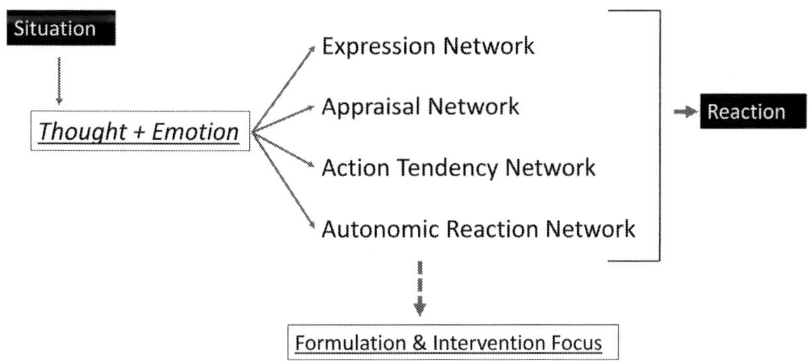

Figure 5.5 Thought-Emotion-Reaction Pathways

2 **Seek an awareness into their life**: This is necessary for multiple reasons and must be done in a warm and collaborative manner, because at the early stages this might be interpreted as 'prying'. This also helps the client and the practitioner understand the patterns that are currently in play. Helping the client feel safe with a warm, genuine, and empathic style. You can tell the client what you as the practitioner will do and why, so the client knows why this interrogative part of CBT occurs. Sometimes, either the practitioner or the client curtails gathering sufficient details about problems. For instance, some practitioners might believe all information holds value so they do not follow the heat of the problem with enough questions. Socratic questioning allows us to ask questions from different angles so our persistence is necessary. Some questions present more fruitful returns than others, so we might need to work our way around a problem rather than persistently grilling the client.
3 **Go beyond the talking:** If clients struggle to answer a question or questions, they might not know the answer or they might be reluctant to answer. When we consider the problem from the client's perspective, it's likely that they do not attend to the factors about which we are raising questions or their avoidance or safety-seeking behaviours become so effective, they no longer experience negative thoughts or engage in particular behaviours so cannot report them. To gain access, however, we might need a behavioural experiment to gather data for assessment. We might ask a client to create a new situation in which the client does not avoid or engage the usual safety behaviours, then the thoughts and feelings will register anew.
4 **Beyond words:** Some athletes struggle to express their thoughts and feelings with words. Sometimes they have feeling in their body or images in their minds. Some clients like to trace the image and translate it into words as a homework task. At other times, a client's feelings vocabulary might need a list from which to choose the feeling that feels right. Two other issues often arise in the assessment phase. One relates to 'giving the right answer' to avoid disapproval because of what the client wishes to present (i.e., thoughts and feelings about which there might be embarrassment or shame). Sometimes, the practitioner offers suggestions about signs and symptoms other clients reported so it normalises the presentation. Some clients might be worried about what will happen with their disclosure: will the coach find out? Will they drop me from the team if they find out about my diagnosis? The practitioner can reassure the client here about the bounds of confidentiality and privacy.
5 **Diagrams:** Formulation diagrams help the client and practitioner keep everything accessible and understandable as they work through a problem. A simple formulation might include vulnerability factors, beliefs/attitudes, precipitants, problems, maintenance, and strengths (Kennerley et al., 2016).

How does a formulation benefit us?

A formulation describes the current problem(s) while offering an account about how and why these problems developed and the maintaining processes proposed to keep the problems going. A formulation offers several advantages to the practitioner and client (Kennerley et al., 2016).

(a) The client and the practitioner put some order to the collection of information gathered and make inroads, especially when faced with complex problems.

(b) Formulations bridge the gap between theory and practice. At a general level, we hold theoretical knowledge about anxiety, low mood, loss of confidence, and so forth, but we also need to know how this theoretical knowledge fits the specific experience of our client.
(c) Formulation offers a shared understanding for the client and practitioner of the processes causing and maintaining problems. Together, the client and practitioner judge what might work best to address the problems.
(d) Formulation helps the client to view and think differently about their symptoms. The apparent hopelessness or helplessness during an initial session eases as the client discovers new ways of thinking and possibilities for tackling these symptoms.
(e) A sound formulation predicts the pitfalls that lie ahead for a client. For example, a client struggling with issues related to perfectionism, especially self-critical thoughts, may well present difficulties doing homework because the client might feel their efforts are not good enough or do not meet the right standard.
(f) Formulation normalises the client's experience. It is no longer a complex, unknown difficulty, but one that can be seen, sketched, and planned for. This also empowers the client to initiate action and participate in interventions from change.
(g) Formulation promotes client engagement by allowing clients a sense of control of difficulties they are experiencing and how to change to achieve their goals. Even when struggles continue, mastery continues, the situation is more in the know. For example, 'just as we discussed last week, when mum sat quietly, I could feel my chest tightening. I did not like it … I could not stop it, but I understood it, you know' says Annette.
(h) Formulation enables intervention development and high-quality supervision because the practitioner clearly understands all that is going on with the client. During supervision, this allows clarity of reflection and action. This has a knock-on effect on the client interaction itself because supervisory inputs are more easily translated to practice.

In summary, formulations hold several advantages for the practitioner and client; however, we ought to remember that formulation involves as much art as science. The client remains in the foreground of our work together because all plans and interventions involve the client and the client's needs. In sport settings, many issues presented do not fit into a neat protocol or perhaps there is no clear protocol for treatment, so we build a bespoke formulation and develop a course of therapy from that foundation.

6 Measurement in CBT

In previous chapters, we have learned about establishing working alliances and structuring cognitive behaviour therapy (CBT) sessions. Reflecting on your comfort/discomfort with CBT enables you to establish the point where your professional philosophy in practice interacts with CBT techniques. For example, humanistic/psychodynamic/emotion-focused practitioners trained in semi-structured psychotherapeutic practice often find the structure of CBT rigid. Others find it a welcome way to navigate client processes. Where do you stand?

Once the CBT session process has begun, we train the client on how to use the four-factor cognitive model to gauge their reactions. Clients come to the practitioner with various issues and difficulties. Some may struggle with form, some may have performance anxiety, some may have noticed their mental health suffering because of friction in a personal relationship. Each of these situations and the experience of every individual client bring a certain pattern of thoughts, emotions, and behaviours. Measurement, through various metrics, informs the assessment and formulation process (e.g., does the client exhibit stress or is this anxiety? What are the sources of anxiety in a client?). Measurement also establishes the effects of treatment and allows continuous evaluation of practice. In this chapter, we explore different measurements and how measurement can enhance the client's and practitioner's understanding of issues. We then consider the sources of measurement, how to devise effective measures and provide worked examples of implementing measurement in CBT for sport. We will outline how to navigate these actions in practice with case studies.

What is measurement? Types/sources of measurement

Before we dive into the fundamentals of measurement and its sources, we need to connect the empirical nature of CBT to measurement parameters. From the beginning (i.e., the first session), we want to encourage clients to view the therapeutic process as a mutually participatory experiment. In this experiment, thoughts, emotions, behaviours, beliefs, and the relationships between them can all be investigated via certain measures at various points in time. We can then feedback this information to the interventions or 'experiments' the client is conducting to improve their experience.

What are measures?

Measures are single-source, or multimethod approaches to evaluate the current mental state and psychosocial functioning of the individuals. Measurement involves using measures in a planned and structured manner to provide a comprehensive idea of the

DOI: 10.4324/9781003274513-8

levels of the individual over a period. For example, let's consider Sharla, a 16-year-old ice hockey player. She starts sport psychology support because of extreme anxiety before competitive matches, but aces practice. You provide a measurement psychometric to her during her first session, such as the Competitive State Anxiety Inventory (CSAI) (Cox et al., 2003), and then after three weeks of sessions ask her to complete the CSAI again. The results indicate that the physical symptoms of anxiety have reduced significantly, and the cognitive ones have reduced but less so. This then shows Sharla that anxiety is manageable and provides the practitioner with added information to go into the formulation.

Using measurement effectively is the cornerstone for evidence-based therapeutic intervention. There are many reasons to conduct measurement at the beginning of work and periodically throughout to get an adequate picture. Some key reasons for measurement are:

- Regular measures allow the practitioner to obtain a baseline, which provides insight into the mechanisms of the difficulty the client is facing (e.g., Sharla's physical and cognitive sources of anxiety). The same baseline allows us to assess the effects of future interventions (e.g., what changed for Sharla).
- Measurement allows the client to make direct observations in real life. This has therapeutic effects. For example, Sharla was provided with evidence that she has made progress around managing the physical sense of anxiety.
- Clients often lose awareness of how far-reaching and disabling their difficulties were initially. Baseline measures allow the client to assess their progress more accurately and increases their sense of self-efficacy.
- Effective measures provide the practitioner and the client with the 'data' to analyse why the intervention did not secure its predicted effect. For example, Sharla's cognitive anxiety may have remained high because of her school placing high expectations on her to win, which may not have been considered within the measures.

Therefore, practitioners use various measures for many reasons. Common aims when using measures include (a) *Screening* for the presence or absence of mental health conditions, risk/protective factors; (b) *Formulation* for supporting formal assertions on what difficulties the client is experiencing using diagnostic interviews and intake interviews (see Chapter 4); and (c) *Symptom & Intervention Monitoring* to assess changes in severity, level, and intervention outcomes across the course of CBT work with the client.

Types of measurement

With this understanding of the importance of measures and measurement, let's review the various measurements. In counselling, CBT measures typically include client self-report (i.e., the client reports on the various aspects such as cognitive, emotional, behavioural, relational, occupational). Practitioners do this via psychometrics or Socratic questioning. Psychometrics are standardised measures of a particular psychological variable such as anxiety, personality, depression, work life balance and others. They have prescribed instructions for use and scoring (see Rust & Golombok, 2014). Socratic questioning is the process by which the therapist asks probing questions which initiates challenging thoughts and interpretations of an event by the client (Clark & Egan, 2015). Typically, counsellors are restricted within their offices and

Table 6.1 Types of measurement and situations

Measure Type	*Description*	*Situational Example*
Client Observation	Observing the client in training and/or competition environments	Attending a tennis tournament where Annette is competing
Coach & multidisciplinary team (MDT) Feedback	Working with the coach and multi-disciplinary team to support the client and gain multi-dimensional information	Travelling as a practitioner in the staff during a world Cup
Parent Feedback	Sourcing feedback and non-contact time information from parents/ caregivers	Checking in with parents to figure out general behavioural patterns
Performance Analysis	Working with performance analysts to figure out behavioural action patterns in the game	The analyst informs us that the cricket batter is making out consistently around ball 30 during second innings-indicating a concentration dip post exhaustion
Media Sources	Viewing media based external sources including but not limited to print, TV and social media	Client working on identity. Has a bad match, you see the social media abuse, update formulation about stressors, and work on how that affected the client

therapy rooms, where the client brings the 'access' to their lives (i.e., self-report). This limits the measures they can use and apply; however, this is not the case in sport and performance. Practitioners in these contexts have greater access to clients in naturalistic settings (i.e., the setting where the client lives their organic lives). This affords greater access to types and sources of measurement besides psychometrics and Socratic questioning via client self-report. See Table 6.1 for various types of measurement that are accessible in sport and performance.

Psychometric measurement: What is it and considerations?

A psychometric test is employing a standardised test to measure an individual's cognitive, emotional, and behavioural patterns or capabilities at a certain point in time. Often, there are many psychometric measures available for any construct. For example, you can measure mood and emotions with POMS, Brunel Mood Scale, Interactive Profile of Mood States in Sport, and Sport Emotion Questionnaire (SEQ), among others. The question then arises; 'which one do we use?'

Within the CBT framework, the primary aim of using a psychometric test is to determine the extent to which an individual is affected by a condition (e.g., depression) and/or cognitive, emotional, personality, behavioural baselines (e.g., existing strengths of the client). Therefore, we pick the specific psychometric test from options based on the following considerations.

Psychometric characteristics

Validity and reliability

Psychometric tests are validated which means they measure the construct they are aiming to measure (construct validity), they measure the total dimensions of the construct they are trying to measure (content validity), and they can predict the stability of a certain construct over time with behaviour being shown in real life (criterion validity). These tests are designed with the latest theoretical evidence, tested on a large sample to ensure they are measuring the same thing, across individuals, and can predict behaviours based on the scores the individual obtains. A valid measure should also consider the language appropriate to context.

A reliable psychometric achieves the same result or score when given to the same person under similar conditions at another point in time or with another person conducting the assessment. A measure low in reliability produces inconsistent findings. Reliability of the psychometric is reported within scientific papers using Cronbach Alpha coefficients.

Measurement reactivity

The process of measurement often has a positive or negative effect on the dimension being measured in the client, which forms the reactivity of measurement. For example, if we are measuring perfectionistic behaviours, a beneficial reactivity may occur when the client realises the triggers of perfectionism, such as feeling inadequate. The client often responds by inhibiting that response at the beginning of the cycle. Clients can also have a negative reactivity. For example, if we are working on fear of failure, understanding the situational triggers can lead to an increased preoccupation and increase in negative automatic thoughts (NATs) increasing anxiety in the short term.

Relevance and simplicity

Often, psychometric measures do not 'perfectly fit' into the client presentation. Therefore, the choice of a relevant measure is valuable for intervention outcomes and the client experience. For example, the client is unlikely to engage if the psychometric is measuring depressive mood when they feel their main difficulty is anxiety. A helpful way of ensuring relevance is *operationalising* (i.e., assigning clear, defined parameters of measurement). For example, if you are working with a tennis player who loses his temper, you could first say, *'Let's be specific about what we mean when you say, 'losing my temper'. What were you doing when you 'lost it'?'* The client may respond with things like stamping on the court or yelling, which can then be linked to the process of measurement to apply to the issue they are working on.

Clients appreciate simple measures that do not overburden them. Clients often come with a *deficiency* or *difficulty*. Begin with a simple psychometric instead of a battery of tests. As clients understand the value and/or provide encouraging feedback, you can extend the testing protocol to go more in-depth. Provide simple, easy-to-understand instructions before psychometric measurement. For example, if you are providing the client with NEO-FFI, a personality psychometric, explain what personality is, what the Likert scale in the test says, and how to go about responding to it aligned to the instructions in the psychometric testing manual.

All psychometrics must maintain test-client integrity (i.e., psychometric suits the population/situation it applies to), and ensure proper adherence to protocols of administration, scoring, and debrief. Beidas et al. (2015) has compiled and reviewed some validated and open access psychometric measures.

Context of measurement

Using measures in CBT depends on various contextual factors. Some practitioners have a strictly regimented measurement practice whereas others do not think it is necessary nor helpful to be measure-intensive. Factors such as 'I work with kids', 'Athletes don't like filling forms', or 'time is a constraint' are often cited factors. For evidence-based practice, however, integrating research with clinical expertise in client characteristics, culture and preferences is critical (American Psychological Association, 2006). There are two broad considerations for the context and purpose of measurement: time and socioecological levels.

Time of measurement

The time of measurement refers to the frequency and purpose of the use of a specific type of measure. Measures can either be used: (a) consistently at the beginning of each session to monitor weekly changes and guide session plan and/or (b) systematically (but less recurrent) for a broader evaluation of change.

Consider the weekly monitoring measure. A key part of a CBT session structure is the 'mood check'. A mood check with an adult is often as simple as asking the client to rate their specific mood experience on a scale of 1 to 10 or use a psychometric measure such as the Profile of Mood States (POMS). For example, an athlete working through an injury rehabilitation and the associated psychological effects of that, can be asked to rate how they are feeling on the day and how their week has been. This response would allow the practitioner to formulate whether emotional management interventions are needed at the beginning of the session. For children and adolescents, a similar check could be conducted via visual means, such as a Feelings Thermometer (see Figure 6.1). Such weekly measurements allow the practitioner to guide sessions and, over time, track changes in mood with multiple longitudinal data points. If the measure or the questions remain the same every week, clients build up a reflective awareness and can respond quickly.

Other than weekly measures, the practitioner may want to use periodic measures. We typically give them to the client at specific intervals of time (i.e., every three sessions or every month or each time intervention planning is updated). Periodic measures tend to be in-depth assessments that align with the focus of an intervention. For example, if a practitioner has been working with a client on his/her anxiety and perception of situations, they may use a detailed psychometric after the planned period to identify if any changes have occurred. Periodic assessments may also evaluate overall mental health, metacognitive factors, life satisfaction, emotional regulation, or similar global aspects of functioning. These measures, combined with direct client feedback, allow the evolution of formulation and the modification of interventions if necessary. For best practice, the choice of measure should be informed by the initial formulation. Psychometric measures have greater rigour and specific focus than more generic scales (see 'Psychometric Measurement' above).

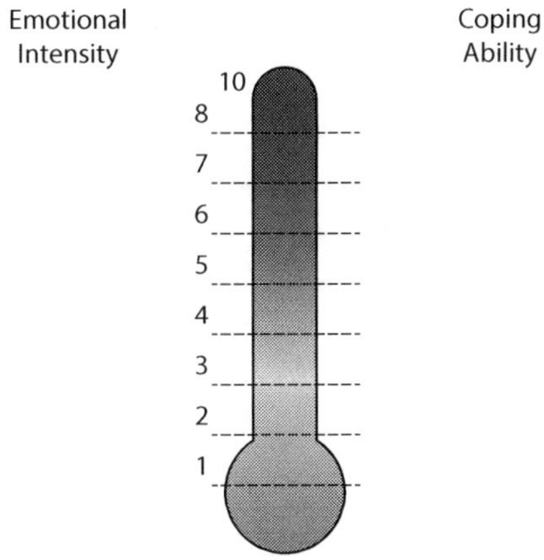

Figure 6.1 Feelings Thermometer

Socioecological factors

Another key consideration which guides measurement is *where* the source of information is coming from. Unlike clinical or counselling settings, sport affords the practitioner the opportunity to gather information from various sources guided by the socio-ecological model of human development (Bronfenbrenner & Ceci, 1994). In this model, the practitioner understands the complex interplay between individual, social, community, and societal factors to understand the wide range of interactions that the client may have. In doing so, we can also access multi-dimensional and holistic measurements. The framework also allows the practitioner to understand where the client exists within the broader organisational culture (Bronfenbrenner, 1992). The levels of the athlete, their microsystem, exosystem, and macrosystem are outlined in Figure 6.2

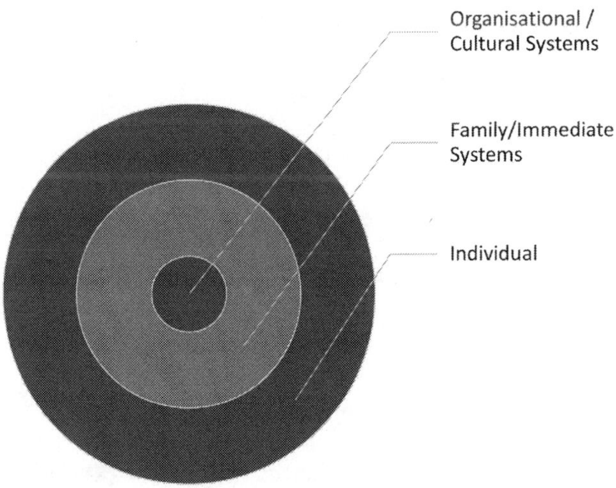

Figure 6.2 Ecological Systems Model

Source: Adapted from Purcell et al. (2019) Ecological system model here (Open Access).

Table 6.2 Socioecological levels, descriptions and measurement questions

Socioecological Level	*Description*	*Measurement Questions*
Microsystem	The microsystem encompasses all the things and relationships that have direct contact with the client in their immediate environment. This includes home, family, partners, sport colleagues, coaches, physiotherapists, sport physicians, teammates, manager and others the individual has daily contact with.	1 How is the athlete interacting with the microsystem? (forms baseline) 2 Does the microsystem provide feedback on behaviours about the athlete to the embedded practitioner? (day-to-day context specific responses)
Exosystem	The exosystem incorporates formal and informal social structures within which the individual resides and interacts. This includes the sporting environment, contextual factors (contracts, living conditions etc), training, travel, competition performance standards and others.	1 What is the nature of the sporting environment and how is it affecting the athlete? 2 Does the training environment allow the athlete to express themselves and align to their motivational orientation? 3 What are the performance standards being placed on the athlete during competition?
Macrosystem	The macrosystem represents the larger cultural beliefs, laws, perceptions and shared values of sport that influence the client. This includes the ethos and culture of the sport ('one for all and all for one' in rugby), beliefs about acceptable social norms, culture where sport exists (e.g., playing sport in a different country growing up before moving as part of transfers) and others.	1 What are the values and beliefs of the sport context the athlete is in? 2 What are the cultural reference points in the athlete's life? 3 What are the acceptable standards of behaviour in the macrosystem of that particular athlete?

(Ecological Systems Model for athlete and sport, adapted from Purcell et al., 2019, Open Access) A detailed overview of the characteristics of each level and examples is provided in Table 6.2 (refer also to Bronfenbrenner & Ceci, 1994).

This framework allows the practitioner to understand within which system their measurement source lies. In sport, the 'data' that arises out of the measure is often located from within these sources. For example, a practitioner working with a team is often told by the coach that a certain player could do with some support because of a different behaviour pattern that the coach has noticed. Often, the sources of psychological distress are location because of factors in the macrosystem. For example, if a client has moved to a different country and is struggling to adapt to the culture, this can result in psychological distress, reducing sport enjoyment and performance, and causing a distress loop.

A major consideration that practitioners need to have while isolating socioecological levels of measurement is the ethical basis of measurement. The measurement process needs to be aligned with guidelines of psychological testing/assessment from the BPS (British Psychological Society, 2019a) and the ethical principles of psychologists (cf. American Psychological Association, 2017). Informed consent must be obtained verbally, and information should not be sourced without the explicit consent of the client. During the process of measurement, client confidentiality must be maintained. The various socioecological levels beyond the athlete are often helpful *additional information* points, adding to the measurement feedback from the athlete. This allows the practitioner to provide a more holistic formulation.

Identifying emotions and automatic thoughts

In Chapter 3, we outlined and understood what automatic thoughts were. In CBT, a cornerstone of measurement is to identify a client's negative thoughts. This helps the practitioner understand the NATs that the client is experiencing and allows an increase in the client's self-awareness.

Measuring NATs requires consideration of the client presentation and their individual differences. NATs are *situation-specific* thoughts that are present on the edge of awareness. Some clients can track their NATs with little or no prompting from the practitioner. For example, a hockey player might report, 'when I missed that shot, I could almost hear my head saying, 'you're not good enough' and I kinda believed it ...'.

On other occasions, individuals may not be aware of them. This is because the NATs are internalised to such a degree that they are part of how the individual views themselves. In such cases, the NATs are not recognised as being distorted or problematic. Here clients are more aware of their feelings arising from a situation. If we take the example of the hockey player who missed a shot, being unaware of their NATs they would report something like, *'I felt extremely annoyed at myself after I missed the shot'*. They would have difficulty connecting the thoughts to the feelings.

In the CBT framework, NATs are the first type of thoughts that clients are taught to detect, examine, and modify; however, clients are unlikely to only recover their NATs when measuring and reflecting upon situation-specific thinking. Core beliefs and underlying assumptions are likely to be found as well. The practitioner must selectively categorise the measured 'cognitive data' with the client to distinguish what are NATs and how they pop-up in response to situations. There are various ways to record this information. Some examples are highlighted and explained below.

Thought diaries

Although having an awareness and understanding about automatic thoughts is the cornerstone of CBT, most clients do not possess an automatic awareness; however, almost every client has specific situations that trigger NATs and lead to dysfunctional feelings and reactions. Typically, this happens extremely quickly, and the client never pauses to notice, be aware of, or question this chain. Thought diaries are a key part of CBT allowing the individual to build this awareness; however, most clients need to understand how to step away from this experience of the event to reflect. This can be done via the 'Time-out' button (see Figure 6.3).

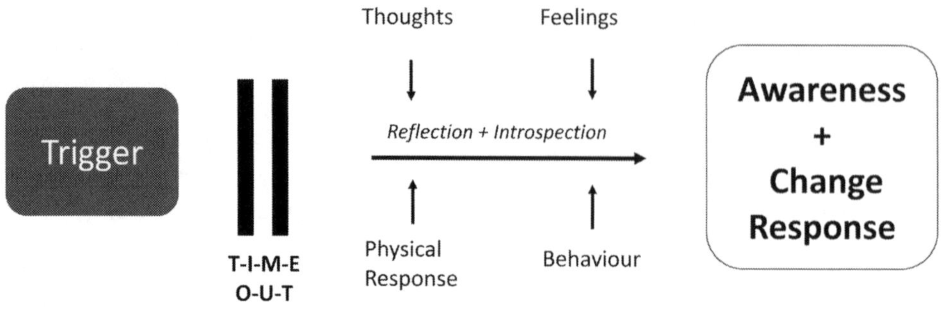

Figure 6.3 Timeout Button

The first step involves the client practising the 'Time-out' (see Figure 6.3). This allows disengagement with the speed of the trigger situation and allows the beginning of the process of self-reflection. The timeout allows the client to pause from the typically overwhelming trigger and take a step back to reflect on the cognitions and emotions associated with it. Let's look at how that works with the case below:

Application Time: Case of Mo

Mo informs you that, 'I am never comfortable in what I am doing … I always feel that there is something more I could do … and every time I see others around me, these big names, all capped international players who regularly play World Cups … I am … uncertain … I keep thinking that I am not good enough'

PRACTITIONER: Of course … it's as if everything has changed?

MO: Yes, and not in a good way because I feel like a little bird in a big city and that is causing problems.

PRACTITIONER: So is the sense that everything is so big, the media and the fans and everything the main source causing some stress?

MO: I think … not sure.

PRACTITIONER: Let's try the timeout! Can you see this picture? (see Figure 6.3, 'Timeout Diagram'). Okay, let's take a breath. We can have a break now, just like in training. Are you feeling steady?

MO NODS.

PRACTITIONER: Can you see that X, is that the main stress thing, can we just pause for a second and think about all the reasons it might cause some stress?

MO: You mean feelings?

PRACTITIONERS [NODS]: and those thoughts.

This then leads to Step B, which helps the client to understand what their situational triggers are by assigning an intensity to them (see Table 6.3). The higher the intensity of the lived experience of the situation, the greater the likelihood that this is a trigger for NATs for the client.

Table 6.3 Situational trigger detecting worksheet

Situation	*Intensity*
	Thoughts/Feelings (Rate from 1 to 10; 1 = not intense; 10 = very intense)

Situational trigger detecting worksheet

A major goal for the practitioner is to identity the specific situation types that are triggers of NATs. This measurement process is also a key part of the formulation. Many clients have a vague, underlying sense of awareness of their triggers; however, they have difficulty identifying the specific trigger situations. For example, clients often say that they are 'always anxious during competition' or 'always lose concentration' but cannot identity the specific situations when this is happening. After the client is comfortable with the 'Time-Out', the 'Situational Trigger Detection Worksheet' can be used. The practitioner should ask the client to monitor tricky situations and the 'unhelpful' or difficult feelings and behaviours that happen during it. Following this, ask the client to rate the intensity on a scale of 1–10. After the client has listed a few, we can start to see patterns. The focus must be on helping the client identify situations that are specific and concrete. Let's look at the case of Mo to get an idea of how to apply it.

Application Time: Case of Mo

[Continuing on from Step 1]

MO: The timeout thing helped! I think majorly it's about those thoughts you know? They are constantly coming in my head!

PRACTITIONER: Are those connected to any situations?

MO: I don't understand *[clients often fail to connect situations to trigger thoughts].*

PRACTITIONER: Well, you see, sometimes specific situations bring certain thoughts. Has that ever happened to you?

MO: Like when I walk by a café with great smelling coffee, and I want coffee?

PRACTITIONER: Yes! Quite like that ... so when those not-so-helpful thoughts arrive, do they arrive in specific situations?

MO [THINKING]: I think so ....

PRACTITIONER: Let's use this sheet to trace them like a detective (see the Situational Trigger Worksheet).

MO [LOOKING OVER]: Hmm ... well, firstly when we are in training and like that it happens ... when I make a mistake ... but that's not much ... maybe 4.

PRACTITIONER: Hmm.

MO: Sometimes out of sport you know ... so I went to dinner, and the waiter also said that it's okay if I did not play well in the cup game, they had high hopes and knew I would do well ... that I was thinking about for a long time ....
PRACTITIONER: Of course, it was all the time, you could not stop?
MO: Yes, like it was an 8 easily.

Mo's situational trigger worksheet

Situation	*Intensity*
	Thoughts/Feelings (Rate from 1 to 10; 1 = not intense; 10 = very intense)
When other people tell me they expect me to do well, and I will do good things for their club when they barely know me	Thought – 'I must always do well' = 8

This brings us to step three: understanding internal reactions. We use the 'Understand your Internal Reaction' worksheet, which served as a thought-recording tool to help the client identify and record reactions (see Table 6.4).

If the client is not used to writing things down or engaging in structured self-reflection, they are likely to find this process awkward. Depending on the client's comfort, all three steps can be done in one session, or step three can be done in a follow-up session using the information the client has gained through step one and step two. The worksheets help the client stop, take a 'time-out' and purposefully reflect, which slows down the often-runaway thoughts. The worksheets also have a value outside the session because the clients intuitively use this structure to make sense of their internal processes in stressful situations. This also helps structure sessions; however, be flexible as a practitioner. For instance, step one to three can also be done orally as part of session dialogue initially to allow the client to get used to it.

W – questions when training (What happened/Who was involved? Where did it happen? When did it happen?) – think like a detective or a journalist. But with empathy

Table 6.4 Understanding your internal reactions

Understanding Your Internal Reactions				
Situations	*Thoughts*	*Feelings (rate 1–10)*	*Physical Reactions (rate 1–10)*	*Behaviours*
Who? What? Where? When?	*What did I think?*	*What did I feel?*	*How did my body react?*	*What did I do? How does this affect me?*

Application Time: Case of Mo

[Continuing on from Step 2]

PRACTITIONER: So, shall we untangle some of those thoughts and situations?
MO [NODS].
PRACTITIONER: So remember, how we discussed situations are present, but the main thing that affects us is our thoughts and our feelings that come from the situation?
MO [NODS].
PRACTITIONER: You have already said how the expectations from so many people at the big club were one of the factors.
MO: Yes, definitely ….
PRACTITIONERS: Let's try to put them on and trace them from the situation, to the thought that came into your head, the feeling you felt and what you do after.
MO: And this will help because how thoughts affect me can be changed?
PRACTITIONERS: Well, yes, that is our goal. But first, before we change something, we need to know what to change.
MO: Oh, like before a pass, you need to know where your teammate is.
PRACTITIONER: Yes, exactly. Shall we?

[Mo starts thinking, reflecting and filling it in. But his first attempt is not specific enough].

PRACTITIONER: You mentioned you thought it was pressure, could you be specific?
MO: How?
PRACTITIONER: Like could you think of the dialogue almost that was fired in your head? You know, the raw direct voice in the head we all have.
MO: Oh … I thought … I was still not settled in the team … so ….
PRACTITIONER: That's a great start! Let's press on that?
[Practitioner empathetically helps Mo reflect and eventually we complete the first row].

Mo's understanding reaction Worksheet

Understanding Your Internal Reactions

Situation	*Thoughts*	*Feelings (rate 1–10)*	*Physical Reactions (rate 1–10)*	*Behaviours*
I was told by my barber that this haircut will look great for the camera when I score next match	I cannot even pass accurately with my new team yet, how will I score?	Anxious (7) Nervous (6) Angry (7) Restless (8)	Felt my neck stiffen when he said that	Got out of there soon, and went for a drive on the highway aimlessly so I could be a little alone

Frequency counts

If the client displays an awareness linking a specific type of thought to a situation, we can aid this process by recording its frequency. Counting is often the most reliable measurement method and one of the simplest. It allows the individual to understand the magnitude of how much that NAT appears and links it to situational triggers; however, the practitioner and client must have clearly outlined parameters that would inform the frequency count. For example, the number of self-critical thoughts during a training session *('that was a poor shot')* or number of times their success on the field was suppressed *('that pass was not clean')* or how many social situations did it pop up in *('the manager did not say hi, he must not like me')*.

The practitioner and client creativity are key in creating a pattern of recording frequency counts contextualised to the situation/specific difficulty the client is facing. It is also important to understand, via Socratic questioning and formulation, what the resulting frequency could be. For example, if the athlete is likely to record a few hundred intrusive self-critical thoughts during training, it is likely to cause an emotional reaction and lower confidence. If the frequency is to be high, the practitioner can ask the client to focus on a particular sample from a relevant time of day. This could be a critical phase of competition, such as teeing off/putting in golf or serving to defend break points for a tennis player. Let's look at how to apply this using the case below:

Application Time: Case of Mo

PRACTITIONER: Shall we look at how many times the 'pressure' feeling has happened?

MO: Yeah … well, it happened twice on Monday ….

PRACTITIONER: The barber and?

MO: The café. It happened once on Tuesday after training. Four times on Thursday-once during our strength session, once with this academic visit and twice when I was at a restaurant.

PRACTITIONER: So I have been counting with you, interestingly it did not happen when you played in Basel on Wednesday?

MO [SURPRISED]: Actually … no it did not.

PRACTITIONER: So it has only been happening out of matchplay then?

MO NODS.

PRACTITIONER: But it's affecting your preparation and mental peace because match days are only three hours?

MO: Yes! You get me! And I want to stop it before it comes a big issue.

Event duration

The duration of an event or experience is also relevant and likely to be a reliable measure, provided the client has a sense of awareness that the NATs exist. The duration measurement allows the client to see the effect of the NAT triggered thought cycle. It also helps facilitate an understanding of when it happens and how it influences the client for the duration it is present. Some examples of event duration measurement of NATs include time able to concentrate on discrete skill practice such as basketball free throw repetition training during anxiety. Another example could be recording the duration of safety behaviours (i.e., behaviours that reduce a NAT). For example, a tennis player who has the NAT of 'I don't want to lose this point' subsequently engages in safety behaviours of moving behind the baseline and looping balls in. This allows her opponent to attack further triggering the NAT. A retrospective measurement of how long the NAT and safety behaviour duration existed would allow the client and practitioner to understand the lived experience of it. Let's look at how to apply this using the case below:

Application Time: Case of Mo

PRACTITIONER: When it does happen, how long does it stay?
MO: Stay?
PRACTITIONER [NODS]: Yes, like stay and you think about it and all that.
MO: Oh … it does quite a bit ….
PRACTITIONER: Of course ….
MO: Like … it will happen, then it will go … but then in training and stuff when I make a mistake it comes again … which is difficult.
PRACTITIONER: Difficult because?
MO: Like it takes away focus from what I want to do: which is play football the best way I can.

Self-rating

Self-rating is one of the most common ways of measuring automatic thoughts in CBT. They capture the experiential quality of internal events and provide an understanding of cognitions. Self-rating operates like a feedback process on the client's experience of the NATs and the situations that triggered them. They are often placed within anchor points, such as a ten-point scale. For example, *'could you rate that thinking of 'I'll never recover from this' on a scale of 1-10, with 1 being not very influential and 10 being it affects me very much?'*

Self-ratings allow the practitioner and the client to monitor discrete events, such as being stressed whenever they play someone they are 'expected' to win against, or when parents come to watch them play. For example, the practitioner can focus on asking the athlete to self-rate their having feelings of inadequacy or 'I am not good enough' every time he goes to training after a new player has joined the club and is competing for his position.

If the phenomenon or NAT being measured has a continuous nature to it (such as chronic low self-efficacy or anxiety) or even if it occurs frequently (such as pre-competitive anxiety), then the practitioner should work with the client to choose a time to rate. Alternatively, there can also be a process of averaged responses. For example, if the athlete has played four competitive events in a day (often the case for u16/u18 individual sport events), the aggregated rating can be obtained, and more detailed information on specific events can be obtained later on in the session. Let's look at Mo's case to understand how to apply it:

Application Time: Case of Mo

[after we implement the Timeout and the Understanding the Reactions Sheet]

PRACTITIONER: Did that make sense?
MO: Yes, I was surprised but yes … the timeout really helped me just you know … stop the thought flow, like we do during a throw-in.
PRACTITIONER: That's an excellent analogy. If I were to ask on a scale of 1–10, how comfortable did it feel using it?
MO: Quite comfortable actually … easy 8.
PRACTITIONER: That's good to hear. Can you see yourself implementing it outside the sessions as well, when those thoughts come?
MO: Umm … to be honest, I hadn't thought of it that way … but it does make sense to do it.

Personal journals/artwork/vlogs

Personal journals, art and, in recent times, Vlogs are excellent measurement sources for the client and practitioner to measure NATs and situations. They also allow the client to reflect upon raw presentations which were recorded at the time to understand the links between various aspects of the issue. For example, a personal journal can allow the client to look at the detail to understand the relationship between particular triggers and the problem. An athlete who keeps a journal of all the times she *'felt she deserved the win'* can review the entries to understand all the factors which she considers made her 'worth it' or deserving of the win, and therefore are direct positive reinforcers related to her self-concept.

A similar detail is also obtained through artwork or vlogs that clients often engage in as a medium of expression. All these sources are multi-faceted and do not have a structure. Focus on working through recordings/making entries with the client, but without over-formalising the process. The goal is to allow the naturalistic expression of internal events but ensure that the client returns information that is consistent and possible for cooperative analysis. A helpful way of engaging in this is to source client feedback about what is relevant and sensible, and when they want to engage in this. Let's look at Annette's case to see how to implement this.

Application Time: Case of Annette

PRACTITIONER: What is tennis to you Annette?

ANNETTE: It's hard to explain.

PRACTITIONER: I completely understand ... no issues take your time ... we can look at other ways of expressing than talking as well!

ANNETTE: 'Really' I thought this was just talking.

PRACTITIONER: Ha ha not so. Well, we can look at different options. Earlier you told me you like to sketch?

ANNETTE: Yes! I get bored during all the travelling. And I carry my little sketchpad around. I am not good though [downcast eyes].

PRACTITIONER: Well, you draw for yourself, why should anyone else need to decide if its good or not? [to counter parental conditions of being perfect].

ANNETTE: I guess ... my grandma always says that.

PRACTITIONER: It seems like you are close to her.

ANNETTE: I really am! She's amazing! She's the one who introduced me to tennis!

PRACTITIONER [SMILED]: Would you like to draw out what tennis is to you?

ANNETTE: Yes. *[practitioner provides a page and a pen. Annette draws and practitioner does not look directly giving her a non-evaluative space].*

ANNETTE: So, this [pointing at the tennis court lines she had drawn] ... is where I ... [drawing a girl with a racquet, books, and long hair] ... feel like me ... because there is just me and the racquet and ... yeah ... that's all there is ... I like moving to the ball and feeling the wind in my hair, the slide and the perfect touch of the ball ... it's simple and it's me.

PRACTITIONER [PAUSES]: That was a really honest and beautiful description.

ANNETTE [SHEEPISHLY SMILES].

PRACTITIONER: I notice it's just you and tennis here ... but tennis now for you is a bit more complex isn't it?
ANNETTE: Yes. That's a little bit of the problem.

[by using art the practitioner has sourced important information on what tennis means to Annette and also what her conflicting issue is]

Psychometric scales and questionnaires

Psychometrics are developed for the measurement of specific aspects of an individual's functioning. Most psychometrics have comparative data across groups, such as a clinical population, across genders and ages. This allows comparison of where your client is compared to the normative score. It is important to note that this does not imply no change can be made but is a helpful starting point. For example, a badminton player reports having recurrent thoughts and ruminating about loss of funding if she does not maintain/improve her ranking. This is causing an unstable mood, which often comes through in high stress moments during competitive matches. She also reports that she is not enjoying a lot of things that she expected to be enjoying. The practitioner could use the 'Ruminative Responses Scale' (Treynor et al., 2003), a 22-item scale that describes self-focus, symptom focus, and focus on possible consequences. The results indicated that her intrusive, ruminative thoughts were primarily focused on possible consequences and self-focused where she scored highest, allowing the practitioner to appropriately inform interventions.

Psychometrics are also used to understand strengths and related automatic thoughts to ensure the extension of desirable thoughts and behaviours. For example, a long-distance swimmer from India seeks help because he reports *'I am struggling with motivation ... everything seems like a task ... especially things that have a long-term timeline and I can see no immediate reward of all this hard work'*. This aligns itself to motivational orientation and also grit (i.e., passion and perseverance for long-term goals). The practitioner uses the three-dimensional grit scale (Kuruveettissery et al., 2021) and understands that the athlete scores higher on Interest-Passion and Perseverance-Commitment but is low on Goal-Directed Resilience. This allows the client to develop an awareness of what element is causing his 'loss of motivation', which also guides intervention. See Table 6.5 for some commonly used validated psychometric scales used in mental health settings and sport.

Distinguishing emotions from automatic thoughts

The CBT framework is founded on the position that it is our cognitive interpretation of situations and events that lead to emotional responses (see Section I). Therefore, clients need to make this connection and build it within their awareness before, during and after measurement. Without a clear distinction, clients are likely to (A) not measure their thoughts and emotions accurately or; (B) attribute their own reactions only to the situation. For example, the client may say 'I feel I am not good enough' or 'My partner makes me angry when she does not check-in after a big tournament'.

Table 6.5 Examples of psychometric scales

Psychological Variable Measured	*Psychometric Scales*
Anxiety	CSAI-2 (Competitive State Anxiety Inventory) SCAT (Sport Competitive Anxiety Test) HAM-A (Hamilton's Anxiety Test)
Mental Health	SMHAT (Sport Mental Health Assessment Test)
	SMHRT (Sport Mental Health Recognition Tool)
Performance Strategies	TOPS (Test of Performance Strategies)
	Psychological Performance Inventory
	PBPSQ (Performance based Performance Strategies Questionnaire)
	PST (Psychological Skills Test)
Stress & Emotional Regulation	PANAS (Positive and Negative Affect Scale)
	POMS (Profile of Mood States)
	Athletic Coping Skills Inventory
	RPE (Rate of Perceived Exertion)
Self-Awareness	Psychological State Test for Athletes (TEP)
	(MCAS-DS) Metacognitive Awareness Scale-Domain Specific
Resilience	+AdaptR
Personality	NEO-FFI
	Sport Personality Questionnaire
Motivation	Sport Motivation Questionnaire Situational Motivation Scale

The thought diary, as 'Understanding Internal Reactions Sheet' is a key part of this process. When introducing the exercise and at check-in points, the practitioner must work with the client to allow them to practise detecting NATs and separating them from the consequent emotions. For example, let's look at the excerpt below in the Application Time box:

Beck and Fleming (2021) and Beck (2020) suggested that clients should put their statements and NATs into the active voice (*'I will never get another chance'*) rather than passive voice *('Another chance will never be given to me'*). This allows the client to detect and express NATs in the form they appear in our cognitions. For some clients, this process is quick. Other clients require some time and conscious effort to learn the differences between the NATs and emotions arising in a situation. Some common mistakes are the jumbling up of thoughts and emotions. For example, a javelin thrower might put *'I feel anxious that I will not be picked for the Commonwealth Games'* in the 'Thoughts' column of the sheet. *'Commonwealth games selection uncertainty'* should be in the 'Situation' column and 'I feel anxious' should be in the 'Feelings' column. The NATs are not clear in this instance. Socratic questions could be used to reflect with the client on what it means to him if he does not get selected. This may lead to his actual 'Thoughts'/NATs such as *'I will be behind in the Olympic cycle, my qualification will be screwed, my career will be over, I'll never be an Olympian'*. In the initial sessions, the clients are guided to build a focus on situations, thoughts and emotions to practise detecting their NATs. These are then

Application Time: Case of Mo

PRACTITIONER: Shall we look at the thoughts that come with these situations?
MO: Yeah, let's take that one ... the one where I had lunch plans with my manager and he cancelled because he had go for another meeting.
PRACTITIONER: Right ... what were the thoughts?
MO: Why the hell is that player more important than me? He should want to have lunch with me, but I feel [confusion of thought with emotion] he doesn't want to because he doesn't rate me as before.
PRACTITIONER: What feelings did that lead to?
MO: Kinda hurt ... felt like I should not be ignored because I made a few mistakes.
PRACTITIONER [NODS]: Of course ... but 'feel' is not the main thing is it? It's those thoughts of he doesn't want to have lunch because I am not valued anymore?
MO [NODDING]: Well yeah ....
PRACTITIONER: And those thoughts made you feel hurt.
MO: Yes definitely ....
PRACTITIONER: So based on this ... we have uncovered an unhelpful thought, that NAT ... can you tell me what it is?
MO: Umm ... I am not valued?
PRACTITIONER [NODDING]: Also perhaps, he does not value me, that is why he is doing things?
MO: Oh ... [pause *insight moment*] ... so the thought was giving ... how you say ... meaning because I felt insecure?
PRACTITIONER: A little bit yes ....
MO: I see ... I did this with the restaurant also .... In that time when I and the team went out, and the manager asked the captain what bottle of wine we would have ... but maybe it's because he was the captain.

[Practitioner guides Mo to review all of his situations and the corresponding NATs so that he can understand the link between situations and NATs]

connected to the unhelpful emotions they experience in specific situations. Let's look at Mo's case outlined above of how the session can be used to guide the client through this process of distinguishing.

One key point that both practitioners and clients should know is that inserting 'feel' into a sentence does not turn the response into an emotional response. Individuals (including practitioners) interchangeably use 'I feel' with 'I think'. For example, a tennis coach might remark, 'I feel like that player and I are drifting apart, especially during this abductor rehab process'. What the coach is actually remarking is 'I think the player and I are drifting apart', with the emotional response subtext, 'which makes me *feel unsettled*'.

Although it may seem like this is a minor issue of semantics, these corrections eventually facilitate client awareness of their dysfunctional thoughts *and* the emotional response that arises because of it. By doing so, clients understand the distinction between thoughts and emotions, especially during distressing emotional responses that are triggered by their NATs. The practitioner must remember to undertake challenging with an empathetic and warm stance. A helpful reminder is to highlight that all their emotions are valid, it is only their NATs and triggering thoughts which are being challenged for examination. This is helpful because,

> *Feelings are not open to dispute; they are phenomenological [subjective] experiences for which only the individual has data. You cannot argue with such subjective states*
> (Walen et al., 1992, p. 98)

So how can the practitioner know whether the statement is truly representative of a thought or an emotion? (Keeping in mind that you will not be immediately familiar with the client's internal frame of reference and way of interacting with their environment.) Greenberger and Padesky (1995) suggest the rule of thumb of mood words. Emotional moods are distilled to one word, such as guilt, anger, anxiety, stress, depression, shame, elated, happy, satisfied, scared, remorseful, helpless, embarrassed, humiliated, and so on. If the client is struggling to distil it to one word, the chances are they are identifying a thought or NAT. For example, a triathlete who is returning to sport after injury may say,

TRIATHLETE: I will never be able to break my personal best any more.
[The practitioner could paraphrase and reframe] Practitioner: You have this … thought that you will never be able to overcome this problem? How do you feel with that thought in your mind?
TRIATHLETE: I feel that no one will be able to help me.
[Practitioner identifies another thought statement package as feel] Practitioner: Is that also an example of thinking? I think no one will be able to help me?
TRIATHLETE: Kinda yeah.
[Practitioner focuses on eliciting emotion]: How do you feel with those two floating thoughts in your mind?
TRIATHLETE: Umm … helpless … sad … angry? I am not sure about the angry.

With emotions, clients may use one-word descriptions due to low emotional awareness. Some classic examples among athletes are 'bad', 'good', 'awful', among others. They have tremendous value in providing the depth of emotion, but the practitioner needs to focus on the underlying thoughts, situations and behaviours from 'crap' or 'hopeless', that is, what was the situation, accompanied by what thought made them feel 'crap' or 'hopeless'.

Note on Cultural Competence

The practitioner ought to remember that not all cultures express emotions in the same manner (see Lim, 2016 for review evidence and further reading). The second author of this book, Sahen Gupta works across the United Kingdom, UAE, Canada, and South Asia. Emotions are expressed in different parameters. Often, the normative or 'expected' emotional reaction in one cultural paradigm may be unavailable in another. This also extends to the semantics used to express emotions. For example, a first-class, male cricketer in England gets out playing a loose ball and is livid with himself. A cricketer of a similar age playing at the first-class level gets out playing a loose ball is also livid with himself. The one from England sulks and is overtly disappointed. The one from India experiences shame. Both their NATs were along the lines of, *'I will not be rated by my coach, and dropped down the batting order'*. Although there are minor individual differences in personality and parental styles, the similarity between them is uncanny, but yet, emotional valence differed. Another example is how languages express the same emotion in different ways. In English, fear is expressed as *'I am afraid'* with a direct connection to self. Whereas in Hindi (roughly translated) it is expressed as *'Fear is present'* with the connection to self being a subtext. A helpful way of going about this as a practitioner is to have regular check-ins with the client about the quality of their emotional expression. Further reading can be sourced from Gupta and Divekar (2022).

NAT specificity and emotions

A common difficulty faced by practitioners is the lack of specificity in client feedback or response to questions. When clients discuss events/situations in general and vague terms, it is difficult for the practitioner and the client to understand the concrete examples where they appear. This issue is exacerbated because emotions are typically felt intensely in specific situations and sport has high emotionality involved. For example, an athlete might tell you, *'I felt scared when I realised, I was going to be late and miss the team bus'*. This prompts a much more intense reaction as compared to a general statement just as *'I get worried about my punctuality'* which would not allow the client nor the practitioner to understand the NATs behind or the emotion.

To engage in NAT specificity and emotional identification, the practitioner must facilitate the client to anchor the general 'issue' presented to a specific context:

CLIENT: There's no situation ... I like things organised and I am a worrier ... I overthink.
PRACTITIONER: Are you worried when you play?
CLIENT: Yes [nodding] ....
PRACTITIONER: What thoughts enter your mind when you play that make you worried?
CLIENT: What if I can't make that shot, or that tackle ... what if the gaffer doesn't rate me ... what if I get dropped?
[Practitioner focuses on drilling through the general feeling of 'worry' into a situational context where the worrying and 'what if' NATs are being triggered].

The client is verbalising thoughts as 'what if's', which indicates Thinking Traps/ Crooked Thinking. The practitioner should also focus on converting those 'what if' statements into clearer statements without questions to remove any ambiguity. This allows us to engage further with the 'cognitive data' from the thoughts and dive deeper into the emotional experience of the client. Any client who has any level of distress or wants to push for improvement will have several automatic thoughts. A lot of those NATs are irrelevant, because they are unfocused reactions to things. They are not drivers of the NAT system (Weishaar, 2001). The practitioner and client need to filter through the overflowing NATs to link the thoughts which are causing emotional distress. Clients often provide their reflections on thinking rather than actual thoughts. For example, *'I thought I was stressed in this situation because I was playing out of my natural position'*. To uncover the actual thoughts, the practitioner and the client could engage in imagery (to recreate the situation), motivational interviewing (a directive, client centred questioning and engagement style that elicits motivational processes linked to thoughts and behaviour i.e., 'why you did what you did?') or Socratic guided discovery. Clients often report a stream of thoughts related to difficulties (like a narrative flow), but consciously or unconsciously omit key disturbances which trigger NATs. Let's look at the same footballer, who has 'worry' and 'what ifs'.

CLIENT: I feel guilty and worried about messing up ... and also about ... the other things such as staying up late, coasting in training, some of the ... em parties ... I think ... what will people think? And when things go bad on the pitch ... they sometimes do right? And these things come back on my mind ... then I think ... what if the coach is also aware of all this? What if they drop me?

[The client has two streams of thoughts. The first is the actual behaviours he engages in, and the second is the cognitive appraisal of those situations that he undertakes himself and those he thinks others are thinking about. The practitioner tries to align with the second stream, and go away from the narrative].

PRACTITIONER: You said you were guilty about what you do? What thoughts make you feel so guilty?

CLIENT: Like ... it's my fault ... to actually live a life ... and that causes me to mess up on the pitch, and not be a good footballer ... like ... if I had not done all that, I would stop making the mistakes I make ... stop having the bad games ....

PRACTITIONER: So what you do ... those thoughts come and say that's responsible for all the mistakes? And makes you think of alternatives and what ifs?

CLIENT: Yeah, actually ... but that's a weird cycle isn't it?

The practitioner engaged in categorising the NAT and fed it back to the client, who then agreed confirming the validity from their experience. This is a process of indirect measurement as well because the practitioner has now measured: (A) What are the parameters and 'specific' descriptions of NATs; (B) What triggers them and which situations keeps them going? This process also allowed the practitioner to go beyond the narrative review of the situation given by the client and to the actual thoughts.

Rating emotions and intensity

> *Emotion is the horse that pulls along the cognitive cart ... provides direction and motivation for cognition ... cognition without emotion is a cart without a horse, which will simply sit going nowhere*
>
> (Power, 2010, p. 149).

Because of the focus on cognitions in CBT, it is often interpreted that CBT does not focus on emotions or works on 'thinking your way out of emotions'. CBT has its critics stating that there is an emphasis on mastering negative emotions instead of accepting them at face value. Practitioners need to know that emotional changes in the real world are subtle, as they move and change both on their own and interdependently with cognitive changes. For example, a basketball player may feel nervous about their free throw because their body is at a high state of arousal at the line which they associate with anxiety. This combines with the fact that the points from the free throw are essential to the teams' chances, leading to a full-blown pre skill execution anxiety process.

Emotional experience and individual differences

Emotions are a complex set of physiological and psychological states that involve cognitions, feelings, and behavioural responses. When experienced briefly, they are termed feelings. When they are experienced chronically, with enduring and predictable patterns, they are termed as mood. Current psychological theory (at the time of writing this chapter) highlights that emotion is best understood as an information guide of events within them or around their environment that require their considered attention. In this sense, emotions are viewed as functional. For example, fear draws attention to possible threats, both short and long-term, in our environment. A footballer fears they will miss the penalty, because it will cost them the game, which will reflect badly on their performance, causing drawbacks on their contract (i.e., livelihood). Since these emotion systems are functional and linked to the individual, they differ across individuals. For example, Player A has a bad backhand, whereas Player B has a great backhand. Player B is more likely to get angry compared to Player A if they mess up their backhand shots.

In psychotherapeutic practice, we broadly work around five basic emotions: sadness, anger, fear, happiness, and disgust (Power & Dalgeish, 2015). Complex emotions come out from a combination of these basic emotions. For example, perfectionism-linked-anxiety comes out of the fear of losing by making mistakes and anger at not being able to be perfect. The identification of such emotional processes is rooted in individual differences and must be employed within sport CBT formulation (see Barlow et al., 2021) (see Chapter 5).

CBT is 'cognitive behavioural', why emotions?

In the CBT four-factor model, emotion has a place, but cognition takes centre stage. So, the question may arise: why should we bother with emotions? Emotions are typically triggered more strongly and quickly than cognitions. Intense emotions are emergency signals and have an 'attention fixating' capacity (i.e., they overpower attention to a specific element of a situation, causing a disruption in the cognitive system). Because of this interference, the cognitive mind functions erratically, triggering NATS and thinking traps. For example, fearing anxiety causes more anxiety. This anxiety increases hypervigilance (i.e., continuous scanning of internal/external stimuli for danger signs). This causes overinterpretations of danger by distorting reality, ultimately leading to short- and long-term consequences.

Emotions have motivational underpinnings for behaviour and cognitions. Specific emotional systems lead to specific thought-behaviour patterns. For example, fear leads to over-engagement or avoidance. Working with the client to focus on uncomfortable emotions can be helpful in understanding the motivational underpinnings and process them better. At times, however, emotional activation is too high for any cognitive work to occur. In these cases, maladaptive emotions need to be addressed to validate and accept emotional processes using techniques of emotional regulation and self-soothing. Some resources have been adopted from beyond the classical 4-factor CBT model, with newer therapeutic modalities. For example, Emotion-Focused Therapy (EFT) can be integrated into a more emotionally grounded version of CBT (Greenberg, 2011), which has found specific blueprints of application in sport psychology (see Gupta & Duncan, in review). Even within the CBT theory, transdiagnostic model for emotional concerns (Barlow et al., 2021), emotional regulation skills (Leahy et al., 2011), metaemotional skills during session (Power, 2010) and compassion focused interventions for defusing and healing extreme emotions (Gilbert, 2010) have arisen.

Measuring and rating emotions are therefore critical to paint an accurate picture of the inner experience of the client and formulate effectively. We work through the following three steps:

Step 1: Identifying emotion type

Emotions have specific types or valences (i.e., the degree to which unpleasantness or pleasantness is derived from an emotional stimulus). See Figure 6.3 for the different valences and arousal levels that each emotion accompanies.

Clients are typically at different levels of emotional awareness. The average client is aware of the basic emotions, and their experience of them, but often lack a suitable emotion vocabulary. Therefore, engaging the client in psychoeducation about multiple emotions and their valences which exist in their daily life is fruitful. Evidence has indicated that there are around 27 distinct emotion categories bridged by gradients (see Cowen & Keltner, 2017). Much like the process of measuring cognitions, it is helpful for the client to identify the specific emotions. Without specificity, there is a vagueness to the emotion reporting which does not match the actual experience. For example, the client who has low self-esteem and continuously lowers their successes may say they're 'satisfied' with their performance, when they actually mean 'delighted' with it. Alternatively, a client may say I was 'angry' about not scoring, when they were actually experiencing 'frustration'.

The practitioner can employ psychoeducation to increase client awareness, and then work to list specific emotions in specific situations. This allows the client to link their emotional experience to both cognitions and situations. Some specific methods to focus on are:

- **'Feeling words'**: Clients typically have their own words or phrases that they use to describe emotion. For example, a table tennis player describes anxiety as 'feelings like I'm unstable, like I am hung in the air … like the ball for a service toss, which doesn't know how I will hit it'. It is important to identify these idiosyncratic expressions of emotion.
- **Body language, facial expressions, voice tone**: This is often neglected, but an important part of the practitioner identifying the emotional changes within clients in session. Typically, emotions are evidenced in tone of voice, words used, specific points of emphasis and facial expressions. Simple reflection is a good way to test this and increase client awareness. For example, the same table tennis player says, 'feelings like I'm unstable, *[sighs]* like I am hung in the air … like the ball for a service toss, which doesn't know how I will hit it [voice trails]'. The practitioner can reflect saying, 'I noticed that there was some emotion attached with what you described … what was the feeling of that experience?'
- **'Think/Feel Dilemma'** (Wills & Sanders): This is a linguistic dilemma where clients mix up thoughts with feelings. 'I feel I will not beat my personal best' says a swimmer. This is actually a cognitive thought prediction, that is, 'I think I will not beat my personal best'. The emotion experienced is probably anxiety or fear. Using thought diaries and empathetically challenging the client facilitates the resolution of this dilemma.

Step 2: Rating emotion intensity

As discussed above, emotions have different valences and intensities. This has a corresponding effect on behaviours and cognitions. For example, fear may be accompanied with avoidance behaviours and avoidant cognitions. Often, clients do not possess an awareness of the intensity of the emotion they are experiencing. Highly intense emotions also have a physiological correlate causing the body to feel different. Most commonly, intense anxiety-based emotions are manifested through stiffness in the chest, heaviness in the head, headaches, nausea, stomach discomfort, and unclear thought processes among others.

Highly intense emotions also cause conflicts and roadblocks between the operations of the different routes of cognition. Because of the stronger nature of intense emotions, our cognitions get overpowered. The balance between the emotion-cognition processing gets highly disrupted. In normal situations, the cognitive system processes information and produces realistic interpretations of risks detected by low-intensity emotions. For example, the player knows he made a mistake leading to a weaker tactical position causing some stress, but the cognitive system knows that they have gotten away with it for this point as the opponent misses, and brings back equilibrium. A balanced cognitive-emotion system allows the individual to actively and consciously evaluate the details of the situation and decide if any action is needed; however, during high-intensity emotions, the cognitive system get completely overridden, and only the negative emotional experience will drive action. This is the common cause when athletes 'play afraid' or report 'my head was telling me to do it, but somehow I did that'.

Self-monitoring of emotional experience is the easiest and most effective way to facilitate measurement of emotional intensity. This allows the client and the practitioner to gain an understanding of the experiences of high-intensity emotions and what happens after. Some major techniques are:

- Emotion logs (List out the situation ≫ list out the emotion ≫ give it a rating intensity out of 10),
- Thought records, that is, Understanding Internal Reactions sheets
- Personal Journals or Diaries or Vlogs (which provide qualitative details on the emotional experience)
- Clients sourcing information about how they behave when they are emotional from people they spend time with (coaches, teammates, partner, rivals, physiotherapist, family and others).

Identifying core beliefs (when do you need to?)

As outlined in Chapter 3, NATs are the gateways to the deeper, more foundational core beliefs that inform cognitions and actions. They are the roots on which the branches of underlying assumptions are steadied and leaves of NATs flutter.

We know from Chapter 3 that the Core Beliefs are typically represented in the Triad of Self, Other and Future/World. These core beliefs are manifested through underlying assumptions and NATs. For example, a cricketer who has the core belief that 'I' *'need to be better and improve constantly'* (Core belief directed at self), leads to underlying assumption that 'I need to look for ways to better myself and constantly

Table 6.6 Examples of core beliefs

Core Belief Examples		
Self (I)	*Others*	*Future/World*
Incompetent/Stupid	Untrustworthy / Out to get me	Unsafe/ hostile
Loser	Unhelpful / Exploitative	Luck is the only reason for my success
Unlovable/Unsuccessful	Manipulative / Bad	The world will not let me be happy
Unworthy/ Underserving	Always doing things for my benefit	Nothing will happen if I play with my injury
Perfect/Better than everyone	Total reason for my success / my only option	The organisation will never give me a second change
Only worthy if I win	Only going to care if I am successful	The world and luck is against me
Never as good as someone else	Always going to abandon me	No matter what I do, the world will not let me succeed
I don't matter	Going to always look after their own interests	Luck will come back to make me fail in the future
Not trusted to deliver on the field by anyone	Everyone should always put me first in the team sheet	

strive for higher levels' leading to a belief that there is 'a perfect standard I need to attain, or I cannot be good enough'.

So where do these core beliefs come from? Core beliefs are fixed and enduring beliefs which form the bedrock of cognition. They are formed because of early experiences, our attachments and upbringing. These may range from early childhood (ages 3–6 years), all the way to young adulthood (age 20–24). Before we go into how to identify core beliefs, the practitioner needs to know what certain core belief examples look like. This is outlined in Table 6.6.

Beck (2011) proposes that negative core beliefs about the self falls under three main categories;

1 **Helplessness** – core beliefs that fall under the helplessness category are related to inferiority ('I am a hopeless player compared to them', vulnerability ('I have too many weaknesses') and a sense of personal incompetence ('I will always make these mistakes').
2 **Worthlessness** – core beliefs linked to the category of worthlessness includes the idea that the individual is insignificant and a burden to others. 'I am failing to win tournaments despite my parents investing so much into me'.
3 **Unlovability** – is the core belief category represented by the idea that the individual is not likeable, or capable of strong intimate relationships. 'I don't think I can make this work', 'This coach appears to always tell me I am progressing, something is surely wrong'.

These negative core beliefs typically stem from attachment concerns in early childhood. For example, imagine a child who is in a sporting setup at 7 or 8 years of age. They are constantly reminded that the academy to professional conversion is less than 5%

and therefore one has to be good all the time. This creates a perception that the child *must* be good or they are not worthy. Occasionally, when they are not good, they feel helpless, and unsupported if the communication pattern has an absence of relational support elements. Over time, this child secures an academy contract, but is told that is nothing, and not the level. Eventually, they secure a pro contract, but by then their self-esteem is directly linked to what happens in sport because that is the line of messaging that has developed the core belief for 10+ years.

Belief identification: Detective skills

Directly understanding and targeting the beliefs of the client is the best way for change; however, due to the fixation of these beliefs in the cognitive system, there is an understandable resistance. Clients feel that these beliefs have been with them for years (sometimes decades), and letting go of them feels unfamiliar and unsafe. That is why in most CBT work, clients can only focus on detecting their core beliefs (helpful and unhelpful) after they have understood how the cycle of NATs is operating and have managed to uncover some thinking traps. The analogy of a detective is helpful here: much like a detective, the negative spiral cycle, and the NATs provide clues for the client to realise what is going on. These clues form the breadcrumbs to then uncovering the core beliefs, that is, the motives of cognition and behaviour.

In CBT, we (A) Identify the core belief; (B) Focus on investigating and connecting the formative experiences that have shaped the core belief; and (C) Understand and make sense of the formative experiences. How do we do so? Here are some fundamental therapeutic concepts and practitioner skills:

- **Practitioner and client** the practitioner outlined the exact process they will understand to review the clients' rules about the world, verbalise them, and examine them as if they were *hypotheses* about the world rather than fixed rules (Young et al., 2003). As mentioned above, clients have these core beliefs for years, and when the practitioner suggests that the client think against them, it is often anxiety provoking. The goal is not to say core beliefs are 'right or wrong', rather, it is about different viewpoints to see the same valley. The practitioner *must* have empathy, sensitivity and allow the client to lead. The goal is to *work with* clients, *not against* them.
- **Cultural sensitivity** is essential because there are many examples cited by Padesky and Greenberger (1995) of how practitioners from a culture and/or gender easily misinterpret clients from others. Checkbacks and clarification questions are highly encouraged. Where the practitioner is unfamiliar with the sport/culture/gender/age of the client, formulation should aim to incorporate these details to aid the practitioner.
- **Guided Discovery** via Socratic dialogue is a key technique (see Chapter 7). Via the Socratic dialogue of asking key questions, being curious and facilitating the verbalisation of the clients' thoughts, we get closer to the underlying mechanisms, that is, the core beliefs. For example, if a golfer describes a situation where they were anxious before a putt, the instinct is to reply with 'It sounds like you were scared of missing ...?' That is, empathetic paraphrasing. Through guided discovery and Socratic questions, however, the enquiry could be made by saying, 'What would happen? .... Okay ... if you missed ... what would that mean? ... then what? After you lose the round ... how would that be?'

- **Downward Arrow Technique** (Greenberger & Padesky, 1995) should be used to guide the Socratic questioning. NATs can be highlighted, and clients should be encouraged to examine their NATs (e.g., write alternative responses). Following this, the downward arrow should peel off the layers to identify the underlying assumptions and rules. Reflective prompts and linking behaviour in situations to cognitive intentions are helpful ways for this. For example, NAT – 'I need to work harder' is manifested by the underlying rule of 'Working hard is good' manifested in situations across the individual's life. This is then taken further until a bottom line is reached, that is, the core belief 'If I work hard, I will succeed'. The aim is to clarify statements again, and again, until the client has detected their core belief.

This process is a complex one and does not have a fixed timeline for all clients. For example, between two clients who had perfectionistic tendencies, Client A took 2 sessions to uncover their underlying rules and core beliefs aided with out-of-session tasks. Client B took 40 minutes to identify one, and returned for the next session having 'thought deeply about' another core belief pattern. This is hard to predict and is down to individual differences across personality, reflective ability, metacognitive ability and engagement out of session. Let's look at how to apply this with the case of Annette.

Application Time: Case of Annette

[after the client is familiar with Understanding the Reactions Sheet and has a good awareness of their NATs and the situations that trigger them].

PRACTITIONER: Is it okay if we go through a bit of a digging process?

ANNETTE: Digging? Like for treasure?

PRACTITIONER [SMILES]: Sort of. Remember how we talked about core beliefs lying deep within which leads to those assumptions and then finally the NATs? *[refer back to already conducted psychoeducation].*

ANNETTE [NODS]: Yes … the NATs are those like hot thoughts which go by.

PRACTITIONER: Correct … so most of those NATs and assumptions of yours … are they directed towards yourself? Someone else like an other or are they about the future or the larger world?

ANNETTE [THINKING]: Umm … it depends doesn't it?

PRACTITIONER: Go on [encouraging tone].

ANNETTE: Well like … I feel conflicted … sorry think I am conflicted which makes me feel anxious [client demonstrates thought-emotion separation ability] … like its about me at times … but also my parents, especially mum … because ….

PRACTITIONER [EMPATHETIC AFFIRMATION]: It's okay…, take your time.

ANNETTE: It's like she has only ever cared about me when I win and do well … like before I won juniors it was always a pastime for me … that's what she thought anyways … like I am not complaining she always got me whatever I needed and all … but ….

PRACTITIONER: But …?

ANNETTE: I am only good enough for her attention if I am successful, and now that I am I don't get to decide anymore [angrily].

PRACTITIONER: So … if I said … a core belief could be I am only good enough when I win?

ANNETTE NODS.

PRACTITIONER: But that's not always the case though right ...?
ANNETTE [SHAKING HER HEAD]: In tennis you lose ... and I have a long way to go ... learn and develop ... I know that ... and I love it and I want to ... but its scary.
PRACTITIONER: Of course ... I understand ... what part of it is scary?
ANNETTE: That if I lose ... she [mother] will disengage again ... and somehow she will make it that it's all my fault.

[Annette and the practitioner now have a solid understanding of one core belief achieved through guided discovery through Socratic dialogue which is causing her conflict and distress].

Modifying a negative core belief

Once the client and the practitioner have identified core beliefs, they can move onto identifying specific *negative/unhelpful* core beliefs that accelerate distress by causing NATs. Measuring the fallout from the negative core beliefs is a useful way of (A) Keeping track of them and (B) Engaging in the modification process.

Identifying thinking traps

As discussed above, individuals commonly have patterns of cognitive distortions, that is, thinking styles and shortcuts that unhelpfully distort reality. Some examples of cognitive distortions include mind-reading, labelling, and all-or-nothing thinking which are classic consequences of faulty cognitive information processing when an individual is in distress. For a complete list of thinking traps refer to Leahy et al. (2012). These thinking traps start out as normal fluctuations in thought patterns, but become a triggering issue when they become completely biased at the 'extremes' and/or have a chronic presence. For example, in the footballer's case example, 'What if?' was a form of thinking trap. Specifically, the athlete was chronically engaging in 'Future Predicting/Fortune Telling', that is, the assumption that events or situations will end badly for us.

As CBT work progresses, the client begins to become aware of their NATs and also the thinking traps that they spark. This allows them to be aware of their distorted view of reality. For example, after a few sessions, the footballer might say, 'I scored a penalty, that was good, and then I quietly gave a fist bump and returned to my half ... but then those thoughts came, what if the fans get annoyed with me ... but this time, I was like ... no, you're going to the trap man, the fans are just happy its in the net'. The client begins to identify their key thinking traps. See Table 6.6 on how this process unfolds.

The practitioner can also employ certain techniques to aid the client in their process of identification of NATs:

- **Imagery**: The practitioner can use imagery to allow the client to recreate situations that trigger thinking traps to engage in the process of avoiding the thinking traps and seeing what that outcome looks like. For example, if an athlete is catastrophising before the results of a selection game come out, the practitioner may want them to imagine the situation. Identify the thinking traps, which may be along the lines of 'I might not get selected, and that's the end of my career'. This is a *rational* thought process. It *may* be detrimental to their career, so do not dismiss it.

Rather, questioning could allow the athlete that the probability that it will 'end' careers is smaller than the thinking trap is making it seem.

- **Ratings and Percentage Assignment**: The practitioner could also actively encourage the individual to measure the effect of the thinking trap as it happens. For example, if the client is catastrophising, the practitioner could literally ask the client to rate how likely is it that negative outcome will happen (i.e., not selected). Then they could go on to ask the client to rate how likely is that their career will end from this one event. The client might say 30% or 80%. Depending on the rating, the practitioner needs to engage the appropriate intervention.
- **Experiments**: The practitioner could conduct small, immediate experiments to show that the thinking traps can be false. For example, if the client is engaging in Mind-Reading in the form of 'I know that my manager doesn't rate me, and most people do not like me. I can tell what they are thinking when they see me'. The practitioner could conduct an immediate experiment by writing something down (e.g., 'I think X has a great taste in fashion') on a piece of paper, and asking the client to predict what was written down. The client will likely be unable to say what was written down, and therefore disputes the thinking trap. Mind reading is often a form of projection. Clients often believe others see them as they view themselves and this is often present with low or unstable self-esteem and/or self-efficacy. The focus is to dispute the thinking trap to allow the client to be aware of their own thoughts in a non-distorted manner, instead of attempting to predict the thoughts of others. In the example here, the client could find a middle ground of 'I don't know what they are thinking of me unless they tell me'. This reduces the extreme interpretation and also the extreme emotional reaction (McKay et al., 2011).

Most thinking traps either have excessive focus on external things or excessive self-focus. For example, an all-or-nothing thinking trap interprets situations to be extremely positive or extremely negative, whereas, personalising is an excessive self-focus where the individual blames (or credits) themselves for the totality of a situation which had many factors (e.g., I am the only reason my team won/lost).

Avoiding thinking traps: Weighing evidence

The most common method for modifying NATs, thinking traps and ultimately core beliefs is weighing evidence, that is, analysing the outcomes and concrete evidence relating to a situation to challenge distorted pictures of reality. For example, a client catastrophises and remarks, 'nothing ever goes right for me'. They then go on to list current and past setbacks/failures to support this thinking trap, thereby falling further into the cycle. This then makes them 'prove' their case and conclude that their future endeavours will also fail. This thought pattern then turns into a self-fulfilling prophecy where the belief drives behaviour causing performance instability and low confidence. This causes a few setbacks, which triggers the thinking trap again.

The practitioner needs to engage in a step-by-step process to facilitate the client to weigh the evidence. A helpful metaphor is that the practitioner and client are walking down the grocery store aisle of evidence. The client has already determined that what they need is not available here. But the practitioner points out each specific shelf, and eventually takes some evidence items into the basket to challenge the thinking trap in an empathetic manner. Let's look at Mo's case.

Application Time: Case of Mo

[this is to be conducted after the client has measured some of their thinking traps. The practitioner works to build a system of refuting and avoiding some of those thinking traps.]

PRACTITIONER: So now we are going to engage in a different type of thinking ....
MO: You mean like positive thinking?
PRACTITIONER [SMILING]: Well ... not exactly ... the more accurate term is realistic thinking because we will try to consider all areas of proof on those thoughts and thinking traps that pop into your head.
MO: Like argument?
PRACTITIONER: Yes indeed!
MO: Okay ... this should be interesting, but I am game.
PRACTITIONER: So, could you tell me one of the core beliefs we have uncovered?
MO: I always have to push to find that extra 1% to be better.
PRACTITIONER: Absolutely, and this belief in and of itself is not bad because it has motivated and pushed you to achieve a great many things.
MO: Yes ... but its over pushing if that makes sense?
PRACTITIONER: Yes ... so when did you move to the new club and the big contract?
MO: Three months ago.
PRACTITIONER: How would you describe how the club and team management and the players have responded to you?
MO: Very good actually ... I know what is expected of me ... I feel welcomed, they take care of me.
PRACTITIONER: How many matches have you played?
MO: Umm ... good question [laughs] ... I think six maybe, not sure.
PRACTITIONER: No issues, let's take 6 ... what is your role in the team?
MO: Playmaker and finisher from the attacking midfield.
PRACTITIONER: What would you say your passing percentage has been?
MO: No clue sorry [smiles].
PRACTITIONER: Hear me out, I pulled up some numbers ... compared to last year ... you are 2.1% down .... Your shots on target is 1.17% up ... but your goals to shots on target ratio is about 8% down.
MO: Hmm ... seems about right ... I haven't scored my first goal yet ... but I did get a couple of assists.
PRACTITIONER: 3 actually.
MO: Oh ....
PRACTITIONER: So have you been as you described 'off the pace'?
MO: Umm ... not really ... but there are areas to improve ... but not really ... so uh ... hmm ... [confused] why was I thinking that way?

[Mo refutes his own thinking trap of personalising and black-white thinking caused by his drive to perfectionism core belief. Practitioner uses performance indicator evidence, see below].

Often, difficulties arise over what is the 'evidence' and the process of weighing out thinking traps. Typically, the client has a resistance to the process of weighing the evidence. This often represents itself with 'I understand but ...' or 'That makes sense but ...'. The therapist is seeking facts to support and/or disconfirm the thinking traps.

This information can be gained in a structured way with the forms of evidence measured by either the client or practitioner or both. They are listed below:

- **Conjectural Data:** Thehe practitioner works with the client to evaluate potential alternate scenarios and situations from impressions and general trends of what the client focuses on. For example, the client may engage in all-or-nothing thinking by stating 'I must get that contract or it will go downhill'. The practitioner could engage in a line of questioning on 'What might happen if you get the contract?' and follow that up with 'What might happen if you don't?' and weigh both sides.
- **Observational Data:** What the client/practitioner has noticed which may point to an indisputable fact that the client is making incorrect inferences. In sport this may be a match performance analysis video/highlight/news article/interviews/game or training observation.
- **Confirmational Data:** This is the process where the client is encouraged to find indisputable facts to support their thinking traps. The practitioner then challenges and finds flaws in the evidence that the client comes up with to support distorted thinking like a lawyer conducting a cross-examination; however, this process must be grounded in empathy, affirmation and must be preceded by clear goals of why the practitioner is engaging in this process. For example, the client says 'I am no good under the pressure of competition. I had to throw 80 m or above to be safe, I bottled it'. The client displays the event reports where they threw the javelin 79.6 m, 79.8 m, and 79.9 m in successive throws securing gold. The practitioner disputes that by identifying that 'bottling it' implies a complete failure, not a miss by 0.1 m. They could also highlight that the silver medallist threw 79.7 m as their best, and therefore the client was better than the competition.

Confirmational evidence is the best practice recommendation for weighing thinking traps; however, it may not always be available. The practitioner is recommended to go step-by-step, starting from Conjectural to Observational to Confirmation to thoroughly disconfirm and dispute the thinking trap together with the client.

Reflective Task – can you go through the case example above to isolate the types of data sourced and how it was used to dispute the thinking trap?

The goal is to weigh and balance out the thinking traps. This aligns thinking and cognitions accurately with the reality of the external world. That is – the reality of an event A, matches with the perception of event A. This reduces distorted thinking and consequent emotional distress. The goal is to explore the inner experience and perception via thinking traps and disputing them to enable the client to gain a realistic assumption of the world around them (Dobson and Dobson, 2018).

Developing a new core belief

After the practitioner and the client have sufficiently disputed and modified the unhelpful, negative belief, there is a gap in the belief system. This gap is to be supplemented by a new belief which is more helpful to the client and allows a more functional belief system to operationalise, which helps regulate the pre-existing negative core belief and thinking traps even more. A useful metaphor to understand this process is to imagine

Table 6.7 Existing core beliefs – Mo's case

Existing Core Belief (Mo's case): 'I have to be perfect all the time'	
Advantages	*Disadvantages*
1 I will always have an extra gear	1 Not every day will be a highlight reel in sport, so I put extra pressure on myself 2 I can't be my own self 3 I feel stressed a lot and struggle to switch off from sport

a bucket containing blue liquid (negative core belief). Once the process of modifying has begun, we have poked holes at the bottom. The blue liquid is leaking out, but with the process of developing new core beliefs, we are pouring yellow liquid in. There will be a crossover point where both blue and yellow liquids are present, before the holes in the bottom are closed, and only the yellow liquid remains. There are specific therapeutic techniques to engage the client in this process of developing a new core belief.

Thought-balancing

Imagine a see-saw or a pros-cons list. Using the thought-balancing technique, the practitioner facilitates the client to isolate the advantages and disadvantages of both the existing, under modification negative thought, and the new core belief that is being developed. Through this, clients learn to revise their self-defeating, and triggered NATs and beliefs to alter core beliefs in subtle but important ways. This can be done in a rudimentary manner using a whiteboard or a chart with the client leading the way (see Table 6.7).

The practitioner asks the client for examples at every point that they make until they run out of points for either side. The client gains an understanding that 'I have to be perfect all the time' is actually not completely helpful, which allows them to actively focus on disputing the thinking traps associated with it. The practitioner can then explore what could be an alternative belief.

Application Time: Case of Annette

PRACTITIONER: Why do you think you have the urge to be perfect all the time?

ANNETTE: Because … mistakes finish people off in this sport … I gotta be on it every single time.

PRACTITIONER: I understand. To you, what does being 'on it' look like?

ANNETTE: Umm … talking to my coaches, understanding my role, being physically and mentally ready for the match … knowing the opposition … working on the tactics ….

PRACTITIONER: Right yes … so do you have to be (emphasis) absolutely perfect in every single one of those things to be successful?

ANNETTE: Umm … no … you actually will not be … there will always be a better way but that comes in hindsight you know … you have left something out there that could've been better … but you gotta try you know what I mean?

PRACTITIONER: So, the emphasis is more on to be perfect?

ANNETTE: Kinda yeah, push to be perfect.

PRACTITIONER: What if we develop that belief then?

ANNETTE: I don't follow.

PRACTITIONER: What if instead of the belief being 'I have to be perfect all the time', we tweak it to 'I will always work hard to do everything I can to strive for perfection'.

ANNETTE: So ... I still push ... and be relentless ... but I know being perfect won't always be possible?

PRACTITIONER: Yes ... to use a metaphor, you know the car's top speed is 250 km/h. And you will do everything to reach it ... but sometimes you won't quite get to the perfect top speed ... but doing everything you can to get there puts you in a better position anyways.

ANNETTE: Ah ... I get it ... also takes some pressure off me.

Through that process, the client understands that the idea of perfection was striving for perfection, not being perfect in outcome. By doing so, we have modified the negative belief and developed an authentic core belief. This belief will also allow the development of a growth mindset because the client will adopt a high motivational drive to strive for perfection, but failing to do so will aim to understand areas to improve.

Some clients find the advantages and disadvantages technique of thought balancing to be oversimplistic and difficult to engage with. An alternative technique is the Intention v/s Counter-intentions process (Hanna, 2002). Intentions are actions that align with beliefs, whereas counter-intentions are unintended, non-aligned actions that reflect conflicting values and goals in the individual's life. For example, a racing driver pushes too hard despite being in the lead and eventually crashes out of the race. This is a counter-intention coming through trying to be perfect and finish P1. The intention and counter-intention is then discussed in detail and re-evaluated.

Let us look at the Annette's case to understand how this unfolds in a session.

Application Time: Case of Annette

[after we have explored Annette's core beliefs and uncovered thinking traps, we try to measure and engage in thought balancing].

PRACTITIONER: So there is a limbo isn't there?

ANNETTE: Yeah ... very much so ....

PRACTITIONER: So when we tried to balance those thoughts, did you feel like there was a tug of war going on in the head?

ANNETTE: Yes ... quite a lot actually ....

PRACTITIONER: So what are your intentions that align with that belief? [i.e., belief of 'I am only worthy if I am successful'].

ANNETTE: Well ... I always push myself to be successful which makes me feel that I am good enough.

PRACTITIONERS: And when you fail?

ANNETTE: I feel like rubbish ... my mum gives me a hard time ... the media gives me a hard time ... they go from 'darling' to 'desperate' [making a face].

PRACTITIONER: Of course ... which affects us doesn't it?

ANNETTE [NODS SADLY]: Yeah ... and it's like that makes that belief stronger like ... like it digs inside my head and goes on and on.

PRACTITIONER: Of course ... but tennis is different for you isn't it? Remember that drawing you made? [data measured before] ....

ANNETTE: Yeah ... it's just me, my racquet, the ball and the court ... it's simple ... it's free.

PRACTITIONER: So ... the belief is pushing one agenda whereas your true need is completely different? *[Intention v/s Counter-intention highlight].*

ANNETTE: Oh my god.

PRACTITIONER [EMPATHETIC AFFIRMATION].

ANNETTE: No wonder it's a fight inside my head! That makes so much sense.

[Annette is then given out-of-session work and a curated intervention so that this verbal learning is put into behavioural practice. The goal is to allow her restructuring to occur where she can accept that life decisions are accompanied by doubts and honesty rather than complete certainty].

Defining and clarifying perception

A key part in developing alternative core beliefs is working with the client's perception of a negative belief-reality link. This is commonly represented by the imprecision and overtly negative language used by the client to describe themselves or their difficulties. For example, the client (a cricketer) was rested by the team for a tour but perceives that 'I've been dropped ... they didn't want me and see me as a failure'.

PRACTITIONER: When you say failure ... because they rested you ... do you mean failure as a cricketer and a person?

CLIENT: As a cricketer.

PRACTITIONER: How does being rested make you feel like a failure?

CLIENT: Well ... makes me feel I've been dropped from the team.

PRACTITIONER: Of course. You really wanted to be with the team, but you mentioned that the selectors had told you specifically that you were being rested to not overload your back?

CLIENT: I mean yeah ... but they were being nice.

PRACTITIONER: How so?

CLIENT: I just feel like they are dropping me.

PRACTITIONER: But we know that feelings are not facts ... could you identify what thinking trap was being triggered?

CLIENT: I guess I am reading their minds ... even though they told me I was being rested.

PRACTITIONER: Yes, we can try to figure out why you think you were dropped ... why was that?

CLIENT: Because I went for loads of runs last over of that last t20 and lost us the game ....

PRACTITIONER: But you had the second-highest wickets and second-best economy in the series ... so what's an accurate description of the situation.

CLIENT: I mean ... okay ... I guess, I felt tired during that last over, probably due to my injury and my physio knows I played through the pain ... the selectors decided to rest me so that I don't get back on the physio bed and have me fit for the next series.

As we can see, the terms used by the client were leading to the maintenance of the negative core belief. Clients may complain that these are semantic games (e.g., 'we are just using different words'). This is crucial, however, because using negative words to define ourselves are overgeneralisations and self-labelling, which reinforce the negative core belief. Semantics also tell the practitioner the extent to which the new belief developed is stable or not. Being semantically precise helps the clients to be clear and accurate about events ('I have been rested' not 'dropped'), and what can be done about it ('I can focus on rehabbing my back and preparing for the next tour'). Negative semantic self-labelling directly compromises the metacognitive evaluation of a situation leading to threat perceptions. This reduces goal-directed behaviour and lowers resilience in the face of setbacks.

Reframing: Playing different tactics/Constructing alternative explanations

Reframing is noticing thinking patterns and constructing alternative interpretations/explanations about any situation. The client is typically asked to (A) Describe the situation; (B) Highlight 2 or more alternative explanations of a situation; and (C) Assign realistic probability of the likelihood of that situation being real. Let us look at Mo's case example;

Application Time: Case of Mo

PRACTITIONER: What makes you think it was as you said a 'flop'?
MO: I did not score.
PRACTITIONER: Fair enough … but you got an assist, played the full 90 minutes and the team won 2–0.
MO: Yeah, but I missed an easy goal ….
PRACTITIONER: What was your role in the team?
MO: Playmaker and finisher … okay I get it … I did the first part not the second ….
PRACTITIONER: So it maybe was not as bad as I thought it was.
MO: But people are still feeling sorry for me … at the hairdressers … the restaurant.
PRACTITIONER: Hmm … okay … but are there no other explanations for getting those responses?
MO: Well … maybe they appreciated me and wanted to support me before I got my first goal.
PRACTITIONER: I get the sense you don't really believe that statement.
MO: Not yet … but I mean … I want to get goals.
PRACTITIONER: To sum up … just stay with me here … you had assists, high accuracy passing, played full 90 … but did not get a goal … and the thought focused on others thinking you were not good enough … any thoughts on that summary?
MO: It wasn't really others … I am putting pressure on myself for more …too much too quick which is … being difficult.

Reattribution

Reattribution is to process of facilitating clients to remove themselves from the situation and review the many contributions to a good/adverse outcome. It is important to remember both good and bad outcomes here, because sometimes high-functioning individuals undersell their contributions to a good result as well. On the other hand, clients with self-critical thoughts often blame themselves for causing the bad outcome seeing themselves as 'fully responsible'. This process of self-blame is often common in negative emotions and/or guilt-based presentations. For example, a badminton player may say she is guilty that she is 'injured and not on it yet because it's unfair to my doubles partner' and has a cognition that she is failing her partner. This is also reflected in the client's assumption of control (i.e., she controls all that her doubles partner does).

Attribution theory states that individuals perceive the causes of everyday events to be attributed to two broad factors:

1 **Internal Factors** (i.e., behaviour/outcome is caused by something within the person). This is known as Dispositional Attribution and is typically linked to intelligence, ability, talent, personality, attitude, effort and other internal characteristics. For example, the client trains as hard as everyone else in the squad, had better training adherence, but thinks 'I cannot succeed because I do not work hard enough'.
2 **External Factors** (i.e., behaviour/outcome is caused by something outside the person such as the environment or situation). This is known as Situational Attribution and is typically linked to group/team dynamics, norms, luck, weather, equipment, turf and other external characteristics which may not have a relation. For example, a cricket batsman loses his wicket and says 'The pitch was bad, I did not make a mistake', even when he was aware of how the pitch would play.

The maladaptive core beliefs typically attribute events to either extreme of dispositional or situational attribution and distort reality. In the example above, the pitch may not have been that bad, but the cricketer engages in situational attribution to protect self-esteem. When we are developing a new belief with the client, we actively engage in the process of reattribution. This strengthens the new adaptive core belief. During the process of modification of maladaptive core beliefs and replacement with new core beliefs, there is often resistance. This is natural because although the older belief system is maladaptive, it is familiar and provides the impression that it is more controllable. Reattribution allows *appropriate accountability*, that is, the client does not label themselves to be causing an outcome when it is not relevant. It does not mean that they are to let themselves off the hook for every behaviour and outcome. A helpful technique to facilitate the client through the process of reattribution is through attribution mapping (see Figure 7.2).

Strengthening a new core belief

Once we have moulded a new core belief, there is still work to do; however, unlike muscles which can be strengthened via a gym program, the cognitive system is more tricky to work with. So why do we need to strengthen beliefs? And equally (if not more importantly), how do we do it?

The new core belief is fragile, and often fallible in triggering situations as the client defaults to the familiar older belief system to guide cognitions and behaviour. The process is quite similar to skill acquisition in a way. Let's imagine that a tennis player changes their grip. During intense moments in training and in competition, they forget their new grip and revert to the older one. This is not because they are not trying nor are they unaware, but simply because they have not become habituated yet. Replace the 'grip' with 'belief system', and we understand why clients sometime struggle to automatically change their default beliefs and use the newer belief systems.

Developing and strengthening new core beliefs often go hand in hand, but we have separated them here for clarity for the practitioner as they develop these skills. The following sections highlight processes that the practitioner must adopt to help strengthen their clients' beliefs.

Practice before exposure

Athletes spend hours *training* and developing a new skill before executing it in competitive match play. Similarly, in CBT work, we must see how the newly developed core belief works in contained, protected simulated practice phases with the client before triggering situations. *This is the process of measurement and intervention in equal measure.*

The empathetic and strong relational contact between the practitioner and the client (see Chapter 4) provides a safe 'training' space for this. At this stage of CBT work, both the client and the practitioner should have an effective grasp of the nature of triggers and triggering situations for the client. The therapist can engage in the following techniques to allow the client to take their newly developed belief system for a test drive within the safe and non-threatening environment of a session. Some examples of techniques (listed in order of application) are:

- **Verbal discussion** is the space where the client and practitioner engage in a verbal, non-judgemental, dialogue about hypothetical situations on how they may respond to a specific trigger situation with (A) their old belief system and then (B) their new belief system. They can then review what the differences in responses are and some challenges. For example, if the old belief system was extremely perfectionistic and rigid, how would the client respond with their new belief system of viewing perfection as a process and failure as a part of that process when they make a major mistake?
- **Metaphors** are a highly efficient way of extending the verbal discussion to having deeper meaning and experiential elements. For example, if the client with the perfectionistic tendencies keeps stating that 'it's a game of inches and I'm missing them' as part of his older core belief, the newer belief system could replace that with, 'It's a game of inches, and I am inching closer to where I want to be'. By metaphorically replacing just the outcome ('I am missing them') with process ('Inching closer to where I want to be') the client shrinks the uncontrollable and has a structured plan to work with.
- **Imagery** is used because verbal discussions often cannot replicate the emotional upheaval from triggering emotions. Working with the client's imagery is a situationally relevant way to identify how the client can apply their new belief system to the situation. For the example above, the practitioner can create a vivid imagery of the client actually committing the mistake, before inviting the client to continue that imagery and its aftermath, but looking at how the new core belief functions. *In certain cases, once the core belief is strong enough, the practitioner may also use videos to replicate the situation.*

- **Role-play**. Sport is a visceral setting, and role plays are part of simulations. Role-plays can take many forms and can be used after the client is comfortable with applying their new core belief at the verbal discussion, metaphor and imagery level. Role plays can replicate dialogue with the practitioner taking up the role of a parent, coach, rival, fan, negative internal voice, or anything relevant to the client. Role plays can also be simulated within the sporting environment where the client engages in a low-intensity sport skills training in a naturalistic manner with the practitioner observing. When a triggering situation arrives (i.e., making a mistake), the practitioner intervenes becoming the older belief system as the client debates and pauses before applying their new belief system.

The techniques listed above *must* be applied in the order of sequence. This is because they are progressively deeper in their level of immersion. If the client is finding it difficult to engage their new core belief at the verbal discussion level, it is unlikely that they will do it at the imagery or role play level. The key is not to rush the client because doing so will cause anxiety from the older core belief and regress the client into questioning their new core belief and reverting to the use of the older core belief.

7 Interventions

Cognitive behaviour therapy (CBT) tools and interventions are used to facilitate change in an enduring and meaningful way. Designing and implementing interventions is how the practitioner enacts that change with clients. This enables the client to understand and work beneficially on unhelpful thoughts, feelings, and behaviours. Interventions in CBT can be directed at the cognitive, behavioural, or at the emotional/physiological level, depending on the particular client presentation. It is important to customise and tailor the tools and interventions for the unique situations of the client and the formulation (see Chapter 5). We now examine each of these elements and showcase how to apply them through the case applications.

Introduction to facilitating change in CBT

Facilitating change through intervention in CBT needs to begin from the client formulation and reference to the literature. As practitioners working in a sporting context, often what we need is more information on the 'how' than the 'why' to *practise effectively* and apply CBT. This is also the case for our clients who are not necessarily interested in what the academic literature says about the use of CBT in sport and performance. They need clear processes and strategies that make sense for them and their situation. For example, knowing that the literature demonstrates the effectiveness of CBT for perfectionism in sporting contexts isn't as useful to a client as being able to highlight to them that their negative automatic thoughts (NATs) around perfectionism (e.g., *'I must be the best'* or *'I should make every shot'*) are a fruitful area for therapeutic work in which we can help them alter that negative Self-Talk and to understand how such thoughts are maintaining psychological difficulties that translate into performance issues (see McArdle & Moore, 2012, for a full example of how CBT works in perfectionism in sport). As trainee and practitioner sport psychologists, what you really want to know is what is it about your work with someone that brings sustainable positive change and how can you ensure that outcome for those with whom you work? We need to develop an individual specific case formulation and then draw on techniques that focus on the individual client's need. The following sections in this chapter will provide you with clear guidance and information on how to use a variety of tools and techniques, effectively resulting in a transition to client self-help.

By employing interventions aimed at behavioural and cognitive aspects of the client's experience, we use the process of guided discovery, allowing the client to see those links between the four factors outlined in Chapters 3, 4, and 5. As a practitioner, you will need to decide where to aim your intervention work and that will depend on

DOI: 10.4324/9781003274513-9

the client's presentation and your relationship with them. You could choose to start with cognitive elements of your client's presentation or you could choose to work with the behavioural aspects. Running alongside these, you'll also need to consider the role of physical strategies and the use of homework.

The following sections consider these different approaches and will also provide guidance on when and why you would use them. For each area of intervention, we follow the same structure for ease of application in applied practice: (1) What is this intervention? (2) When to use it? (3) Things to do for implementing it; and (4) Analysis of application using a case.

Behavioural interventions

Let's consider the 'B' in 'CBT' for a while. As we have outlined already (see Chapter 3, 4, and 5) there are links between our thoughts, feelings, physical reactions and behaviours. Knowing this link exists helps individuals to be aware of and understand their own reactions. It supplies them with a clear map or structure to navigate, reflect on, understand, and change their situation and experience. The Behavioural Principle, which CBT inherited from Behavioural Therapy, is that behaviour (what we do) is crucial in maintaining or in changing psychological states (see Chapter 1). From an intervention perspective, starting with behaviour is often a good strategy because behaviour has a strong influence on thought and emotion. Crucially, changing what you do (your behaviour) is often a powerful way of changing how you think and feel. For clients in the sporting arena who are used to the focus being on their behaviour or their performance, this can also be a comfortable place to begin. This can also be a good place to start with your own self-practice and self-reflection because as Christine Padesky (1996) says '*To fully understand the process of the therapy, there is no substitute for using cognitive therapy methods on oneself*'.

Behavioural activation

Lewinsohn developed behavioural activation (BA) to treat depression. Lewinsohn's theory is based on instrumental behaviour where behaviours typical of depressed mood do not allow room for positive reinforcement and are maintained by the individual's withdrawal from positive reinforcement opportunities. To enact change you want to engage in incremental positive reinforcement to alter behaviour for a knock-on effect on cognition. Practitioners in sport will frequently encounter athletes who are experiencing anxiety associated with major life events and depressive symptoms, with some leading to a full-blown major depressive diagnosis. These could be within their sporting career such as an acute injury, or a transitional phase of their sporting career, or major contractual loss or could even be placed outside that sporting arena in their everyday life. These are presentations that are suitable for behavioural work from the outset.

BA is a structured, brief psychotherapeutic approach. BA increases the client's engagement with activities that are related to mastery and pleasure while decreasing their engagement with activities that are maintaining the low mood. We start with working with the client to identify and modify issues that are limiting them or preventing them from increasing their control beliefs and pleasure related activities. BA works at the level of changing behaviours, promoting the idea that changing what people do can change how they feel. BA also highlights that sometimes the way we cope with events can lead to more difficulties over time, with decisions about what activities to engage in based on how we're feeling leading to continued depression. For a thorough coverage of BA, Dimidjian et al.'s (2011) paper is a good resource.

When using BA as an intervention with the client, a clear understanding of the behavioural maintenance activities is needed within the formulation process (see the CB-Sport Formulation model in Chapter 5), because the short-term coping strategies that people chose will ultimately lead to the maintenance of their depressed mood (e.g., isolating from partner). The emphasis will be on activity monitoring and scheduling, on avoidance and escape behaviours (e.g., starting with a reduction of complete isolation from partner, and being in the same physical space as them), on emphasising a routine and on behavioural strategies for targeting worry and rumination. This works as restructuring behaviour through small doses of positive reinforcement to facilitate change. We have split some processes of BA as intervention below:

- Understanding and educating the client on their avoidance strategies is important as a first step. There are tools you can use to help clients to identify their avoidance strategies and to help them build more reinforcing behaviours into their everyday lives. Measures are readily available for your use on recognising avoidance, activity scheduling and triggers (see Chapter 6). See the resources on TRAP/TRAC, Avoidance and Activity Scheduling below as well. Some avoidance strategies may not be conceived as avoidance strategies by the client. For example, athletes often overcompensate their depressive feelings by overtraining. When this does not lead to an automatic improvement, they hyper-focus on their low mood. Overtraining also causes greater tiredness, which when combined with low emotional mood, maintains the behaviours and depressive symptoms complicating mental health problems.
- Rather than expect that your client will need to feel motivated before making a change, what you are asking them to do is to make that change and increase their level of and ability to act from the outside. So, we ask clients to follow a written plan, for example, an activity schedule and we monitor their progress, highlighting consequences of increased activation. This is the process of *Activity Scheduling*. In this way, we work with the client using scheduling and functional analysis to assign incrementally more difficult tasks to move them towards full participation in activities.
- When working with BA the plan will be individualised to your client. You can begin with psychoeducation around depression and low mood and explain your reasons for working behaviourally (cf. Beck, 1979a; 1979b). Work with reflective questions to help the client understand where their unhelpful behaviours are placed within the CBT four-factor model and how it is causing the distress to continue.

TRAP ≫ TRAC intervention technique

TRAP stands for **T**rigger, **R**esponse, **A**voidance, **P**attern and, using this mnemonic with clients, can help them identify their own TRAPs. To engage in the TRAP technique within BA, we use the following steps (but customise it for the client!):

1. **Identify** the Trigger (see Chapters 5–6 for measures and techniques)
2. Understand *all* the dimensions of the **Response** (responses may be singular or have multiple component elements)

3 Explore **Avoidance** (i.e., the behaviours the client engages in to avoid the negative consequences of the trigger). Note: the avoidance pattern is any behaviour that delays or protects the client from the negative consequences (i.e., allows them to *avoid it).* It may manifest as over engagement as well.
4 Discovery and brief on the **Pattern** (i.e., the sequence that leads to the trigger-response and avoidance, and the behaviours that follow and maintain the cycle).

Once you've helped your client to identify their TRAPs, you can help them get back on **TRAC**. This change requires using the 'doses' of BA, to change the pattern to *Alternate Coping Strategies (i.e.,* what they engage with instead of avoiding). Let's look at the case of Annette to understand this in practice. This work can then lead to *Activity Scheduling* where you work with the client to plan what to do and when. This is especially effective with athletes who are used to training plans and targets. The practitioner then asks the client to carry out those behaviours at those times whether or not they feel motivated to do them. By doing so, we use the principles of BA to direct their behaviour and their ability to act from the outside. A continuous self and practitioner monitoring loop is also tracking their progress and the effect that changing their behaviour has on their mood. See Lundqvist (2020) for a case report on using BA for an elite athlete following career termination.

Application Time: Case of Annette

If you remember, Annette is a star performer in junior tennis. She has competed well, and is currently waiting on a wildcard for a 'Futures' competition, but is not sure if she will get it and does not feel fully ready for it yet. Her mother insists that this is the perfect time to transition both from a sport and commercial perspective. The practitioner uses the TRAP > TRAC to see the avoidance in Annette's response to the situation. She has been avoiding her coach, mother and reports that she has not put her full effort into training for a few days. Using Socratic questioning (see Chapter 6) the practitioner finds examples of avoidance, while also being mindful of the client keeping 'busy' to avoid something else. These include spending time with her friends and inviting them to her training environment, and going to her physio and stating that her side strain is paining her more than it actually is. Annette is engaging in these avoidance activities because in the short-term avoidance can make her feel better, and she justifies it to herself as being the reason she does not get the wildcard. Annette thinks *'If I try to train now I'll only mess it up, so I'm better to wait'* and *'I'll feel more like planning what to do tomorrow'*. In the short-term, avoidance helps and prevents Annette from feeling overwhelmed and guilty; however, there are longer term more negative consequences in that she will fall further behind and this will affect her overall wellbeing. What Annette is doing is falling into a **TRAP** due to low mood and anxious apprehension.

Following questioning with Annette, she identified the Trigger was the unknown of the wildcard; her Response was ruminating on the problem and avoiding considering it. This response included feeling overwhelmed and thinking negatively. Her Avoidance Pattern was to postpone engaging with her training to the intensity she usually does, which also reduced her enjoyment of tennis. In the short term, she could then put things out of her mind, but the longer-term consequences were that she felt behind with her training and the time left to her to work on improving her level of play. The result of this was increased anxiety.

The practitioner now moved to help Annette get on TRAC. Annette's triggers and responses remained the same, but through questioning and discussion helped Annette to develop Alternative Coping strategies, (i.e., what she could do instead of avoiding). In Annette's case, this was speaking to her coach and asking her friends to be a normal support system instead of discussing tennis all the time as well as understanding how she would respond and plan in case she got the wildcard. Using activity scheduling, Annette used her fitness tracker to check her exertion level and heart-rate variability to confirm that she was giving it her all in training. This also led to an improvement in her skills, which acted as the positive reinforcement.

Note: Three months later, Annette did indeed gain the wildcard. She has used the TRAC to plan for the tournament and also agreed with her mother to keep commercial engagements and the 'hype' to a minimum. She ended up going till the Quarters and achieving her target of executing what she trained for.

Reflective Exercise

- Reflecting on situations or major events in your own life over the last twelve months, try to write out your own TRAP and TRAC forms. Would your response to these events have been different had you taken a behavioural approach?
- Think about a client you've worked with in the past and try to map out TRAC and TRAP forms for them. Can you see how these could have changed how you worked with the client?

Behavioural experiments

Behavioural experiements through the CBT process serve an important cognitive and behavioural purpose testing the validity of the client's thoughts, beliefs, and actions. Our clients continue with the behaviour and thoughts because they have helped in some way. This makes the client feel that their thoughts or behaviour are valid in some way. Behavioural experiments are planned experiential activities to test the validity and helpfulness of these thoughts and actions. They are an information-gathering process to confirm older beliefs/thoughts or check how the newer restructured ones are operating. Much like science experiments, they show evidence to support theories- both to the practitioner and the client. We adhere to the following steps to design behavioural activities and then use Table 7.1 to implement and track them:

1. **Select target:** This may be a cognition or behaviour. But the practitioner needs to clearly and collaboratively define it with the client.
2. **Design an experiment:** Thehe experiments can be of any kind. It may expose the client to a controlled, specific, situation that will cause an interaction between their cognitive/behavioural systems and the environment. For example, a client might think that they are not good enough to win. The practitioner designs an experiment where the client looks at the statistics of her previous record to validate whether that thought is accurate. The focus is to *design an experiment that is aligned with the target*. For further reading, see 'Oxford Guide to Behavioural Experiments in Cognitive Therapy' (Bennett-Levy et al., 2004).

Table 7.1 Behavioural experiment tracker worksheet

Target	*Experiment*	*Prediction (How Likely It Will Happen 0–10)*	*Actual Outcome in Sport and Life*	*What Did We Learn?*
Mo's performance pressure	Using instructional Self-Talk process before training	It will make a little difference The fans and team will still expect stuff from me	Mo runs instructional Self-Talk and sees that he is less concerned about how fans will react compared to before.	Mo reports that 'I could think about what was going on the pitch and not in the stands. It sort of … reduces that tightness and stress a bit'

3 **Pre-experiment prediction:** This is the process where the individual is asked to predict the outcome of the experiment before the experiment is actually conducted. This allows the individual's pre-conceived notions that are attached to the unhelpful action/thoughts to be clearly stated. When the experiment results arrive, it is easier to check back on how those pre-conceived notions stand up with the evidence.
4 **Set a timeline for the experiment:** Often having a timeline for these experiments ensures clarity and increases adherence to the experiment. It also provides a clear roadmap of when to conduct it and to discuss any issues. For example, for pre-competitive anxiety, it is hardly relevant to conduct experiments to challenge self-critical thoughts post-competition if the target is pre-competition triggers.
5 **Set multiple trials of the experiment:** If only conducted once the strongly held pre-conceived notions may be seen as a 'one-time thing' and may not be sufficient for change post intervention.
6 **Measure the outcome of the experiment:** This allows the client to understand that where the pre-conceived notions and the actual evidence mismatch and how to proceed. The measurement should be done with established measures (see Chapter 6).
7 **Compare to prediction:** This allows the individual to see how their predictions may be faulty and not match up to the reality of a situation and its corresponding thoughts and behaviours (see Figure 7.1).
8 **Lessons learned:** This allows the individual to review the discrepancy which allows the shift and restructuring of the alternative thoughts and behaviours.

The practitioner should never assume that just because the behavioural experiment has proved a success, the change will be permanent. While evaluating the data from the experience, the client may just deflect and return to their maintenance cycle. Therefore, avoid constructing behavioural experiments in absolute success or failure terms. The outcome of the success/failure alone should not determine it. The protocol must state that information gathered from the experiment should reveal new aspects of the maintenance cycle or elements that could road test the process (see Bennett-Levy et al., 2004). Another process of experimentation could be observation oriented instead of the client conducting the action themselves. For example, Mo and the practitioner could watch the game highlights focusing on how the crowd reacts to Mo's mistakes and successes. This can dispute Mo's belief that he is letting down the fans.

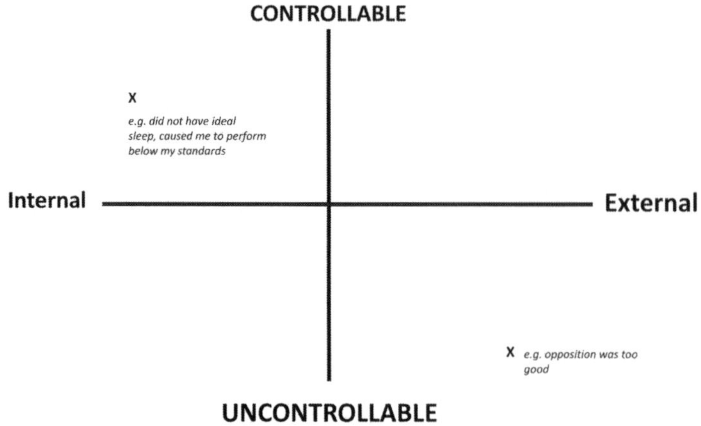

Figure 7.1 Attribution Graph

Tinkering with thoughts: Cognitive interventions

In the previous section, we were working from the premise that changing behaviour can change thoughts and feelings. In this section, we go beyond actions and into the thoughts that fuel them. Through cognitive interventions, we understand what the cognitive thought process is, the underlying assumptions and core beliefs that are fuelling it and attempt to restructure these. We will outline many cognitive interventions and showcase how to apply them. It is up to the practitioner to review their client specific formulation (see Chapter 5) to understand which one is an appropriate intervention technique. At times, cognitive interventions may involve multiple techniques, each more complex than the other diving deeper into the cognitive system. Thinking of it like working with your client to teach them how to play the piano. You start simple, by learning the positioning of the keys and the notes they represent, then learn simple melodies before progressing to play short pieces, then ultimately concertos. Similarly, we engage in the following sequence:

1 Building awareness reflectively;
2 Engaging client-led awareness in real time;
   - Identification of problematic cognitions;
   - Identification of cognitive distortions in these thoughts;
3 Understanding core beliefs;
4 Client-led understanding of how core beliefs affect behaviour;
5 Identifying maladaptive core beliefs;
6 Providing alternatives and restructuring interventions;
   - Rational argument or disputing of these automatic thoughts using Socratic dialogue; and finally
   - The development of alternative thinking;
7 Maintaining new belief structures;
   - By testing them out in triggering situations and strengthening them.

When we work with clients in this way, we are following this broad series of steps. We use the methods described in Chapter 6 to identify automatic thoughts and then we help our clients to evaluate these. This process of identification is an intervention itself. If the formulation indicates that thoughts are unhelpful and possibility distorted, then we work with the client on challenging these with the end goal of generating alternative balanced thoughts to replace them. There are different ways of implementing cognitive interventions with clients. We now look at each of them.

SITs and SATs

A common sign of troubled times in the cognitive system are SITs (i.e., Stress inducing thoughts) which increase the cycle of stress because of the interpretation of the event. For example, the athlete hyper focuses on a potential penalty situation in a cup final before the game has even begun, causing it to become a SIT pattern (See Figure 7.2). Contrastingly, there are SATs (i.e., stress alleviating thoughts) which are more functional patterns that reduce the stress cycle and promote adaptive thoughts. For example, the athlete shakes his head off and notes that the penalty situation will only occur if they cannot close out the match in the 120 minutes. He looks around at the locker room and has a SAT that his team is capable of that. We all have SITs and SATs that are in the cognitive system. It is often useful to use a scaling measure to help the athlete measure how bad the SIT is by rating it between 1 and 10. Then, the intervention process encourages them to develop a SAT and then rate it out of ten as well. The goal is to increase the strength rating of the SAT compared to the SIT and therefore reduce the interfering effect of the negative cognition. SITs and SATs allow brief, solution focused interventions that are highly effective in field situations such as before a match, during breaks within competition, or during event transitions in a day where a full-blown session process might not be possible; however, it is crucial that the SITs and SATs are informed through an effective formulation so that the practitioner is aware of potential SITs and can help develop effective SATs.

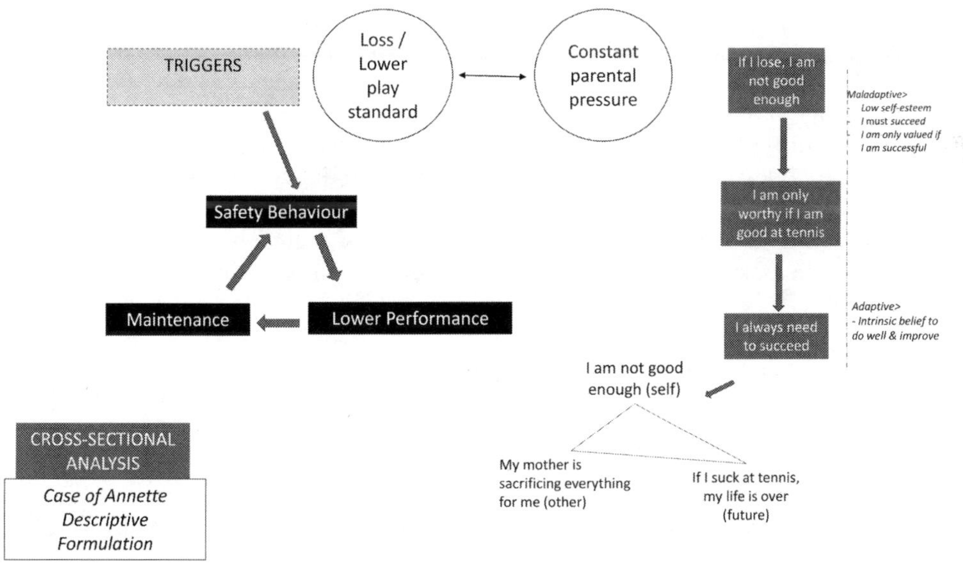

Figure 7.2 Maintenance Cycle and Core Belief of Case

PITs and PETs

PITs are performance interfering thoughts (i.e., thoughts and thinking cycles that interfere with the execution of a particular skill). For example, the athlete has the PIT that *'you are going to mess up today'*, which acts as the trigger for a maintenance cycle that eventually culminates in a pre-competitive anxiety presentation. This makes the athlete go through a PIT or a downward spiral that ultimately compromises performance, development, and mental health. PETs are performance enhancing thoughts that aid the individual to find the mental space that allows seamless execution of skill sometimes under performance pressure. For example, the individual challenges the PET with *'I have trained hard, and I will just execute that'*. This transition from PIT to PET allows the athlete to stay focused, avoid self-sabotage, and use experiences to plan positively for the future. This transition to PETs does not automatically erase the PIT. Rather, it allows the individual to understand their distressing thoughts and learn to coexist with the PIT and PET also featuring prominently in their cognitive system. PETs as an intervention should focus on the following broad thematic areas of intervention in sport psychology:

- Challenge-Threat model (Jones et al., 2009) by making the PIT of threat combat with the PET-based challenge;
- Resilience Trajectory (Gupta & McCarty, 2022) by ensuring that PETs feature the time to be resilient instead of the catastrophising PIT of failure;
- Self-Talk to replace the negative cycle PITs with self-affirming PETs;
- Active Coping PETs to counter the often-Passive Coping PITs.

Socratic dialogue

As we have highlighted in previous chapters, clients do not always know what is going on - they do not have sufficient self-awareness. Therefore, we engage in discovery with the client. Due to low awareness, this process must be guided. Guided discovery is a process where the practitioner acts as a guide to facilitate clients to uncover, examine and reality-test their cognitions and make improved problem-solving decisions. Appropriate questioning and engaging in Socratic dialogue are one way to facilitate this. You might wonder how is a dialogue an intervention? This dialogue serves to bring subliminal thoughts and actions to the surface which enhances clarity. To use a metaphor, the object under the water is just seen as a shadow, but as we pull it to the surface, we can see it for what it is with clarity, which allows us to decide what to do with it.

Greenberger and Padesky (1995) listed such questions to assist here, e.g., 'When you're not feeling this way, do you think about this kind of situation differently?' or 'Are there any strengths or positives in you or the situation that you're ignoring?' or 'Can you think of anything you've learned from experience that could help you now?'. Maybe you want a structure that gives you more space, detail and more opportunity to gain detailed information about the situation and if this is the case, then using longer, more focused thought diaries is a good technique. Socratic questions should be phrased in such a way that they stimulate thought and increase awareness. There is *no requirement for a correct or perfect answer.* This form of Socratic questioning allows the client to provide their own answers. There is no need to rely on the answers or interpretations that might be offered. Some key elements that Socratic questions require are (refer also to Clark & Egan, 2015):

- There is no requirement to have one concrete answer.
- Clients need to think and interact with the questions and answers from their own viewpoint of reality.
- It is not an attacking mental torture; Socratic dialogue needs to be facilitative for the client to answer the questions and understand the many elements of any situation.
- 'Productive discomfort' needs to be a fundamental part of the process where the client understands the *why* of the dialogue that is being undertaken.
- Be mindful of power imbalance, and also of underlying competition between the client and practitioner. There should not be a direction of finding who is right, which may lead to combative dialogue which is unproductive.

The Socratic technique explores thoughts and responses in-depth. Practitioners use it to promote independent thinking where clients can think, discuss, debate, disagree, evaluate and analyse content through their thinking. We have outlined certain fundamental tips for using Socratic questioning:

- **Plan** the significant questions that will provide the client direction to continue the dialogue. Basing this upon the client formulation allows a higher degree of effectiveness.
- Clock the **Wait-Time** before the client responses. Do not jump in to fill the silences, allow the client to take ownership of their dialogue.
- Regularly summarise what is said and use open questions
- Follow-up with appropriate probing questions which are (a) short; (b) clear; and (c) on the topic
- Socratic questions can be asked with the 'Ws' and how,
    - **WHO** is involved?
    - **WHAT** happened?
    - **WHEN** did it happen?
    - **WHERE** did it happen?
    - **WHY** did it happen?
    - **HOW** did it happen?

There are many forms of Socratic questions as well. We have summarised a few of them commonly used in the applied world of sport in Table 7.2.

Let us look at the following worked out case example to see:

Application Time: Case of Mo

MO: So, I was sitting at home, doc, and something weird happened. Looking out the window, and it was raining. I suddenly felt a wave of depression. I do not really know what caused me to feel like that.

PRACTITIONER: Shall we see if we can uncover something? [Mo nods] – Can you remember what thoughts were running through your head at that point? [Question about Initial Issue]

MO: It was just a rubbish night.

PRACTITIONER: Why? [Clarification Question]

MO: Transfer window just closed, and we did not get the midfielder we were seeking.

PRACTITIONER: And? [Clarification Question]

MO: I mean … it sucks?

PRACTITIONER: Why? What caused you to feel that way? [Assumption Questions]

MO: Umm … I felt more expectations?

PRACTITIONER: Of?

MO: Like I am the only senior midfielder in the team, the team will look forward to me.

PRACTITIONER: So, that combined with your recent return to previous levels is causing …?

MO: A bit of pressure I guess.

PRACTITIONER: Could you take me through that reasoning and what would happen? [Reasoning Question & Implication Question]

MO: Like, If I don't pull my socks up and start hitting the ground well, the team would lose the midfield, and eventually we would lose the matches, and then the championship.

PRACTITIONER: Where did you get that idea? [Origin Question]

MO: Pretty obvious, isn't it?

PRACTITIONER: Not to me, but you are the football expert why don't you explain your reasoning to me? [Reason & Evidence Question]

A-B-C-D-E

Ellis et al. (1997) classified most cognitive patterns into an A-B-C-D-E format where:

A = Activating event;
B = Beliefs about the event or others triggered by the event;
C = Consequences of your beliefs (both emotional and behavioural);
D = Disputations to challenge your beliefs to create new consequence;
E = Effective new beliefs are adopted and implemented.

Using this structure, you can work with athletes to create new, more beneficial thinking and to improve their overall mental health. To give an example, you might work with an athlete through the steps below:

(A) An athlete is preparing for a key sporting event (their **activating** event).
(B) Their thoughts during the final run up to the event might be around them believing they won't win even one game (their **beliefs** triggered by the event).

Table 7.2 Examples of applied Socratic questions

Socratic Question Types	*Example*
Questions about Initial Issue	• Is this question relevant to you? • Is this question easy to answer or difficult? • Why do you have that opinion? • Does this question prompt other important questions?
Clarification Questions	• What do you mean by …? • Could you describe that differently so I could understand? • What about an example of that? • Could you expand on that particular point further?
Assumption Question	• Why are you making that assumption? • What are you assuming here? • You seem to assume that _____ lead to _____ outcome • Did I understand you correctly?
Evidence Checker Questions	• What could be an example? • Why do you think this is true? • What other information could we draw upon? • Could you explain or list down the reasoning for us? • What led you to that pattern of thought? • Is there any reason to doubt that evidence or what happened?
Origin Questions	• Have you always thought this? • Where did that thought originate or start from? • What caused you to feel that way? • Did you hear it from someplace else? • Has your opinion been influenced somehow recently?
Implication-Consequence Questions	• What effect could that have? • What is an alternative to that? • What are you implying with that? • What else could happen after that? • If we changed_____ could _____ change and happen as well?
Viewpoint Question	• Is there another way of looking at that situation? • If I put someone else in your position, how would they respond? • Imagine that you were watching the 'highlights' broadcast of what happened, what could be an alternative way to understand it?
Challenge Questions	• Could you explore a different point of view? • What assumptions are you making here? • Is there a possibility that _____ could be wrong? • What do you think was really important there? • Is there another _____ question we can ask there?
Reasoning Questions	• What is the thought process behind …? • If I was the one in that position, how do you expect me to think? • If we were to draw a chain of thought or reasoning, how would that be?

(C) The **consequences** here could be a deterioration in their usual level of play; an avoidance of their training; anxiety; fear and anger.

(D) **Disputing** this thinking, the athlete could be mindful of how often they have won early rounds before; they could view their knowledge of the environment where they've played before as an advantage; they could use past performance and the estimates of coaches and team members, too.

(E) This can result in **effective** new beliefs where their thinking is related to using past knowledge and experience to gain wins and the outcome they want is within their reach (see Figure 7.2).

A common way to work through this A-B-C-D-E framework with your client is through the use of thought diaries (see Chapter 6). You can use these with your client, but the aim will be for them to use these themselves moving towards their independent use first with the structure of the diary and then later once they have internalised the process without having to write everything out. The thought diary starts with recording the event that has led to the automatic thought. The second step is where you record the automatic thought(s) and the third is for you to identify the emotions that are linked to that thought. When you are starting out with a client, just using these three columns can be beneficial and can help them to see the links between events, thoughts and emotions (i.e., the A-B-C). The next step would then be to introduce additional columns. The fourth would be where you identify whether there is any evidence to support or dispute the thought. The fifth is where you record the alternative thought and the final column is where you note down how to use this in future and what the consequences of these new thoughts are.

Through following this structure, clients will become more self-aware, more used to recognising and challenging their negative thinking and more able to see the benefits of taking time to seek alternative ways of viewing events. Scaling and rating are used frequently in CBT and the thought record is no exception (see Chapter 6). You can ask clients to rate on a scale of 1–10 the extent of the emotions the thoughts are triggering. You can also ask them to rate on a scale of 1–10 the effect on their sporting performance. This is technically a process of measurement, but when placed within the A-B-C-D-E framework (see Table 7.3), we can work during the session to support them in evaluating their thinking, restructuring it and implementing new thinking. The practitioner can do this in a number of ways:

a Try asking three key questions about their automatic thought: *Is it true? Is it logical? Is it helpful?* You can also gain positive results from presenting thought-challenging as if you and the client were approaching the end of a court case. You are asking them to sum up the argument for the prosecution and the defence as though preparing closing arguments. In this way, they can get a balanced view of the automatic thought versus the alternative adaptive thought.

b Use synthesising questions to help clients such as *'How does this fit with your belief that you will never recover from this injury?'* or *'How do you think you could use what you've discovered through completing this thought record?'* Be collaborative, curious, neutral, and open to staying with your client's train of thought. Try to avoid appearing as if you know the answer, coercing or having your own agenda (see Figure 7.2).

Psychological skills training (PST)-based interventions

As we know, PST is a major area of focus in sport psychology interventions research and applied practice, which can also contribute to improving focus, managing emotions and pressure, building confidence and coping with injury and setbacks with clients. Psychological skills training (PST) is the *'systematic and consistent practice of mental or psychological skills for the purpose of enhancing performance, increasing enjoyment or achieving greater sport and physical activity satisfaction'* (Weinberg, 2019, p. 230). Recent evidence (Barker et al. 2020) showed that PST based on cognitive behavioural principles was effective in enhancing key areas, such as psychological,

Table 7.3 A-B-C-D-E thought-diary-based cognitive intervention – Case of Annette

A.	*B.*	*C.*	*D.*	*E.*	*F.*
Activating Event (Situation or Behaviour)	*Beliefs or Automatic Thoughts*	*Emotions 'How Did I Feel?' (Rate It Out of Ten)*	*Evidence for and against This Thought(s)*	*Alternative More Helpful Thoughts*	*Future Learning or Resulting Consequences (How Do I Feel Now and How to Use This in Future?)*
Important qualifying round coming up	I won't be able to win even one game	Fearful 7/10, anxious 8/10, impending doom 8/10, embarrassment 8/10	For: I've seen others lose in that way. Against: I've never competed and not won a single game.	I'm going to focus on the match day, remember my training and give it my all.	If I think I'm going to lose I tense up, and my performance decreases. I feel more positive and will try to beat my overall score at the last event.
Stress strain of wrist	I will never play again	Despair 9/10, worry, lack of focus, anxiety,	For: Other players have suffered career ending injuries. Against: The Dr thinks I can recover from this. My coach has seen this injury before and expects me to recover.	I will work hard, follow advice from my coach and Dr and get back to where I was.	Negative thinking doesn't help me. I feel hopeful now 7/10. I feel I have a clear direction and I'm focused 8/10.

behavioural, and performance outcomes. If athletes can feel that they are in control of managing their psychological state, this can increase self-confidence wellbeing and performance. Primarily, you are aiming to work with your client to ensure that they feel the necessary level of mastery over their psychological state to enable them to perform optimally. Through implementing these skills, athletes you work with can reduce their anxiety and improve their concentration. The ability to concentrate is key in several sports (e.g., football, where a lack of concentration can lead to match loss).

Most PST interventions are also implicitly cognitive-behavioural. In most sports, certain levels of anxiety or stress are necessary to performance. This is especially true of high-risk sports such as skiing, motor sports and gymnastics, where eliminating anxiety would not be desirable or realistic as a goal and could in fact be detrimental and potentially dangerous. To ensure safety and optimal performance, what the practitioner aims for is a balance where anxiety or extreme emotions are (a) well managed; (b) in conscious awareness and (c) actually contribute to performance and safety. We accept that in competitive sports extreme emotions will be experienced and need to be recognised, but our role is not to eliminate these experiences but to work with athletes to ensure they can perform well while experiencing them. Through implementing PST interventions within the CBT process, we can help athletes improve their mental aspects of preparation and practice. We have focused primarily on two PST techniques, namely Self-Talk and Imagery. We direct the reader to further PST-based resources (see Durand-Bush et al., 2022; Hanrahan & Andersen, 2010; Schinke et al., 2016).

Self-Talk

Self-Talk is a widely used performance enhancing strategy in sport and its effectiveness has been shown for a range of tasks across a range of athletes and sports. Its effectiveness in exercise has also been demonstrated for example, with those who take part in aerobics, walking and running. Self-Talk occurs when the sender of a message intends that message for themselves, and the message can be conveyed internally (silently) or externally (out loud). Self-Talk is a cognitive strategy and can be seen to have its origins in Cognitive Therapy where Self-Talk was seen as linked to emotional dysfunctions and was a person's way of describing a situation to him or herself.

The individual's belief systems are represented in Self-Talk. Therefore, the underlying assumptions and core beliefs of the individual are often manifested within it. Self-Talk can be viewed as a means by which, as a practitioner, you can explore the athlete's automatic Self-Talk and learn from that, and it can also be seen as a cognitive intervention strategy. Both approaches give an 'in' for you as a practitioner to work directly with a client. The first would align well with the use of thought records or diaries and is often referred to as organic or automatic Self-Talk and can include spontaneous as well as controlled or deliberately used thoughts. The second is often referred to as strategic Self-Talk and is focused on performance improvement and the achievement of goals. Three aspects of Self-Talk that are worth considering within CBT intervention are its function, valence, and overtness. These can reinforce the cognitive belief restructuring and thought balancing interventions that are being conducted (see Table 7.4).

Table 7.4 Use of Self-Talk aspects within CBT intervention

Self-Talk Aspect	*Type and Description*	*Example*
Function	Instructional Self-Talk has been shown to improve performance, especially when it is task relevant. It can also help with skill acquisition and learning.	'Set, bounce, bounce, toss, serve'
	Instructional Self-Talk can increase confidence levels and performance by focusing attention on technique and strategy.	
	Motivational Self-Talk occurs more frequently during competition and often relates to mental preparation and being 'psyched up'.	'You have trained for this - let's go execute!' 'Time to be awesome'
	Motivational Self-Talk acts to improve performance through increasing confidence and creating a positive mood.	
Valence	Positive Self-Talk could encompass praise (e.g., 'go you!' and 'I can') and has the benefit of helping athletes to stay focused on the here and now.	'Let's go man, we got this'
	Negative Self-Talk tends more toward criticism (e.g., 'I'm an idiot' or 'I'm rubbish at this'). It's important to note though that some negative Self-Talk can actually be facilitative of improved performance so focusing on the meaning of Self-Talk to the individual can be seen as more important than the overall valence or the outcome produced. For some athletes their negative Self-Talk might have qualities that they perceive as motivational.	'What the hell are you doing? Get your head out of your ass' 'I should go home'
Overtness relates to whether the Self-Talk is sub vocal, so heard only as a voice inside the mind of the client or athlete or whether it's more overt and spoken out loud, articulated so that others can also hear what is being said.		Athletes (such as Nick Kyrgios) often scream out their Self-Talk. Others may whisper it, or have it internally in their head

There is extensive consideration of the theory underlying Self-Talk in sport. This has included, for example, self-determination theory, self-efficacy theory, and dual processing theory. To give an example, one approach suggests that there are two processing systems, 1 and 2 involved in Self-Talk.

- System 1 is quick autonomous processing, including things like gut feelings and emotions.
- System 2 Self-Talk is concerned with using working memory. This is the slow and deliberate system bound by rules and consciously monitored. It's also the place for assigned Self-Talk tasks aimed at performance enhancement.

As System 2 uses effort and energy, it can become depleted and actually lead to worsening performance. This then leads us to rely on System 1 and our intuition, gut feeling, and emotion. See van Raalte et al. (2016) for a thorough review and sport-specific model of Self-Talk that encompasses Systems 1 and 2, personal, contextual, and behavioural factors.

Before we move on to look at how you could work with Self-Talk as a practitioner, it's worth outlining the concept of Self-Talk dissonance, which results from the sport-specific model. This is when there is a lack of alignment between the gut feelings or automatic Self-Talk thoughts (System 1) and the more planned and energy intensive System 2 Self-Talk. This conflict between System 2 Self-Talk and System 1 gut feelings creates a reduction in cognitive resources and a resulting negative effect on performance. An example here would that the System 2 thinking 'I am the best' can conflict with System 1 thinking like 'I'm rubbish at this' resulting in dissonance. More work in needed to discover what moderating factors are involved in this and how to best work with Self-Talk dissonance to mediate the effects of this on performance and how core beliefs are manifested through that (see Figure 7.2).

The role of context and culture are highlighted by the sport - specific model. We can learn from how others use Self-Talk and the cultural norms within teams can also have an effect. Some considerations include:

- When you are working as a practitioner, you'll need to consider the clients current level of awareness of Self-Talk and use that as a starting point.
- Understanding their 'default' language for Self-Talk. Often athletes may not feel completely comfortable with English as their Self-Talk language (see Gupta & Divekar, 2022). For example, Roger Federer uses motivational Self-Talk (though rarely) as 'allez' which means 'come on'.
- Ask questions and elicit information on what Self-Talk the client already uses and combine this if possible with observational data.
- There are several ways to collect data on Self-Talk as a starting point for any work in this area. You can observe play, you can video record and watch back the feed with the player to help elicit their Self-Talk. You can instruct them to talk out loud during the performance or to write what was going through their head during their last match or performance. There are obvious limitations to these techniques, including people's tendency towards social desirability and their concerns over sharing private thoughts, so building an effective foundational relationship with the client will be a necessary first step. There are also other options to access this information. For example, you can use Descriptive Experience Sampling (DES) or established validated questionnaires. DES is a means of accessing and exploring inner thoughts. The athlete is asked to carry a beeper and when it sounds, they write or record their thoughts or Self-Talk. So, this is an idiographic method and can be successfully employed during sport performance.
- There are also validated psychometrics such as the Psychological Skills Inventory for Sport (PSIS); the Test of Performance Strategies-2 (TOPS-2), the Thought Occurrence Questionnaire for Sports (TOQS), or the Automatic Self Talk Questionnaire for Sports (ASTQS). As an example, the ASTQS includes measures of four types of positive and four types of negative Self-Talk. The positive Self-Talk measures include motivational, confidence building, instructional and anxiety controlling statements. The negative Self-Talk measures include worries, disengagement, fatigue, and irrelevant thinking.

Gathering this data will allow you to begin work on identifying maladaptive thinking in those you are working with. It can provide data for you to then work with your client to see how they currently use Self-Talk, to raise their awareness of the role of

Self-Talk and to start to implement some guided Self-Talk into their performance routines monitoring any performance - related changes.

Imagery

Imagery is a key PST and a longstanding key element of CBT. Imagery is different to visualisation because it is practitioner guided. Imagery is a key PST that can be used in CBT because cognitive thoughts often have associated images. For example, 'Annette has an image of her mom shaking her head when she double faulted' which for her is the biggest representation of the pressure of having her mother there, and all the expectations she brings. Using imagery allows the clients to:

- Relive unhelpful situations in the past in a safe manner;
- Figure out cognitive patterns and emotions that took place;
- Understand why those thoughts were unhelpful and where they came from;
- Consider how to implement change.

This allows the client to mentally look at the situation like a puzzle. We can follow the clues with the client and facilitate the space where they can put it together and make sense of an otherwise seemingly unsolvable situation. Below are some forms by which imagery can be used in CBT:

(A) **Worst-case imagery:** Often, the clients have their NATs or triggering thoughts as a situational image. For example, Mo imagines the crowd booing him because he has not lived up to expectations. In such cases, it is useful to go with the imagery and see where it leads. Socratic questioning with clarification and outcome questions are useful in this space. While this procedure leads to some stress, in the long run, it allows the individual to see that the negative imagery may not be that bad, or if it is bad, it is just a thought, not reality. In doing so, this becomes a behavioural experiment as well. The client's imagery journal will go through the worst case and demonstrate that it is not necessarily the 'worst deal'.

(B) **Coping imagery:** Refers to the imagery process where clients are facilitated to imagine themselves in their most feared situations; however, in this position, they not only face up to the unpleasant outcome, but also engage in the imagery process to view what they will do to cope. This allows the client to go beyond the emergency response to the threat and find out alternative actions that they undertake. For example, Annette imagines that in times of stress in a match, she will look to her racquet, not to her mother, because it is her racquet that will be with her in the game, and her mother can only be with her outside the court.

(C) **Action imagery**: A common feature in highly unhelpful or triggering situations is a sense of 'this is what is meant to happen' or engagement in safety behaviours. Clients, therefore, are undermotivated or do not know how to effectively problem-solve, and therefore remain stuck in the problem-perpetuating cycle. This triggers further thinking traps of catastrophising and all or nothing thinking (see 'Thinking Traps', Chapter 4). Action imagery involves making a short list of things that the client wants to do at a specific time in the future and a daily process of imagery where they view themselves as doing those things. This reduces the 'impossibility' of the situation, and increases motivation. This is highly effective when working with athletes recovering from an injury through the process of return to sport.

Emotional/physiological interventions

In this section, we have categorised emotion and physiological regulation-based interventions together. Emotional and physiological responsiveness are one of the interacting systems of CBT. They often conflate and combine with each other as well. Once you have identified an emotional element to the maintenance cycle, it is likely that there is a physiological output associated as well. This is most commonly seen in anxiety, fear, or arousal-based emotions. This can then be the starting point for defusing this emotion-physiological consequence through interventions. The overall purpose of emotional- and physiological-based interventions is *deregulation*, the process by which the individual's emotional and physiological responses are returned to their normal base level from under or over activation. This is the basis of planning ways of disrupting the cycle via deregulation. The client is taught a skill of deregulation and this proves to the client that the often-overburdening emotions they experience are things they can take charge of and control.

Defusing emotional intensity to manageable levels

An extremely high emotional intensity is infertile ground for CBT work. This is because rational cognitive processes are being constantly disrupted by the emotional system. The first step that the practitioner needs to undertake is to facilitate the client to return to a lower intensity of emotion. This is *not ignoring emotions and their effect*, rather it is pausing the 'CBT' work until the client can find a low intensity, stable emotion base. Some specific methods to measure and modify extreme emotion intensity are:

- **Validation**: Most individuals, including athletes are often in invalidating environments. There are 6 levels of validation, (1) Listening; (2) Restating (accurate, non-judgemental reflection); (3) Observing (the unspoken and nonverbal cues); (4) Causation (focus on causes of emotion past and present, but let the client elaborate the process); (5) Assessing (focus on history and how current responses may not be effective); and (6) Compassion (total acceptance and response while showing a genuine belief that the individual is capable of change) (see details in Kocabas & Üstündağ-Budak, 2017).
- **Self-Soothing**: The skills of self-soothing are focused on comforting oneself and being self-compassionate. This is relevant when extreme emotions are coming from highly self-critical positions ('I'm not good enough' and 'I will be dropped and my career is ruined'). Soothing is visceral, and should use sensory modalities that are calming to the client. Some in session examples are: Smell ('I can smell the watered and rolled cricket pitch before a match calming me') or Touch ('Rapping my chest gives me the feeling I am not alone' or Hearing 'stadiums that have burst the roof off when I do well, and think others believe I can').
- **Cognitive Defusing**: Extreme emotional intensity is typically accompanied with negative future-oriented predictions about the self or outcomes. An example would be a tennis player working through post injury anxiety saying, 'If I mess up, I am finished as a tennis player … this injury would have killed me off'. These statements are also linked to threatening core beliefs. Edelman (2006) suggests two ways of helping the client defuse these cognitive bombs, (A) 90+% of the what if statements never happen. The practitioner can point to an instance in

the past where the client went through the same thinking process which never happened, that is, keep a record of these catastrophic predictions and how many of them happened; (B) Working with the client to show that the consequences are manageable. This could be done by pointing out other examples in their sport. For example, an athlete who sees others in their age category make their international debuts while they are not getting a chance may catastrophise *'my' career as an international player is never going to happen'.* The practitioner could point out examples of individuals who made their international debuts in their late 20s, showing that it is manageable with a plan. A creative challenge could also be asking them to outline a positive consequence, What if? Since clients rarely engage in that.

Once the client is at a manageable emotional intensity, and the NATs are identified, the practitioner needs to work on identifying their core beliefs.

Emotion/physiological trigger management

High levels or extremely low levels of arousal often cause a major effect on sport and performance. The obvious examples include anxiety presentations that manifest in shaking, tensions, tremors, and sweating; however, being under-aroused also causes low cortical arousal which does not prepare the body mentally and physically for the demands of sport which may cause risk exposure and injuries. Fundamentally, high or low arousal causes interference with task execution in the short - term and may escalate to a mental health concern in the long run.

Often, when arousal is high or low, they have idiosyncratic meaning for the client. For example, in pre-competitive anxiety presentations, the anxiety arousal is only occurring when there is a competitive consequence associated with the upcoming match. It does not show up during a friendly or in a training situation where the game-day squads are not being picked. Therefore, the emotional arousal is linked to the trigger of being externally evaluated. This interpretation of the situation is cognitive, but leads to an emotional and physiological reaction. The individual is unlikely to respond to cognitive interventions until we can manage their arousal level. This is an obvious place for the use of relaxation,- which manages arousal to a controllable level. When clients first begin to practise relaxation during such triggers, they pick up previously unaware small body changes, which allows them to understand how those situations cause a knock-on effect on their emotions and physiological arousal. In these cases, *Awareness Interventions*, that is, those that are designed to ensure that the individual records and is aware of their emotional experience, have great effect. For example, the athlete with pre-competitive anxiety gets the awareness that their full-blown panic attack starts in the morning when they watch the match previews on the television which causes nervous sweats and butterflies in the stomach. In the following section, we outline progressive muscle relaxation technique and its use.

Progressive muscle relaxation (PMR)

PMR teaches clients to gradually relax their muscles in sequence. PMR can be used to raise self-awareness and to achieve relaxation of the muscles and the mind bringing tension into conscious awareness and selectively relaxing muscles on command.

This voluntary tensing and relaxing of major muscle groups can be carried out easily by athletes on their own once they have been taught the skill. There are many different scripts available for PMR and these are easily accessed online. You might choose to direct clients to these already existing resources or you might choose to record your own version as clients will be familiar with your voice and may engage more readily with this. The time required for PMR varies but usually takes around 10 to 20 minutes. During this time, clients are asked to contract or tense muscle groups for 5 seconds, then to relax them for between 5 and 10 seconds. This is repeated twice before moving to a different muscle group. Most practitioners recommend tensing and relaxing the muscle groups one at a time in a specified order. Usually, you'd ask clients to begin with their lower extremities and end with the stomach, chest and then face. Some clients will be more comfortable practising this seated or lying down and it should always be done in a quiet setting where there is no distraction; however, once the first trial has been run, the emphasis should be to transfer this onto the sporting context with whatever sport-based kit they may have for in situ usage. For example, a footballer would wear his guards and cleats, a cricket batter would pad up.

Application Time: PMR Script Model

We're going to carry out a relaxation exercise now. This involves working through muscle groups first tensing and then relaxing them and noticing the different feelings associated with both. We'll start at the feet and then work slowly up the body. Please tense your muscles when instructed but be careful not to overdo it. You should practise this exercise frequently and with practice you'll start to notice and be more aware of when you're tense and be able to use these skills to relax.

Before we begin I'd like you to get as comfortable as you can. That might be lying on the floor with a pillow or cushion under your head or sitting back in a comfortable chair. You can take off your shoes, loosen any tight clothing and remove glasses if you wear them. Close your eyes if you feel comfortable doing so and if any thoughts enter your mind try to just acknowledge them and let them go before refocusing on relaxing.

Before we start tensing and relaxing specific muscle groups we're just going to work on relaxing and breathing deeply. Please take a deep breath in and be aware of the feeling of the air filling your lungs. Hold that for a few seconds ... and now breathe out slowly letting any tension leave your body .... Repeat that, breathing in deeply .... And breathing out slowly feeling yourself relax and your body feeling heavier. Keep breathing this way for a minute or two ....

Now we're going to start at your feet. Think about your feet and ankles moving your attention to these and when you're ready tense the muscles around these. Notice the tension when you curl your toes towards your head, or curl your toes and the arch of your foot. Feel that tension in your feet and ankles, hold it there and then relax letting the tension dissipate and your feet relax growing heavier and feeling as though they are sinking into the floor. Now repeat that noticing the difference between the tense and relaxed states. Focus on the changes that you experience when the muscle group is relaxed. It might help to use imagery with this, for example, picture stressful feelings and tension flowing out of your body as you relax the muscle group.

The practitioner would then facilitate the athlete to move onto the next muscle group, the calves and lower legs before progressing up the body slowly and gradually covering the upper leg and pelvis then the stomach and chest, then the back, the arms and shoulders and then the final group, the neck, head, and face. To finish, you can instruct the client to tense their entire body and then release. Then, before opening their eyes, ask them to slowly move their muscles. Often after the first few trials, the athlete will prefer a specific muscle group that they would like to relax. The practitioner should facilitate this because it allows client ownership in the intervention itself. Once clients gain proficiency, they can perform a shortened version and some people find they can then relax their muscle groups quickly without the need for tensing first as they become aware of the feelings associated with tension and relaxation.

Reflective Exercise

- Try monitoring your own Self-Talk using at least two different methods. Reflect on how you found the experience, what you learned and whether making changes to your Self-Talk would be easy.
- Spend time online trying out different relaxation techniques. Do you have a personal preference for some over others, and why might that be? How could that knowledge affect your practice and the work you suggest for clients?

Controlled breathing

Breathing is the body's natural cycle of preparation and reduction as part of the sympathetic and parasympathetic nervous system. During high arousal triggers, rapid, shallow over breathing is the natural part of the body's preparation for action. In sport, this is often triggered due to exertion and the physical effort associated with it. Generally speaking, athletes are aware of their breathing patterns and being physically fit, engage in effective rapid breathing when they are in control of physiological arousal; however, when they are experiencing out-of-control arousal they are *overbreathing*, that is, a form of hyperventilating triggered by shortness of breath accompanied by (a) feeling that you cannot get oxygen needed; (b) higher than normative heart rate; and (c) dizzy spells or a feeling of being overstimulated. This over breathing leads to lowering levels of carbon dioxide in the blood due to continuous hyper-exhalation. The feelings of light-headedness, dizzy spells, breath shortness, and tingles add to the maintenance cycle that is causing and keeping the anxiety going – often this leads to an increase in the level of anxiety. At other times, the athletes are feeling a little nervous, but may have a catastrophising thinking trap misinterpreting an elevated heart rate as the beginning of a panic attack when it was because they were doing yo-yo sprints.

These emotion-based physiological responses are most commonly seen in anxiety and fear presentations. They seem overwhelming for the client. But, once the practitioner understands the why of their cause through formulation, the overwhelming physical response can be controlled via controlled breathing. Control breathing by implementing the following steps:

- Relax the thorax and upper body region which are typically tightened without conscious awareness during high anxiety arousal.
- Physically touch the diaphragm with one hand to feel its expansion and contraction.

- Physically place the other hand on the nostrils to understand inhalation and exhalation.
    - Step 1: Fully breathe out slowly with the nose and diaphragm (5 seconds).
    - Step 2: Inhale deeply but slowly through nose to fill lungs until the diaphragm feels like it cannot expand anymore.
    - Step 3: Be conscious of the heart rate that is accompanying the breathing.
    - Step 4: Repeat four to five times.
- Eventually, once the client understands how to engage this controlled breathing and the sensations associated with the nose and diaphragm, they can remove their physical touching of these body parts.

Controlled breathing has several benefits: (a) It slows down the maintenance cycle and prevents thinking traps from being activated during times of high emotion; (b) it reduces the feeling of being overwhelmed through hyperventilation; and (c) it manages the actual physiological arousal of the body which reduces the extremity of the emotional experience. Below is a practitioner directed script of a controlled breathing intervention:

Application Time: Controlled Breathing Intervention Template

1 Ask the client to hyperventilate – but do not tell them why (take consent and give the overall aims of the intervention);

Let's do an experiment, lets stand up, and breathe like this [demonstrate hyperventilation], let's be rapid with it;

2 Continue for 2+ minutes and then reflect on the physical state changes, see similarities and differences to actual anxiety provoking situations;

Could you compare that experience of the body to your experience of anxiety?

3 Engage in controlled breathing training;
4 Initiate hyperventilation again, but follow-up with controlled breathing;
5 Reflect on the change in the experience;
6 Design a behavioural experiment to transfer learning to an anxiety provoking situation.

Sleep and sleep hygiene

Emotions and physiological reactions often manifest in sleep problems for individuals in sport. This is often initiated due to travel, continued stress, and being away from stable home environments (e.g., hotels and airports). When combined with underlying cognitive distortions and high emotion negative events, this can become a major emotional and physiological issue. For example, Annette loses a tennis match, then listens to her mother scold her afterwards on the way to the airport, where she takes a flight to another city, with a time zone change, and sleeps in a hotel, waking up to a completely unfamiliar view. This fast-paced change triggers her sense of com-discomfort with herself.

CBT can be used to work with a structured program that at the cognitive level identifies and replaces inflammatory thoughts that trigger cycles; at the emotional level manages arousal and at the behavioural level promotes habits that are conducive to sleep. Poor sleep can be a physiological *cause* (bad sleep causes greater tiredness and poorer neuronal connectivity in the brain, causing lower cognitive-emotional-behavioural regulation) or *consequence* (stress and negative thoughts, poor coping behaviour such as partying for example causing poor sleep). We do not go too much into depth, but outline some areas for the reader to explore:

- **Location Restriction:** The process by which the normal sleeping space and its characteristics (usually the bed) is used only for sleeping. This uses classical conditioning to associate the location with sleep functions. For athletes who do not sleep in the same room it could be an object such as a blanket/sleep clothing or stimuli such as music or lighting.
- **Stimulus Control:** The process which removes stimuli that force brain activation and resist sleep. Simple examples are removal of electronic devices and social media pre-sleep; consistent sleep-wake routine; comfortable and quiet sleeping environments. A common theme with athletes struggling with pre-match night sleep is a process of thinking about 'what should I do tomorrow' which is a cognitive cycle keeping the individual awake. This is the most literal version of 'my thoughts kept me up'.
- **Sleep Hygiene:** This refers to the lifestyle habits that influences sleep. Common detrimental habits involve stimulants such as caffeine, nicotine, exercise close to sleep time, high emotional/cognitive activation pre-bedtime. Often a helpful process may be working with individuals to create a plan or a 'sleep protocol'. This allows the athlete to prepare and control factors that can harmfully affect their sleep hygiene ahead of time.

Autonomous CBT training

One of the recognised contributing factors to the success of CBT is the use of between session 'Autonomous CBT Training' tasks. Tied to that though is that compliance with between session tasks can be poor and increasing this compliance is often more problematic than you would expect. There are different types of autonomous training tasks or between session tasks. The practitioner needs to consider which are most appropriate to the stage of your work with your clients. We would recommend collaboratively setting these autonomous tasks at every session and then reviewing the training outcomes at the start of the next session. Getting clients into the habit of doing this has several benefits:

1. It will allow the development of a clear structure to your sessions.
2. It will help clients to apply the insight, new skills and strategies they are learning in session.
3. It will help clients to try out things they are learning and show them that they are in control of the changes they make.
4. *Practice Effect & Skill Acquisition* – CBT work involves the development of cognitive and behavioural skills. The autonomous sessions facilitate this process. Use the analogy of a coach – they give the drills, but if the athlete does not practise them,

there will be no change. Similarly, the athlete needs to engage and reinforce the mental *skills* as well.

5 If they only see you once a week for 50 minutes, then there is the potential for a large loss of learning between one session and the next if the client isn't engaging with that content in between sessions.
6 If you are showing a genuine interest in how the client has got on with their homework then that can help to build the relationship. It's often the case that we need to know something in our heads before we really see the benefit in practice.
7 Setting autonomous training allows for that translation of cognitive change or insight into emotional change.
8 Importantly engaging in this training also helps the client move towards becoming their own therapist and being self-sufficient going forward. This can help to ameliorate any dependence on the psychologist and foster independence in the client.

There are many types of autonomous training that you can set. We have outlined the major categories and their application uses in Table 7.5. The aim of any type of autonomous training is to allow practice of new skills and reinforce learning from within sessions.

Table 7.5 Autonomous training tasks in CBT and their application

Autonomous Training Tasks	*Description*	*Use and Training*
Psychoeducational Homework	Practitioner provides reading/audio-visual materials or suggesting areas of information that the client can use to educate themselves.	Use in early sessions or when client has travel periods where they show an inclination to learn.
Self-Assessment	These include out-of-session, real world, sport-based measurement and awareness generation in the form of thought records, self-monitoring activities and tasks that help clients to really see that feeling, thought, behaviour link in their own individual context.	Use throughout the CBT process to (a) secure data, (b) uncover patterns, and (c) measure change.
Exercise Practice	This involves asking the client to practise the exercises developed during sessions in training and competition environments. For example, you can ask your client to practise relaxation or breathing exercises or to use imagery.	Implemented at various stages and combined with self-assessment to see what is working and what needs work.
Simulations	These involve creating artificial environments that mimic the demands that the client goes through in their environment to simulate 'pressure' and built-in difficulties. This provides an in-situ attempt to practise the CBT-based skills such as how to overcome triggers, how to implement PETs and how to road-test new core beliefs.	Creating a pressure training/systematic desensitisation/exposure-based stimulation to create the conditions that would allow the unhelpful actions and cognitions to be triggered and work on managing them through adaptive interventions.

You will find that some clients respond positively to all and any of these and others find their completion much more difficult. For some clients, this can involve stepping out of their comfort zone and spending time with your client finding the right type of homework for them can improve the chances of completion and thereby the overall outcomes of your practice with them. It is important to leave time within each session for the setting of homework and for the review of previous homework. There are several reasons why autonomous training is not completed;

- Practitioner characteristics (e.g., the confidence of the practitioner);
- Task characteristics (e.g., the perceived difficulty of the task);
- Client characteristics (e.g., perfectionistic tendencies or lack of conscientiousness);
- Schedule and infrastructure (for example, a busy training-competition-travel schedule).

The emphasis is to set the right quantity and quality of homework and ensure you provide a clear rationale for the activity. This preparation puts the client in the best position to achieve the task that was collaboratively set. It is also necessary to be transparent about the outcome and to discuss the client's perception of progress from completing the autonomous training. Often clients may mistake autonomous training tasks as a 'magic bullet' that will lead to immediate change. Therefore, do not rush, but take time to really explain it and make sure that your client understands what you are asking of them. The collaborative element is vital to success, and research shows us that clients who set their own autonomous tasks are more likely to continue their practice after the practitioner input has ceased. Often beginning the training task in session, especially in early sessions, can increase the likelihood of completion. Helping to set up reminders for clients to do their homework can be beneficial. To allow the client the best conditions to complete the task, the practitioner must:

1 Take time to explain the task they want the client to complete;
2 Make sure that there is time for the client to do this;
3 If possible, provide a written explanation alongside a verbal one;
4 Set the work in collaboration with the client, explaining to them the role of homework in your work with them;
5 Ensure that clients have the skills and the space to do it;
6 Include the review of the training task on the agenda for the start of your next session, and note down what you asked them to do.

Reviewing autonomous training has been shown to increase compliance with the subsequent task that you set. There are measures of client adherence with autonomous training such as the Homework Rating Scale-Revised which looks at engagement; beliefs and perceived consequences of homework completion. Often, clients will not complete the tasks. It is imperative to approach this with them in a non-judgemental manner. Find out why they are not engaging with work between sessions and consider with them whether alternative forms or versions would be easier for them to process and engage with. Sometimes making really small changes such as renaming homework between session tasks or skills practice can be enough to remove a barrier. At other times, it may be due to client characteristics or the specific client presentation that is operational (e.g., depressive symptoms and amotivation).

Some clients might not complete the autonomous training tasks and others might hate them stating that 'I am coming to you to solve my problem', but on the whole clients will engage in the autonomous tasks and they should be set. You should start from the stance that if you set the tasks collaboratively and clearly then the work will be done.

Reflective Exercise

- Have you completed all the reflective exercises suggested so far in this book and if not, why not? Use this to reflect on why clients might or might not complete homework and what you have learned from that.
- Try setting yourself homework, perhaps incorporating Self-Talk or completing thought records. At the end of a week, review your progress and consider any difficulties you encountered. Try to think about what could have prevented those obstacles.

Reinforcing the foundations of the new core belief

The new core belief is developed and slowly starting to be applied in simulated 'practice environments'; however, often clients get stuck or feel stuck because the older core belief is familiar and 'feels safe' whereas the new core belief 'feels unproven'. The following techniques can be applied continuously with the client to ease this process:

- **Reattribution:** When the negative core belief is operational, the client selectively stops at their view of reality that fits that negative core belief. Like a camera, it only captures the frame you point it at. Clients attribute such causes as fixed and unchangeable and therefore create a mental imagery that is unhelpful to their growth (See Figure 7.1). Wells et al. (1997) highlights the techniques of finishing out the images and taking them beyond their worst point. This reduces distress accompanied by the situation and using the newer core belief, and shifts the mindset away from looking for 'danger'. For example, for the perfectionistic client, finishing out the image could be to review the consequences of learning from mistakes. The client with their older core belief would stop at something like 'mistakes will mean I will never reach the next level'. Instead, finishing out the mistake with their new core belief could show them that mistakes are not the end of the world. Therefore, they have changed their attribution of mistakes and where they fit within their perfectionistic core belief.
- **Exaggeration and Humour:** Humour and exaggeration is a creative and disruptive shift to the functioning and maintenance of the old core belief. The goal is *not to make the client's beliefs the focal point of humour and jokes*, but rather work to a point where the client looks at them as 'funny' or 'weird' or 'silly'. Humour by exaggeration, that is, taking older, self-defeating core beliefs to extreme conclusions to show the weirdness or absurdity of ideas are useful to generate realistic interpretations of what will happen if they let their older core beliefs go. For example, for the perfectionistic client who is triggered by mistakes may say (See Figure 7.1)

CLIENT: It will all go horribly.

PRACTITIONER: Yes, that will lose you the match, then the tournament, that will make you forget how to play tennis, and you will have to start learning how to serve from scratch.

CLIENT: No, of course not, how can I forget to play tennis … it is impossible to go that way.

PRACTITIONER: You did say 'go horribly'.

Clients' [laughs] 'Fair point … so mistakes are not necessarily bad all the time … its what my coach says too, if we know what's going wrong, we can fix it'.

Humour should only be used after a strong therapeutic relationship is established and should be avoided in cases where the client is highly self-critical and has self-esteem concerns linked to the opinion of others. The practitioner can also humorously view their own work with the client to show that humour can be applied to any situation and in that way normalise it.

- **Behavioural Experiments:** They are active interventions that forms a foundational part of CBT. When used to strengthen new core beliefs, they allow the client to *do* and *experience* alternatives, which reinforces the new core belief pattern. The proof that the client *can do* these things and *feel/act* differently is powerful evidence that expands the clients' problem solving. This allows the new core belief to be strengthened. See above.

Reflective Exercise

- Try to complete a thought record for yourself. Use Socratic questioning to help you to identify the event, automatic thoughts, consequences, disputations and alternative thoughts. Reflect on how easy or difficult you found the experience, the extent to which using a thought record column sheet helped and whether over time you find this easier to do.
- Practise replacing SITs and PITs with SATs and PETs, can you do this more easily over time?
- Think of a client you've worked with or choose a case study example from a book and try to complete a thought record for that presentation. Reflect on how helpful you found it.

Section III

Reflecting and Enhancing Practice

8 Education Issues

The education issues we portray in this chapter embrace matters typical of any cognitive behaviour therapy (CBT) process with clients. We converge on the usefulness of education issues to aid the reader in learning, applying, reflecting, and evaluating in a reflective feedback loop to maintain the learning process. Specifically, we shall illuminate critical issues in the session process and a how-to guide to secure session agreement by educating the clients on the timeline of change by organising mental shortcuts in the thought-emotion-behaviour matrix. We will also trace strategies to forestall relapse and facilitate psychological stability in high performance using worked examples from cases.

What are you doing and why you are doing it?

Manoeuvring towards best practice as a sport psychology consultant seems axiomatic, yet without guides, principles, education, and reflective practice, we have a propensity to reproduce our mistakes in a therapeutic merry-go-round. When we understand what we do and why we do what we do, we can lay the foundation from which we can deliver best practices to clients. Our deeper motives for working as a practitioner might tumble into several categories. We often consider these motives as those from within and those from without. From within, we might wish to help others to understand themselves or help others to manage their own lives. We might wish to understand others better or perhaps help others in how others helped you. From without, our motives might propagate from others (e.g., parents and coaches) recognising our empathy and willingness to help those in need.

There is another category of motives that many sport psychology consultants might not wish to consider: shadow motives. Shadow motives are the shadow side of our impulse to help and reveal much about how we meet our needs through helping others. Hawkins and McMahon (2020) presented four common 'shadow motives': (1) the drive for power, (2) meeting our needs through others, (3) the need to be liked, and (4) the wish to heal. In sport and exercise settings, as in life, many of us hold a hidden need for power and to be in control of our lives and the world in which we live. Some examples of shadow motives are:

- Be in a position of control as a practitioner to clients who appear worse off than us because they have requested our assistance. We might not see how we create dependency and undermine a client's worth because we cannot recognise our shadow motive for power and control.

DOI: 10.4324/9781003274513-11

- Another 'shadow' side of helping is meeting our own needs. Whether we recognise these needs, these needs remain. We need clients to need help from us if we are to gain the esteem we generate from our capacity to help. If we deny this need, it would remain in the shadows of our helping work and express itself as a demand to be fulfilled.
- A third 'shadow' motive is the need to be liked and valued. As psychologists, we might believe others see us as 'a good person' who 'always does the right thing'. This superimposed image might not sit well with us because it might not be how we see ourselves. Alternatively, a client might see us as untrustworthy, distant, and misusing our role and power. This superimposed image might hurt us because it is not how we see ourselves. The need to be liked in this circumstance might mean working to 'please' the client, deny this interpretation of you or seek a way out for 'plausible' reasons.

Whatever the client presents to us about ourselves, we can reflect upon it rather than deny it and explore it in supervision because when one feels vulnerable and in need as the client may be, projecting these feelings to make the psychologist feel inadequate as the client feels. The final 'shadow' motive is the wish to heal. If we argue our needs are only dangerous when we deny them, then knowing ourselves and our motives means we can be of the utmost help to our clients. For example, if we are denied our wish to work with senior professional players in a football club, we may unwittingly use the academy players to show our competency and worth to achieve our desired but denied motive. We might project parts of ourselves we cannot endure (e.g., lack of preparation, low conscientiousness) onto our clients claiming, 'they don't do the work so how can they improve'.

Our helping behaviour above the ground has its roots beneath. We witness our actions, but our motives remain hidden. If we do not explore our core beliefs (those roots underground), we cannot know for sure why we do what we do; but this excavating work means we can help clients better and manage our reactions and judgements better as we progress in our profession. Your core beliefs and basic assumptions might seem hidden, but when we scrape beneath the surface, we see them in the way you work, the values and assumptions you hold about people, how you believe people ought to be helped and how you believe change happens. For instance, if you spend your time telling your clients what to do, your behaviour might reflect a core belief that clients cannot help themselves and need expert guidance to change. We need to unearth these guiding values we hold so we can examine and change them as our knowledge and experience grow.

Let us explore three basic assumptions a practitioner might hold:

1. **People are experts on themselves:** If we hold a basic assumption that people are experts on themselves, it means we believe clients know themselves best. They know how it feels to lose a championship final; they know what they most want to achieve in their athletic lives. Yet as athletes, they may have spent much of their lives being told what they want, what they need, what's best for them and how they feel.
2. **People create their own meaning:** If we believe clients create their own meaning, we can understand how, for example, they might construct their own downfall by setting targets that are unachievable just now and confirm themselves as 'failures'.

Their 'failure' confirms the belief they hold about themselves. Together with your client, you can explore these attributions about their experiences and open new and enlightening interpretations.

3 **People can change:** If we believe clients can change, then they can exchange unhelpful ways of behaving for more helpful ones. The client learned ways of behaving that offered a sense of protection from harm, ridicule, or rejection, but brought other problems into play. Within your compassionate and understanding environment, the client can discover options offering better returns.

Non-verbal, paraverbal, and performance behaviour

When we communicate, we use three types of messages. Verbal messages which are the words we use; paraverbal (or paralinguistic) messages reflects how we say the words we use (e.g., tone of voice, pitch, delivery and rate of speech) and nonverbal messages reflects our body language (e.g., posture, proximity, personal space, facial expressions, eye contact). Sometimes a client 'performs' for the psychologist because this interaction with a power broker (i.e., the psychologist) reflects the typical hierarchy in sport settings. This power imbalance, even in a relatively collaborative model of CBT, is clear in the non-reciprocal therapeutic relationship. For instance, the client self-discloses extensively while the psychologist self-discloses little and the emotional neediness of the client presents in stark contrast to the typical exclusion of the psychologist's emotional needs. People in the community often acknowledge those in the helping professions with great admiration and adulation. In sport settings, however, the psychologist might feel exploited by their more powerful client who manipulates to meet their needs.

The goal of this section is to explore communication beyond the words we hear. To achieve this goal, we need a framework upon which we can capture the context of a CBT session and the processes of communication between the psychologist and the client. The practitioner fulfils the role of guide or mentor rather than instructor, so the practitioner is 'walking with' the client who explores her options for new ways of thinking, feeling and behaving with the psychologist asking questions or offering information where relevant. To know the client's world, practitioners actively enquire with genuine care, respect, and non-judgement of the client's feelings and perspectives. We tread a fine line here because we know clients present cognitive errors (e.g., mind reading) that distort the picture presented. Therefore, we occasionally offer psychoeducation. The collaborative nature of the therapeutic relationship in CBT means the psychologist and client are working together to plan and problem-solve together.

In this collaborative relationship, the client speaks for about 60–70% of the session. The psychologist is actively listening to the idiosyncratic details in communication; to what the client says and does not say. The Socratic method is a process comprising concrete questioning, empathic listening, summarising and synthesising or analysing. In the empathic listening process, we attend to what the client is saying and how the client is saying it. Our careful, non-judgemental attention adds to the richness of our hypotheses and the questions that follow. Without knowing, we might press ahead in our questioning to confirm our hypotheses without empathic pacing and allowing the client to make sense of the story unfolding. Our desire to press ahead means we might miss hearing what is not being expressed (i.e., the emotions hiding behind the words) and the silent language of the body, a client's internal experience.

When we attend to our client, we witness changes in posture, eye movements, facial expressions, and breathing. We might witness hand gestures that correspond with stressed words and phrases. As we move from thinking (e.g., observing, categorising, judging, rationalising, summarising) to feeling (e.g., emotional or gut response, immediate, neither true nor false, restless, smiling), we enrich our lives. As we develop our therapeutic skills in CBT, we can move beyond them and allow them to coalesce in active listening, harness our attention, understand from the speaker's frame of reference, limit our talking, notice the paralinguistics – those ways of speaking, utterances, pitch, volume and intonation. Clients present themselves as they see themselves; perhaps unknowingly, we sometimes try to get our clients to see themselves from our perspective. We might need this direction and control because we see our work as evaluating, influencing, controlling and directing rather than listening to understand. In sport settings that are awash with evaluation, influence, direction and control, it is easy to miss this way of our working when working with athletes. Many trainee sport and exercise psychologists share their feelings of strain in supervision, shouldering responsibility for their client. This well-meaning act substitutes clients from the problem-solving process rather than involving them and harnessing their thinking processes to solve the problem. A helpful learning process is recording sessions (with consent). This can be used for discussion and professional development in supervision. We also remember that clients' personal growth thrives on unconditional acceptance. Yet, we might stray into non-acceptance by advising, giving solutions, analysing, lecturing, praising, preaching and probing. By entering the client's frame of reference, we listen for the content and feeling to hear and respond appropriately.

Educating clients in the model and processes with the aim of insight and awareness

There is a role for psychoeducation in CBT. The precise place, time and delivery of psychoeducation depends on the several factors (e.g., presenting issues, client preferences, knowledge gaps) but from first principles, one ought to help the client understand the model of CBT and the processes within it because much distress accrues for clients who do not know and understand the CBT process and the general processes in therapy.

Clients don't know you – Make them feel welcome

It is a daunting prospect to share any part of ourselves with a stranger, so we need courage and trust to do so. This is the reality clients enter to. Knowing this circumstance means our first thought must be to help clients feel safe, at ease, and accepted when they meet you for the first time. This less travelled road for a client brings nervousness or anxiety, but the psychologist might also feel apprehensive about meeting a client for the first time. Knowing these challenges, the psychologist can work to reduce a feeling of vulnerability and build an atmosphere of safety, trust and equality. For a psychologist delivering services in sport, we find ourselves on a training pitch, in a canteen, in an airport lounge and so on because what remains paramount is that we engage the client where the client feels at ease. For example, away from coaches or others, where confidentiality may be at risk. We might also work from our private practice in which we control the environment, but we tip the balance of neutrality in favour of the psychologist. The safety, trust and neutrality the client seeks is also necessary for us, the psychologists, to do good work. We earn trust through active listening, sensitive responding, empathy, and genuineness. We can also model trust and respect through openness, honesty, and reliability. Sowing these seeds of trust at the beginning of a therapeutic relationship brings a bountiful harvest in personal growth for the client. We need to remember that we are building a relationship (see Chapter 4) with the client and our work together is meaningful as a process.

Drawing the lines: Boundaries

Most sports have lines demarcating the field of play- this should also be done to set the boundaries of CBT work. Part of the safety and trust we develop with a client depends on constructing clear boundaries. Some people present with rigid boundaries to protect themselves but also, they limit emotional contact while others present with few boundaries, leaving them open to being hurt. Rigid boundaries present a person as self-sufficient with others kept at a distance and the rigid boundaries mean the person remains relatively unknown to others. Through hurt or rejection, the person learns to protect oneself and they created this distance to protect oneself from further pain. With porous or enmeshed boundaries, people do not have a sense of their separateness in a relationship. An athlete might encourage a close relationship with a coach and overtrain to avoid an emptiness inside from a troublesome home life. The boundaries we learn as children and young people shape the boundaries we hold later as adults.

Without boundaries, we do not know when others cross our boundaries or when we cross others' boundaries. A frantic desire for love and affection might mean a client cannot see how others might manipulate them. We cannot see our boundaries, but we can know they are there, so we establish a sense of who we are and our identity. With healthy boundaries, we respect ours and others'. With healthy boundaries, we generate safety, security, self-respect, and a healthy possibility for emotional connection with others. When others traverse our healthy boundaries, we know through being upset, irritated, or angry. This emotional feedback tells us about ourselves and our boundaries. To set healthy boundaries, we set what we feel is acceptable to us and we take responsibility for our safety (e.g., emotional, physical, and sexual); in doing so, others witness our self-respect and know the limits of what we allow when they are in our company. This goes for both the client and practitioner.

As psychologists, we set boundaries through confidentiality, session times, number and length of sessions, location, responding to correspondence, and so on. We can present our boundaries in information sheets or on a website and then, with a written contract, to work together. Contracting shows respect for both parties so we know where we shall attend sessions, understand confidentiality, GDPR, fees, late fees, frequency of sessions, goals of the sessions, homework, and so forth.

Working with athletes, coaches and teams in a sport setting might feel wholly unstructured because competitions often occur when everyone else is enjoying leisure time. We might receive text messages (or Instagram DM) from an athlete without the athlete seeking our permission or perhaps a client turning up at our private offices without an appointment. In these cases, the client is stretching the boundaries of the psychologist-client relationship, but often without knowing. The client might try to meet psychological needs (e.g., love, belongingness, esteem) in these ways. When a psychologist blurs the boundaries with a client, the psychologist muddles roles and expectations, might create unhealthy dependence, or emotionally or psychologically harm the client.

From this vantage, building rapport and safe boundaries allows the client to stretch and grow personally through the CBT therapeutic modality. Using the analogy of a garden and the gardening process in the client's mind, together, we have tilled the soil to allow insight and awareness available through CBT to grow. Through self-awareness, clients can recognise how they meet psychological needs or not within their lives. For example, one might meet one's esteem needs through professional rewards or belongingness needs by being a member of a club. Our (practitioner) security needs might be met through a salary or an insurance policy.

'Dilemmas', 'traps', 'snags', or 'facilitators'

The process of CBT rarely runs smooth because the dilemmas, traps, and snags we encounter stop us from fulfilling the change process. Knowing about these challenges at the beginning of a therapeutic process means we can prepare for them when they arise. We find dilemmas, traps, and snags in cognitive analytic therapy and they represent a useful understanding about the behaviour of athletes. Dilemmas present polarised choices where one follows the least objectionable option or alternates between them. For example, these false choices keep us in difficult situations because we worry the alternative will be worse. An athlete might believe she has no choice but to keep on training at her limit because taking breaks does not epitomise the 'hardworking athlete who never stops working' and who reaches the top. Traps maintain negative beliefs because they generate forms of behaviour which appear to confirm the negative beliefs. For instance, an athlete might binge eat because he feels bad about himself and feels worse because he binged. Finally, we abandon or sabotage goals because achieving them might be dangerous to oneself or others or disallowed. For example, *'I really want to change but …'*. Sometimes these snags – things we think about that prevent us from changing the behaviours that displease us – emerge through our families *'We were never any good at …'* or when a family member behaves aggressively as we pursue positive changes for us. We see many snags in sport settings because athletes fear doing things that might bring them success or perhaps that their happiness will be taken away or they feel they do not deserve what they wish to pursue. A clear formulation is the bedrock to identify these traps and then design interventions to take care of it (see Chapter 5).

Relapse prevention and performance facilitation

Even when we strive towards change and plant a firm footing in more adaptive behaviours, we can relapse. Part of one's successful behaviour change depends upon knowing the levers of change and the possibilities of challenges that sabotage our progress. One simple method in applied psychology to notice the traps along the road towards our goals is *mental contrasting*. Mental contrasting is comparing your ideal outcome with the hurdles of everyday life. We are more likely to achieve our goals when we focus on the outcome we want and the trials we face, and plan for both. The practitioner and client can theorise about what might get in our way while pursuing our goals; then, with this list, we can assemble an implementation intention *'if-then'* or *'when-then'* contingency plan to prevent the obstacle from derailing our plans. A 'when-then' plan means 'when

X happens, then I will do Y'. This concrete approach to problem-solving is much less cognitively taxing than an abstract approach such as 'collaborate to solve the problem'.

In a more general sense, we need to know more about relapse and what a relapse means in the CBT to manage it. Managing a relapse is a skill for life because, regardless of our worthwhile intentions, we fall back on our promises. One goal of our CBT practice remains to support the client in becoming independent of the psychologist with a toolbox of techniques to apply following a setback. Staying on track represents a skill one can learn early in the therapeutic process, develop, and refine it. Following a setback or a relapse, we try to explain what happened. In a therapeutic setting, the psychologist might set forth the following questions as a tool to recovery. For instance, how can we understand what happened? How can we learn from what happened? What can we learn from this experience if the situation arises again? In short, we tell a story of what happened (i.e., experience) but the story has a moral (i.e., something to learn) and guidance for next time round (i.e., a plan).

From this perspective, our relapse creates resources to draw on because we learn from our experiences. Starting an exercise regime, or healthy eating process, might appear as a dichotomous position for some people: *'I'm exercising or I'm not'* or *'I'm eating healthily or I'm not'* with no position in between. This dichotomy strains most people because the vagaries of life mean we slip out of control occasionally and these slips do not represent the failure one might feel: *'I broke my diet – now I'm a total failure; I can't do anything right'*. We encourage grasping a more pragmatic view that occasionally we will slip from our intentions; however, we can learn from our experiences and approach a similar challenge with greater resources. By learning from our experiences, we might spot the signs or triggers of this event happening and plan for how we might lose control and limit the damage. Many cars present early warning lights on the dashboard (e.g., low fuel level, low tyre pressure) which give us time and perhaps a choice about what to do next (e.g., refuel, inflate tyres at the filling station). In a similar way, we can attend to the environment and situations in which we find ourselves: Will I be hungry on this long journey this afternoon? What food would be best for me? Let's prepare now.

For some clients, writing their plans in a session is helpful to minimise relapse. Many of our clients store their plans on their mobile phone. Distress often means our memory falters, so planning for relapse with plans on your phone is a sensible strategy. One golfer who felt quite miserable while travelling on tour away from her family could see what lay ahead for her. This *at-risk situation* was highly likely, so the client had to develop better cognitive and behavioural coping strategies and plan to put these into action. These strategies and action plans form part of the CBT process and need to be accessible for use when the need arises. Self-statements encourage clients to acknowledge their efficacy to help themselves. For instance, *'My thinking creates these traps for me; however, I know what I can do to help myself when I get stuck. I have my strategies and plans ready to go'*. Cognitive restructuring and cognitive reappraisal are helpful techniques (see Chapter 7).

Psychologist and client problems

Relapses occur for several reasons. Some of these reasons relate to the psychologist and some relate to the client and the circumstances in which the clients find themselves. Although the goal of therapy might be to help clients to help themselves, some psychologists might be reluctant to let go of the role of expert and some clients are reluctant to let go of the 'fixing' from the psychologist. A second issue that arises is that we might not focus on the need for relapse management from the beginning of treatment; however, any lapse during treatment is an excellent opportunity to review and learn from the experience.

CBT is a learning process, and we educate clients in the model and methods of CBT. To remember what we learned, we need to remember facts and skills. As students in applied psychology training programmes, for example, we normally learn by keeping notes, reviewing our notes, making study plans and learning material that comprises knowledge (knows), competence (knows how), performance (shows how) and action (does). We encourage clients to learn through experiences, observe and reflect upon those experiences, and plan for next time. In the adult learning cycle (Kolb, 1984), we learn through observation, reflection, and planning from our experiences and test these again through our experiences. A critical issue for a client is not just learning (i.e., acquiring knowledge) but also keeping what they learn and retrieving it when required. We need to bridge these gaps with reason, focus, repetition, and memory aids.

There are two steps to meaningful learning. First, we need to think abstractly to understand new concepts and ideas and second, apply these concepts and ideas to challenging tasks (e.g., a behavioural experiment). We need our memory to store, organise, and retrieve information to manage life's everyday challenges. But human memory is fallible. Rather than a literal process, it is inferential and reconstructive (Bjork et al., 2013). This inferential process means we store interpretations of events rather than the events themselves, so memories are a smorgasbord of fact and fiction. Because our brains are hard-wired to generate connections, new information reminds of things we know. Spacing our learning means we can add new information to our existing knowledge.

In therapeutic sessions, we can encourage clients to search for meaning in the concepts and ideas we share. This search for meaning is the deepest level of processing to encode information. Asking questions is a clever method to aid encoding of new information. New skills require repetition to enhance their storage. This practice of new skills can form part of the homework challenge for clients. Finally, the retrieval of stored information when it is most needed (e.g., facts, experience, skills) often depends upon a cue. We know people remember information better when the attempted recall occurs in a context similar to the one in which it was learned originally. This context-dependency of memory retrieval means that athletes might need to test themselves under competition-like conditions as often as possible to learn how to cope with the stress of competition.

Our ability to interpret, explain, or impose meaning on things is our understanding. We can fill in gaps in our understanding by using our knowledge and imagination profitably. When clients are learning in therapy sessions, we can encourage questioning to deepen their level of processing and encoding information. Clients can pay special attention to what they are learning as they learn it and develop schemas to organise the material in their own minds. They can link what they are learning to what they already know and, together with the psychologist, can check in to monitor their comprehension of the material. Finally, clients can practise learning and retrieving their new skills in contexts in which they wish to use them. Mnemonics like rhymes and acronyms are especially useful for learning. One useful mnemonic is *Method of*

Loci: walking through your 'mind palace'. For instance, the client places each item they wish to remember in a place in a familiar setting, such as their home. They might wish to remember the sequence of thoughts, feelings, physiological responses and behaviours. They could place each of these elements in a familiar place, from your kitchen to your front door or place your thoughts hanging on the door of your fridge, your feelings draped over your hall mirror, your physiological responses hanging by your coat on your hall stand and your behaviours a hook on the back of your front door. Alternatively, you might use an acrostic device – a sentence in which the first letters of each word represent the items you wish to remember. In music, most people are familiar with the names of the notes on the treble clef (E, G, B, D, F) by the sentence 'Every Good Boy Deserves Favour'.

9 Evaluation and Transition to Client Self-Help

When we work with a client, our long-term goal is to work effectively with them, to (a) make a clear and positive influence on their performance or presenting issue and then (b) to leave them with the skills they need to work on their own once our relationship with them finishes. As practitioners, we are not there to 'fix' our clients. We are there in an educational and facilitative role, helping our clients to see how their thoughts, feelings, and actions are all inter-related and how the knowledge of that interaction and the ability to alter it, can influence sport performance. We work collaboratively, introduce our clients to new ways of thinking and new tools and techniques that can help them work towards their goals. A key guiding principle of our work is to leave clients with new knowledge and a sense of confidence and competence which fosters a belief that they can use what they have learned with us, on their own.

To achieve that goal, we actively discourage emotional dependency on us as practitioners and strive to work alongside them reassuringly. Not that cognitive behaviour therapy (CBT) is 'easy', it's not because we expect our clients to unlearn long-term habitual behaviours and patterns of thinking and to trust in us, and the CBT process, and commit to trying new ways of doing and thinking about their experiences. Though it is complicated, the evidence shows that CBT is effective so what we need to ensure is that we communicate that to our clients. We can help them see the benefit and outcome of the interventions they are engaging with, and that we leave them with tools and strategies that are tried and tested for them alongside a curiosity and a desire to keep making improvements and working on themselves. This chapter will consider how we can demonstrate evidence of value to our client, how we can monitor or evaluate our own practice, what to do when things do not go to plan and offer practical advice on making sure you leave your client with the strategies, techniques, and confidence to keep making positive changes.

Assessing the outcome of your work – The client's perspective

As a practitioner, you will need to decide the type of techniques that you use in sessions with clients to gauge progress and success. There are many ways to do this, and you will need to ensure that you are tailoring your outcome measures to your client and their individual formulation. Goals change as the therapeutic relationship establishes itself and discoveries are made, so you will need to view formulation as an ongoing and collaborative endeavour. Following on from this agile response, you might also need to choose different measures to indicate improvement and facilitate ongoing collaborative working.

DOI: 10.4324/9781003274513-12

As well as re-formulation leading to changes in your practice, changes will occur because of ongoing monitoring of client progress (see Chapter 5). If clients are not progressing as you had expected, then you should raise this concern and intervene. To know if clients are making progress, you need to include some measures of routine outcome monitoring so that you are aware of the level of progress and can intervene if necessary. Research has shown that not all practitioners use outcome measures in their work, but within a CBT context this would be expected as part of your practice, so if you have not been using CBT routinely then incorporating outcome measures could be a change that is required for you. Your theoretical orientation and approach as a practitioner who used cognitive behavioural techniques would require that you do this. There are a vast range of measures that you can use and again, this will need to be specific to the client you are working with and the goals that you have set with that client. Using measures and discussing progress with clients ensures you are meeting ethical obligations to provide beneficial services to clients. Their use can also help you establish good working practices with clients where you are working collaboratively to assess what strategies and tools have helped and which have not. This strategy can foster a good collaborative working relationship and highlight the need for clients to be accountable for their progress.

You should consider the reliability and validity of measures that you use - most measures will have reliability and validity (see Chapter 6); but the same is not always true for performance outcome measures – which are specific to your client and their sport. For a good explanation of this area, we direct you to Schweizer et al. (2020) who consider the reliability of sport - specific outcome measures such as the golf putt, dart throws, and basketball free throw and guidance on how to improve reliability for sport-specific performance outcome measures.

Many of the scales that you employ will depend on self-report and there are clear issues inherent in these. As a practitioner, much of your work will be with performance issues and you will need to *link* mental or psychological wellbeing in your client with their performance. If you can demonstrate this relationship between the two factors (in formulation), then your intervention will follow from that, so you need there to be a strong evidence base to the measures that you are employing to establish that relationship. Many of the performance measures you use (golf putt, number of shots made, accuracy of service, speed over distance) will be easy to measure and will be reliable and valid. It is the measures of psychological states that you might want to spend more time considering (see Chapter 6). What you will want to consider with your client is the perceived effectiveness and usefulness of these measures and also the *timing* of their deployment. If you are working with an athlete and want to record or measure psychological wellbeing prior to and immediately following a competition, then you need to consider the time the measure takes to complete and also consider the extent to which it might interfere with usual pre-competition preparation. You want to ensure that the collection of information for you to establish progress on client's goals is not itself having a negative effect on the psychology-performance correlation.

Choosing efficacy measures

Choosing measures to use with clients can be difficult because of the range of options open to you. You should review those that are available and consider how you could use them within a CBT framework. The measures you choose will depend on how you are as a practitioner and what you feel is beneficial to your client and their chosen outcomes.

To give some examples, you could consider using various measures of mental/psychological wellbeing such as the CORE Measurement Tools. CORE stands for Clinical Outcomes in Routine Evaluation and the CORE-10 is something that you might use on a session by session basis to monitor any changes in your client and their psychological wellbeing and health. If your interest lies in depressive symptoms, then you could consider using the PHQ which is a short instrument used to monitor the severity of depressive symptoms. Alternatively, you might consider a measure specific to anxiety, such as the anxiety subscale of the DASS, or a sport specific anxiety measure such as the Sport Anxiety Scale, which measures trait anxiety (see Chapter 6). The measure you employ will depend on the goals you have set with your client and how you have chosen together to look at progress. The sheer choice can be daunting, but spending time really looking at what these scales measure and its relevance to the client presentation is crucial

The presenting issue and the goals set following assessment and formulation will inform your choices. For example, if your client is a gymnast who is presenting with anxiety around competition, then you could consider the Sport Competition Anxiety Test (SCAT); or if you are working with a younger athlete who is part of an academy football team and presents with concerns around their relationships with key members of their team, peers, and coaches, then you could consider the Student Athlete Relationship Instrument. A body of work has demonstrated the effectiveness of measuring mood states in athletes and of the use of profiles such as the 'iceberg profile' using the Profile of Mood States (POMS) or the Brunel Mood Scale (BRUMS). There are established norms around these types of scales so that you can compare an individual's profiles with established norms. So not only are you gaining individual information, but you can also use these established mood profiles in a psychoeducational manner and help explain relationships between mood, performance, and psychological wellbeing of athletes. Lochbaum et al. (2021) in their meta-analysis of published studies of POMS and athletic performance, concluded that this is a reliable predictor of sport performance among competitive athletes. While working with a tennis player to improve their psychological skills, then using the Test of Performance Strategies (TOPS) scale would be appropriate, as would the Mental Toughness Questionnaire (MTQ) or the +AdaptR (see Chapter 6).

Avoid using any measure *without good reason* and be sure that your client understands *why* you are gathering this information, *what* it will be used for, and *how* you and your client collaboratively use this information to check on progress and make any alterations to your work together that are deemed necessary. Some other examples of measures are:

- As well as these scales that measure specific areas that you might work on, you will also gather data through autonomous tasks or between session tasks on cognitive distortions, activity scheduling, behavioural activation and general reflections. These too are valuable sources of information that can play a key role in highlighting change and progress, so make sure that you use these sources with your client.
- Scaling or grading is common in CBT and should be introduced from the start of your sessions with clients. This can form part of your socialisation process with clients where you explain to them the underlying principles of CBT and why assessment and measurement form key aspects of CBT work. During this

socialisation process, you will explain CBT, the methods you are going to use, and the elements that are within your client's control. You can also introduce the idea of scaling or grading here.

The data you gather doesn't have to be complex and often in CBT what we use are ten-point scales that help us and the client to really understand what is going on for them and can contribute to our intervention design and our evaluation of our work. Asking clients to rate aspects on a scale can help us and them in several ways. It can help to move clients away from black and white thinking (see Chapter 7), help them to gain a sense of perspective and also enable interventions to be developed that target that aspect where you can clearly see progress. If we return to Annette from Chapter 3 her thought was *'I am a failure'*. Asking Annette to rate how much she believes that statement can help us gather more specific information, which can then feed into intervention planning. *'So on a scale of 1–10 can you tell me …'*. Gaining an initial number can help us question the client and discover what is going on for them. We can ask follow-up questions such as '*What would need to be different to move you from that 3 to a 5'* or *'What's preventing you from being a 5'*. In this way, numbers help us to breakdown issues into steps we can plan interventions for. Using regular simple measures allows you to get an idea of a baseline for your client and you can use this information to assess the effects of any interventions that you then use. These baseline measures are also important when you are evaluating the outcome of your work together. Clients make progress during CBT and once that happens, it can be difficult for them to remember how distressing their initial issues were. Having these baseline measures can help you demonstrate to the client the progress they have made.

Reflective Exercise

- Think about a previous client and their presenting issue. What measures would seem appropriate for using with that client? How would you have introduced these measures? How would you have used them in your work with the client?
- Look at the thought records you have completed for yourself following reflective exercises in Chapter 7. How does looking back at these help you plan for the future and see your progress? How could you use this with clients?
- Carry out some reading around mood profiles and consider how you could use this information with previous clients to help explain relationships or educate them.

Assessing the outcome of your work – Therapist competence

Measuring the outcome of practitioner work and competence as you progress as a CBT practitioner is also important. There's a large body of evidence outlining competence as a practitioner generally but less so that is specific to the competence of practitioners using CBT. Some *fundamentals* are (a) ethical practice; (b) reflective practice; (c) awareness of sport context and culture; (d) developing a working alliance; and (e) design and deliver of appropriate and effective interventions (see Hutter et al., 2015).

Many of these are also relevant to your competence as a practitioner, but there are additional variables to be considered when reflecting on and working towards competence as a practitioner. Given the emphasis that we have shown throughout this book on phenomena that are observable and measurable, it is not surprising that measures of therapist behaviours have been developed. Recent advances have included the development of reliable and valid measures of competence that provide clarity around behavioural anchors and can be readily used in formative feedback (Muse et al., 2017). The scales mentioned here are all developed in adult mental health work, so you can reflect on their applicability to your own sporting context. There are several scales you can use here to assess your own competence and these include the Cognitive Therapy Rating Scale (www.beckinstitute.org); the Cognitive Therapy Rating Scale Revised (Blackburn et al., 2001); the Cognitive Therapy Adherence and Competence Scale (CTACS) (Barber et al., 2003); the Assessment of Core CBT Skills (ACCS) (Muse et al., 2017); the UCL Centre for Outcome Research and Effectiveness scales and competence frameworks (Roth & Pilling, 2007) and the UCL scale for structured observation of CBT (Roth, 2016). In this section, we will give more detail on two of these and how you can incorporate them into your practice to aid your professional development.

UCL competence framework

The UCL competence framework is designed for practitioners working with depression and anxiety using CBT methods. Since these presentations are common in sport – they are also relevant to practitioner development.

The UCL framework is based on five competence domains: generic competences; behavioural and cognitive competences; specific cognitive and behavioural techniques; problem specific techniques and meta-competences. These are all arranged in a 'map' showing how they all fit together and outlining the competencies within each domain. For example, generic competence comprises three knowledge competencies; four competencies relating to building and maintaining the therapeutic relationship; competence in assessment and competence in making use of supervision. You can download the competencies, the map and self-assessment tools and guide from the website of the CORE (www.ucl.ac.uk/CORE). The framework can be applied in several ways, including supervision, service development, training and self-assessment. The key here for your development is the self-assessment tool, which can give a clear indication of your current level of competence based on the elements of the framework. It can help you plan which areas of your practice you can focus development on, too. You can download the self-assessment tool from the website and along with that instructions on how to use the tool for your own self-development purposes.

Self-assessment scales

- **CTSR: The Cognitive Therapy Scale** Revised is frequently used in research investigating outcomes in CBT work. It is based on the Cognitive Cycle and the therapist's ability to work with thoughts, feelings, physiology and behaviour. Overlaid on this is the Dreyfus scale of competence, encompassing a range of performance/competence from 0 or incompetent to 6 or expert. The items in the CTSR define the skills needed to move a client around the cognitive cycle effectively. The twelve items outlined in the manual of the CTS-R (Blackburn et al., 2001) are agenda setting and adherence; feedback; collaboration; pacing and efficient time use; interpersonal effectiveness; eliciting appropriate emotional expression; eliciting key cognitions; eliciting behaviours; guided discovery; conceptual integration; application of change methods and homework setting. For each item, what is expected of the practitioner is outlined and a set of checklist questions for raters to ask themselves is provided. As with many of the scales available, this can be quite time-consuming and so shorter versions have been developed which have good criterion validity, such as the CTSR-4. This can be used to assess competence using shorter session samples and so is a lower cost option for therapist training. In place of the twelve items listed above, they have four: Structure; Therapeutic relation; Conceptual integration and Therapeutic change.

- **ACCS:** This is from Muse and colleagues and is not specific to a particular disorder or treatment protocol and because of that can be considered trans-diagnostic and may seem more applicable to the sport and performance context. The ACCS has eight competence domains measured by 22 items. The domains are agenda setting; formulation; CBT interventions; homework; assessing change; effective use of time; fostering therapeutic relations and effective two-way communication. Items within each domain are rated on a four-point scale of 1 limited clinical skill to 4 advanced clinical skill. This scale is developmental and has space for formative feedback that is narrative to help build on and explain the numerical rating scale information. The ACCS has a manual that can be used to familiarise individuals with the scale and how to use it. It offers concrete examples of behaviours considered consistent with each item and these can give guidance on what sort of performance is expected for each of the items that make up the scale. A key feature of the ACCS and one that is relevant here is that it has been designed so that it can be used as a self-assessment tool. So, you could either choose to record a middle session with a client and take that to supervision, requesting your supervisor to rate you using the ACCS or you could rate yourself using this scale as a self-development exercise. Although a self-rating of a session will not necessarily be used as a stand-alone measure of competence or a formal measure of your competence, it can be developmental and can help you reflect on your current skill set and identify development areas.

Reflective Exercise

- Find copies of one or two of these scales. Using a previously recorded CBT session that you can find online, try to rate the therapists. Reflect on how useful you found this and what it highlighted for you.

What isn't working and why – Troubleshooting tips?

Sometimes it is difficult to pinpoint exactly what is or is not working well in your CBT client work. The following sections briefly touch on some common pitfalls or problems that are encountered during CBT work that you could consider if you feel things aren't going as smoothly as you'd like or if progress isn't being made.

- **Is it me?** When you feel that something is not working in the sessions or with your client, it might be worth considering if the source of that is the client or you. It can be that as a novice CBT practitioner, you yourself are having some cognitive distortions, automatic thoughts and worries about how you are being perceived and this could influence the outcome of the therapy or on your perception of that. We suggest that running alongside your client's homework, fill out thought records for yourself, reflecting on the session and noticing what was going through your mind.

For example, thoughts like *'I bet he won't do this homework'* or *'I don't feel like I've set this session up well'* or *'Am I being too directive'* are all things that you can work on through the use of cognitive interventions and reflective practice. You want to be aware of yourself as a practitioner and work to ensure that your own biases aren't affecting your practice. So, use the tools yourself to be cognisant of your own position and how that might affect your practice (see Chapter 10 for troubleshooting options).

- **Check In:** If you find clients are not making the progress that you had set goals around, check in with them to discover why. Speak with your client to uncover what might be behind this lack of progress. For example, perhaps they do not understand how to fill out the forms you have suggested in which case you could use session time explaining the task further and working collaboratively with the client to complete the form before expecting them to do more on their own. At times, we may realise that the client does not fully understand/buy-in to the process and structure of CBT sessions. In such cases a psychoeducation process and a frank discussion around how to measure thoughts, check-in and work around the agenda is needed. When there is a lack of progress/major roadblocks, such as scheduling or adherence, it is helpful to add them to the agenda to work through them.
- **Too much or too little**: Some clients might be talkative, and you might find it difficult to get a word in. With others, you might feel you are dragging out even the shortest sentence to keep the conversation going. Here, you need to employ your questioning and listening skills to make sure the balance struck is appropriate and that it leads to clear objectives. If a client seems unfocused and is just talking at you, then you will need to interrupt politely and try to get them back on track. You can be quite clear that you are doing this, for example, *'Do you think you could sum up your week for me in just two or three sentences'* or *'I'm just going to interrupt you there because being mindful of the time we have together today I want to get a quick overview of your progress since we last met so that we can finish off our agenda for today'*. In a similar way, try to be clear with clients who are not giving you enough information. For example, *'You seem to find it difficult to verbalise how your week was. Can you tell me a bit about what was going through your head when I asked about your week?'* Maybe their automatic thought can give you a clear starting point to move to problem solving.
- **Autonomous tasks, which ones?** Remember to review the client's autonomous tasks or between session tasks at the start of the following session. It can be a good idea to keep a note of what you asked each client to do so that you have that clearly in-front of you at the next session. Maybe your genuine interest in how the client got on with an event or with a particular issue with a coach mean that you skip to that instead of maintaining structure and starting with a review of the tasks. If you don't ask about it though, the message you are sending the client is that you don't really care and that the tasks was not important. That will decrease the chance of them completing it in future and also damage the relationship between you.
- **Balancing demands:** The demands on you as a practitioner can be high and should not be underestimated. You are (a) learning a set of techniques and applying them; (b) you are having to do this in a fast-moving competitive environment with factors like travel to competition, relationships with coaches, family issues and the client's life outside of their sport to contend with; and (c) these techniques must be individualised to your client and specific to their context and sport. This means you must be

continually up to date, able to apply the theory to your practice flexibly and meet the expectations of not only your client, but their wider team. You also have to consider your own emotional and psychological wellbeing and maintaining that can be difficult in the sport and performance psychology profession. It is therefore crucial to develop effective coping techniques to ensure that one is able to manage all the competing demands placed during CBT applied practice. You can look to the wider professional domain for coping strategies, considering those most employed by psychologists and those used specifically by sport psychology consultants (see, for example, Cropley et al., 2016) whose interviews with sport psychology consultants revealed that sharing experiences, supervision, research output, and case study exploration could be a useful means of problem-focused coping. Keeping this firmly in the CBT domain, we suggest you use supervision effectively securing a supervisor who also practises CBT so that your supervision will mirror the structure you are employing with clients. Reading research outputs on CBT in sport and performance psychology and related case study examples will also help you, as will discussions with other CBT practitioners.

- **Lack of clear goals or motivation:** There is a large evidence base to CBT approaches and their effectiveness in various settings. One thing that can be problematic though is when a client comes to you but can't identify clear goals to work on or doesn't seem to be motivated to take the steps to enact strategies that will lead to change. This might occur when they have been referred through a coach or organisation but might also occur when they self-refer to you. One area that can help here is that of combining *motivational interviewing (MI)* with CBT. At its heart it aims to help clients overcome ambivalence and can therefore be a useful adjunct to CBT if you feel the readiness for change is not there in your client. Theoretically, MI takes its basis from the trans-theoretical model which considers pre-contemplation, contemplation, preparation, action and maintenance. It has been successfully incorporated into CBT practice because it aligns with an empathetic approach and with the process of CBT at a theoretical and practical level. A large body of research has looked at the efficacy of MI as an add-on to CBT for anxiety, and a similarly positive effect of MI with CBT has been demonstrated for exercise adoption too. Recently, work has also been fruitful in sport and performance, where conclusions drawn indicate it is a useful approach to blend with CBT in sporting contexts. We refer you to Mack et al. (2019) for an overview of how to enhance athlete engagement in interventions using MI. This case study also provides clear indicators of how MI can help with complex dual relationships often involved in sporting contexts, such as relationships with coaches or teammates.

Reflective Exercise

- Reflect on a client you've worked with before and try to identify potential areas that could have worked better. What might have caused these issues and could any of the areas outline above have contributed? How would you raise these with a client in future?
- Choose one area highlighted above, perhaps the use of supervision or MI and try to discover more about how you could use this to develop your own skills in CBT work.

Transition to client self-sufficiency: Leaving your client with the tools they need

For your client to move forward with the tools and techniques that you've helped them to learn and implement, you need to ensure that you are attributing their progress to their actions and their work. Keep highlighting in your dialogue when the client is making positive changes and keep the focus of these results clearly on them.

PRACTITIONER: I notice that you've been able to much more easily work with your automatic thoughts around your relationship with your coach this week. Why do you think that is?

ATHLETE: I don't know.

PRACTITIONER: Did you do anything differently this week that could have played a role here?

Then, in drawing out what the client did, reinforce their actions and help them realise they were the agent for change. Clients must understand their agency in the changes and progress that they make if they are to take forward what they've learned with you and use it on their own.

You are working in sport, and performance arenas and this can give you an advantage over other practitioners. The athletes you work with understand emotional experience, motivation, and focus. They also tend to have a life that's filled with travel and training and will be used to having to be flexible. These are all advantages that you can work with.

What can the client take away?

There will be several tools and techniques that you have used with clients. They have used these for autonomous training tasks and can take forward with them without you being there. When we introduce the tools, we should highlight that these can be implemented post CBT sessions as well. For this reason, discuss the efficacy of tools used and the importance of skills developed as you progress through your work with the client. These can be highlighted as *self-support tools* and techniques that the client can take from your work together and will include, for example, the ability to use the four-factor model to consider how thoughts, feelings, behaviours, and physiology are interacting in particular situations. This is a key skill that the client can employ in the future to help them understand complex relationships and demystify the confusion that can accompany distress. Clients can also use a host of tools, such as thought records; behavioural activation; activity scheduling; relaxation activities; TRAP/TRAC worksheets to help them in the future. Working with the client to identify strategies that they have found beneficial and planning how they can use these in the future is key to their ongoing use and the client's development of their own CBT skills.

Plan self-management time

Before you end with the client, spend a bit of time implementing a self-management time plan. Here you would work with your client to identify tools and techniques that they found worked particularly well for them. Then make sure that they schedule in time each week for after you have ceased seeing them to use the skills they have gained, check their progress and work on any negative automatic thoughts (NATs) they can identify. Prepare a self-management worksheet for your client or just speak about how they could do this. Your worksheet could include space for reflection on what current issues in performance are, whether progress made during your work has been maintained; whether they have used any of the tools or techniques during that week that they learnt with you and what their role in positive sporting outcomes were that week.

What you are doing is building in a strategy and scheduling an opportunity for them to transition to their own self-help and away from you but getting them to do that is a way that mirrors the session structure you used. You can introduce the idea of this easily (e.g., '*We only have a few sessions left together so do you think it would be useful to spend some time today talking about how you can retain the skills you've developed recently and use them in the future?*' or '*During our final session it would be useful to focus on how we can make sure that you keep using the skills you've developed during sessions. So we could review how you've changed over the course of our work together, whether there are still areas for improvement and how you might plan to move forward and manage any difficult situations that could arise*'.)

Relapse prevention planning

A primary goal for all CBT work is to ensure that it enabled the client to work towards achieving the goals they have outlined. In sport and performance settings, there are always new goals which arise, both in the 'new issues' to work on or even strive towards new performance gains for athlete development. The client, however, must be independent of the practitioner because they are the ones who have to use the skills and advances made using CBT during difficult situations. After all, the practitioner cannot be with the athlete on the field of play. Therefore, it is crucial to long-term success that clients can tackle difficulties using the new cognitions, helpful emotions, and adaptive behaviours learned during the course of CBT work. One key thing the practitioner needs to focus on during the course of intervention is relapses. Relapses refer to a complete return to a previous stage, where the client uses the same old NATs or protective behaviours to handle a situation. CBT outlines to the client that change is not smooth nor linear, but a tug and push between change and advances, which the course of sessions would have trained them in. As practitioners, we want to *manage* and *reduce* relapses. This is a key point because it is nearly impossible to prevent some level of relapse among clients. Therefore, managing relapses and then chipping away to reduce their occurrence and intensity allows the client to take ownership and apply the CBT skills worked on.

Relapse Reduction means to collaboratively build a strategy that is co-created by the client and practitioner to predict future situations that may trigger a relapse. Once these predictions are made, the practitioner creates simulations to develop plans to handle these situations. These plans comprise tools, techniques, questioning, and reflection methods the client has already been trained in. A helpful metaphor to use with athletes is to present this as situation analysis for an upcoming game where the athlete works on their own strategy based on what the opposing team is predicted to do by the performance analyst.

In CBT, Marlatt and Gordon (2005) are pioneers of relapse, building their model based on addictive behaviour; however, their model has proved relevant across psychological disorders and clinical presentations (Witkiewtiz & Marlatt, 2007). We adapt these to the sport context as well. Some factors which trigger and maintain relapses are:

- **Dichotomous/all-or-nothing appraisal of setbacks**, where the clients perceive themselves as being in complete control or completely failing at the sign of difficulty. Once in the completely failing mindset, they spiral into hopelessness and continue engagement in risk behaviours. For example, the injured athlete gets a minor muscle pull and thinks 'what's the point of this rehab' and ceases doing it. Practitioners need to encourage a more *continuous* view of control, where success and failure are small pendulum swings.
- **Permanency View** means clients feel any setback is absolutely permanent and cannot be corrected at any point in the future. For example, 'I lost a set, I will lose the match'
- **No Planned Coping Strategy** leads the client to be confused and overwhelmed when they find themselves in the situations where they might relapse. This leads to thoughts of self-criticism ('I am worthless') leading to lowered self-efficacy.
- **Abstinence Violation Effect (AVE)** (Curry et al., 1987) is the effect where clients live from problem behaviour to problem behaviour struggling to abstain from those being caught up in a powerful cycle of unhelpful thoughts. This makes the client unable to break away from the relapse situations because of continuous NATs and triggers. For example, the injured athlete says 'I will never get better, what's the point?' leading to negative emotional affect, social withdrawal, and anger. They then try to resist, but have a small failure, 'I don't have what it takes' and engage in different behaviours such as drinking alcohol, withdrawal from support and so on.
- **High-Risk Situations** are those where the stress, pressure and intensity of emotions associated with potential relapse is high. This is extremely common in sport (especially high-performance and elite sport) where the outcome and stakes are high. The practitioner needs to monitor and predict these situations. In sport, these situations are often unavoidable (the player has to play the match). In these instances, the practitioner needs to engage in predicting when the worst is to come and work their way back to plan a systematic desensitisation process in the time leading up to it.

We recommend that relapse management and reduction is introduced from the initial stages of the intervention itself with small challenges. For example, while isolating NATs with thought diaries, the practitioner could review some challenges to completing the thought diary. This allows the relapse management skill to be developed in the client as the changes and restructuring gets bigger. We outline some practitioner strategies below.

- **Imagery and client-led prediction**, where the client imagines themselves in these situations and rehearses the actions and thoughts they will take. This strategy mentally prepares them for what's coming. When the situation arrives, they are more familiar with the adversity, and therefore find it easier to manage lapses.
- **Reappraisal – 'lapse is not relapse'**, where the clients are taught to distinguish between small missteps and larger relapses. Reappraisal processes can be taught to the client via self-talk or other messaging techniques to ensure that they understand lapses are part of the process and can be handled.

Working with your client on a relapse prevention or future planning outline is an effective method of helping to ensure they continue to use what they have learnt during CBT. While working with the client, you may have identified specific triggers to performance limiting thoughts or behaviours and using this knowledge gained during CBT to plan for the future can be a clear way to maintain the use of the CBT tools once your consultancy work has ended. In a relapse management plan, you would identify key problem areas for that individual client and plan (using CBT tools and techniques) how the client could use the skills they had learned to prepare them for future issues in performance. This could then lead to a booster session.

Booster sessions

One way to plan for and ensure clients can take forward the tools and techniques of CBT on their own is to plan booster or follow-up sessions. You could, for example, meet with the client at one month and three months following your official termination of sessions. At this booster or follow-up session you can check in with the client in terms of how they are self-managing using CBT techniques, you can refresh any skills that they learned in your sessions that you feel are important to their future progress and you can discuss questions and concerns or help the client review maintenance goals or plans.

Reflective Exercise

- Think about your own use of CBT tools and techniques as you've progressed through this book. How have they helped you to develop or overcome issues? Which particular tools or techniques have resonated with you and will you continue to use? How can you help clients to also identify key tools for their own self-help?
- Try to identify key areas of your own development and issues that CBT has helped you address. What would you need to include in a relapse prevention plan to ensure your continued use of skills gained through CBT?

10 Troubleshooting

We as practitioners want (and sometimes hope) that clients can sail through using cognitive behaviour therapy (CBT) to restructure cognitions and change behaviours smoothly; however, this is often not the case. Being dynamic individuals, who are facing challenges and are interacting with different influences regularly, clients and practitioners often need to troubleshoot 'matters arising'. The troubleshooting is often linked to various issues, ranging from 'getting stuck' to the practitioner feeling confused about how to assist the client. In this chapter, we look at some potential areas where we get stuck, and outline avenues to chase to get unstuck.

Getting stuck: Dig for more information and varied sources of information

'Getting stuck' is a fundamental experience for all practising psychologists. It is often frustrating and extremely confusing. Before we go into how to address it, we need to ask and answer two fundamental questions: (a) What is getting stuck? (b) What does getting stuck look like for the practitioner and the client?'

(A) Getting stuck is also known as 'resistance' in psychotherapy. This has been defined as when the outcome of the method of therapeutic influence and actions are mismatched with the client's propensity to accept the manner in which influence is delivered (Mitchell, 2009). We need to remember that getting stuck is not only about the client. Rather, it is also related to the practitioner because the approach/techniques applied may not be appropriate to manage the responses of the client. The focus should be to understand the *reasons* behind why we (practitioners) and the clients are stuck here.

(B) For the client, getting stuck in therapy may seem like a loop or an elongated emotional traffic jam. Often, stagnation during therapy matches stagnation in life outside. For example, the client may feel that they should unlock some massive mental edge which will help them get into the first team when they have been bench-warming for months. Getting stuck is often accompanied by a feeling of confusion for the clients as well.

For the practitioner, getting stuck with a client may trigger feelings of insecurity, confusion on what approach to take, and may cause them to drift away from the fundamentals of CBT. For example, one author was working with a 23-year-old elite cricketer who was consistently getting out after spending 40 minutes at the crease and 'not playing like himself' (coach description) during the second innings. The formulation was focused

DOI: 10.4324/9781003274513-13

on concentration deficiency, and lack of emotional regulation causing frustration-aggression. This guided intervention; however, after six sessions spread over 55 days, the client had played 14 matches, and the problem persisted. Before the 7th session, the author read a re-tweeted scientific paper on potential effects of COVID-19 on physical endurance and concentration. This 'solved' the case. The practitioner worked with the coach and S&C to ensure that the athlete had a different programme, which allowed him to be functionally fit enough to ensure the concentration and emotion regulation work done during sessions could be carried out. In the next few matches, the client batted for over an hour every innings. When our clients get stuck, we tend towards a blinkered view and over-focus on therapeutic factors and discount the wider environment.

Why do people get stuck?

We will focus on the practitioner in the section below, but first we need to understand the reasons behind why clients get stuck. The reasons for clients getting stuck can be mapped onto internal factors (within themselves/course of CBT work) or external factors (out of session work/their larger life). We have outlined specific reasons for clients getting stuck below with reference to the cases we have analysed above:

1 **Misalignment:** Often through the course of sessions, the practitioner and the client may switch lanes, that is, move away from targets/agendas (see Chapters 4 and 7). At times this is a conscious choice by the practitioner and at times it is due to the client's request; however, clients often get stuck because there may be a misalignment between what they are working on in sessions and what they truly want. In such cases, the focus of work becomes undesired, and clients feel that we are working on the wrong issue or an issue that the client does not really care to work on. For example, the client may think that his pre-competitive anxiety is the main issue to 'fix', but the main maintenance cause for his pre-competitive anxiety is his unstable self-worth and low self-efficacy. On other occasions, misalignment may be due to the speed/intensity of sessions. The practitioner may go too intense too fast by focusing on the client's protective thoughts (even if they are negative automatic thoughts [NATs]), behaviours or sense of responsibility which may be scary for a client. For example, if in the initial session, X's NATs are centred around the coach/their doubles partner being the problem, then the client will not respond positively if the practitioner focuses exclusively on them.
2 **Conflicting life conditions:** Although it is tempting to treat the CBT work undertaken in sessions as if they were conducted in a social vacuum, they are not. Often the conditions in the client's life are unconducive for cognitive change with NATs/core beliefs and/or behavioural change. For example, the pre-competitive anxiety is maintained because the manager speaks to the player before every match and highlights how important it is to perform and the 'stakes' involved. On other occasions, something may have happened which is causing a significant distress needing immediate attention. This may take the session focus away from the target areas and the plan. Upon return to the plan, the practitioner picks up where they left off, but the client needs to start from a few steps back and so feels stuck. For instance, the client has a massive match coming up and just wants to have an emotional debrief, but the practitioner goes ahead to evaluate the effect of the behavioural experiment that was to be conducted.

3 **Appropriateness for CBT:** The nature of client difficulties and client characteristics also determine the appropriateness of CBT. CBT typically requires a moderate readiness for change, high levels of cognitive and emotional reflective ability (Garber et al., 2016) and in certain cognitive restructuring work there is a need for clients to have an ability to engage in abstract thinking and high-order reasoning linking them to situations (Stallard, 2019). For example, with Annette, a developing athlete and teenager, going into abstractions may result in Annette feeling confused and lost. In other instances, the difficulty/issue presented by the client may not be particularly suitable to CBT work. Typically, highly externalised situations which cause intense emotional distress are not suited to core CBT based approaches (Note: although CBT may be used interactively with other approaches). This is because CBT focuses on the individual's capacity to change their cognitions, behaviours and emotions and does not address wider obstacles in systems/families/organisations/teams which may be the source of significant distress. For example, CBT can only help manage the individual level emotions and cognitions but do little to help larger change in the individual's environment such as death in family/friends, contractual termination, and others.

Practitioner strategies to getting unstuck

When we are stuck, we first need to ensure that the three primary reasons clients get stuck are not the issue of the roadblock. We can do this through therapeutic communication and or observing client communication closely. For example, if the client typically says 'Got it' but is suddenly saying 'Hmm' or 'Uh huh', they might not be fully grasping things causing a gap in the relationship between practitioner and client.

It is *equally* important that the practitioner turns the searchlight on themselves. This is because there may be certain biases/practitioner related causes that lead to subtle changes in the practitioner behaviour which may cause the blockage. For example, if the client discusses being separated from their partner and the practitioner too is getting a divorce, it may provoke unnoticed emotions in the practitioner. Other examples of practitioner related change could be because of tiredness (i.e., the practitioner is physically tired/recovering from illness/had an excessive workload which may cause a change in their behaviour). Be aware of these changes, because all practitioners are human themselves too, and self-care is fundamental to effective practice with others (see Quartiroli et al., 2019 and 2021).

On a more holistic level, once the practitioner is aware that there is a sense of getting stuck/being stuck (both practitioner feeling stuck or the client feeling stuck), you can learn to *accept it unconditionally*. If the practitioner engages in denial or keeps trying new things and 'techniques' they are unlikely to work and may well end up alienating the client. Once acceptance has been achieved, engage in positive and collaborative steps to rectify the situation. Below are some steps the practitioner can take, which are highlighted in the order of action:

Clarify and return to evaluate initial goals

When we work with a client for a significant amount of time (8+ sessions and observations/non-session contact), it is rather common to feel stuck. During these long-contact hours, effective practice ensures the client and practitioner have successfully navigated difficulties and achieved initial goals. For example, client X seeks support with perfectionism tendencies causing anxiety. The initial goal was to reduce the pre-competitive anxiety/anxiety after mistakes, which you have now achieved. After this, there is often an impasse, where the client and practitioner need to have *clarity* on how to move forward. This is done in two steps: (A) evaluate the progress made, that is consistent with client's initial goals (e.g., anxiety is managed and no longer debilitating), and (B) what can be some deeper targets for CBT work the client wants to set?

This allows the client to take ownership and understand the specific area of support needed which allows the practitioner to continue work forward. For example, after managing the anxiety, the client might want to understand how his perfectionism itself came about and how to control it so that *'I don't keep being my own worst enemy'*. On occasion, the client may not know exactly what to work on, but have a vague sense – *'the anxiety bits have been super useful … but I feel its temporary, like when a pressure situation comes, I still beat myself up for a small mistake and make more'*. In these situations, the practitioner can suggest areas of work and targets based on their assessment and formulation.

Focus on the therapeutic relationship and new client reality

When work starts with a client, they are in a certain 'normal' where their NATs or maladaptive behaviours are a pattern in life. Because of effective CBT work, the client then restructures these patterns to a great extent by making consistent and/or significant changes. This change forces the client to settle into a new normal where they are challenging their NATs or not engaging in maladaptive protective behaviours. This often reflects in being stuck or feeling slightly lost in sessions as well. A major action the practitioner needs to undertake is understanding this new reality and providing warmth and empathy to the client. This allows clients to go deeper into the expressions of experience by providing a safe, unconditional space where clients can authentically express their successes and their difficulties. The focus should be to empathetically support the client with the *now and new*. By doing so, we orient the client to a new process that they are engaging in their life. There does not need to be a clear and strict 'goal' for this because having another new goal might make the client think the sessions are a forever effort process of continuous change, which is anxiety-provoking. For example, Annette goes from juniors to playing a futures competition which puts greater stress on her. The older goal of managing her self-worth could pause and not be as strict. Rather, we can shift the focus to using a goal-setting based intervention (see McCarthy & Gupta, 2022) to help her prepare for the tournament in a task-focused coping manner.

By focusing on the client's experience during this moment of change, we can deepen the therapeutic relationship. This is a huge advantage to effective work because it allows authentic expression from the client and a deepening of trust. The client may also be stuck because of life-altering experiences outside the session, which may/may not be aligned to the initial goals of the CBT work. These experiences may be both positive and/or negative but come with major life circumstance changes. Some common life-altering experiences in sport include selection to senior/international squads, success/failure in an elite competition stage, deselection, injury, mental health challenges caused by continuous stress, financial gain/loss, abuse/adoration from fans, fracturing/developing relationship with coach and any personal non-sport issues such as relationship status changes, death, marriage, and parenthood among others. Building the strong therapeutic relationship allows the individual to express themselves and share their life as it is, without worrying about further change. Remember, it is the responsibility of the practitioner to be a facilitator not a fixer (see Chapters 2 and 3).

Metacommunication and self-reflection

Metacommunication in psychotherapy refers to the secondary communication that clarifies how a piece of primary information is supposed to be interpreted or asks for more information. Paraphrasing and checking are one of the most common examples of metacommunication in CBT practice.

Metacommunication is useful because during moments of being 'stuck' there is an altered dynamic in the session between the client and practitioner. Typically, the sense of being stuck is implicit and covert. Metacommunication allows the practitioner to be vulnerable and make the issue overt. For example, *'I wanted to say that, lately I get the sense that we are a bit stuck? Things are not changing or perhaps they are not aligning for you well in our sessions'*. This prompts a response from the client and allows an open conversation which affords greater control and participation to the client about the course of their sessions.

Practitioner self-reflection is fundamental to practice, especially when there is a sense of being stuck (see Bennet-Levy & Lee, 2014). Carl Jung theorised that a client can only move beyond the places in therapy that their therapist has moved themselves in their work (see Aoyagi et al., 2012; Cropley et al., 2012). Simply put, the stuckness may be because of practitioner-related reasons. Some reflective questions are highlighted below for the practitioner to ask themselves:

- Is there a misunderstanding/miscommunication that needs to be addressed?
- Are we both (practitioner and client) in the room? Or are our minds elsewhere?
- Is there something I am doing to hold the process back?
- Am I afraid of the emotion in the room/what the client is bringing?
- Is my reaction to being stuck related to something triggering in me about the client and their presenting problem?
- Could the client be facing something I am facing too and left unresolved? Is that bringing countertransference?
- Am I feeling insecure/inadequate/ineffective by being stuck and is this affecting my actions as a practitioner? (Am I trying too hard to force the issue?)
- Am I going through a personal crisis or burnout or dissatisfaction?
- Am I as excited by my client's progress as I used to be?
- Do I feel frustration/any negative emotion/stress from the client?

These reflective questions are also excellent for discussions with the practice supervisor, because it leads to the overall growth and professional development of the practitioner (see Chapter 3). If there are no practitioner-related concerns, some steps for effective troubleshooting by the practitioner for getting unstuck are:

- Remember every client is *unique*, and each client's situation requires a *customised* approach;
- 'Take a step back' – give yourself some perspective;
- Engage in Socratic dialogue with yourself (see Chapter 7);
- By looking at the session process from new angles, ask new questions of yourself, and during sessions, bring it up with clients via metacommunication;

- Role-play: You may ask the clients to have a metaphorical role switch, so the client can decide how to best work with the client, if they were the practitioner, therefore bringing out their needs and providing an authentic experience.

Client as a dynamic system in internal conflict

When the client brings forth an issue/difficulty, it is the job of the practitioner to help the client understand the *why* of the issue and *how* to change; however, the client is never a broken individual who needs to be fixed. The client is also not a static object with a fixed label. It is helpful to view the client as a dynamic system which changes and alters in response to the work conducted in sessions and their life experiences out of it. The client, as this dynamic system, is in constant conflict which causes the stuckness. This conflict leads to an entanglement and rupture which results in (A) The client resisting/not wanting/being able to dig deeper reflectively but the practitioner knowing something is there or (B) The client disengaging to revert to surface level reflections therefore not facilitating any change.

In both scenarios, the practitioner needs to stay in the present and collaboratively work with the client to process the rupture points. Where the client is resisting (e.g., *'I don't think it is that'*) it may be a point to ease off the focus on the particular experience and revert to working on the therapeutic relationship to ensure the client feels trusted and safe. Where the client is sticking to the surface level (e.g., *'yeah, the injury sucks, but that's life'* – but shows clear emotional inhibition as a maladaptive coping mechanism) the practitioner needs to increase the experiential level. An example of this would is outlined below.

CLIENT: I don't know.
PRACTITIONER: Which part of it?
CLIENT: It was easy then so difficult … every time I try to fix it, and I do what coach says, it gets worse ….
PRACTITIONER: What gets worse?
CLIENT: The injury … yeah it sucks … but that's life.
PRACTITIONER: Tell me more … this is your second ACL surgery, how was the first one? *[experiential activation]*
CLIENT: The first one was so long ago … yeah damn, I was 19, it was 12 years ago … it was much easier then.
PRACTITIONER: Easier?
CLIENT: Yeah, less stuff to worry about.
PRACTITIONER: Such as?
CLIENT: Family, didn't have kids then … just had dreams and my two legs to chase em, losing one was hard, but I knew it would come back.
PRACTITIONER: And this time?
CLIENT: Not really sure what happens even if the legs come back ….
PRACTITIONER: What's the 'what if'?
CLIENT: (pause) This is it. I walk away from the game, don't really know who I am or what I do after' *[primary reason for being stuck – overwhelming cognition and emotion of career termination and transition].*

In the case above, we see the practitioner using 'I don't know' from the client as a doorway to go deeper. The practitioner sees the client as the dynamic system in clear conflict (identity related to current injury reality). The practitioner sheds the role of being the 'expert' and allows the client to tell them about their reality. Not having this knowledge, the client is encouraged to analyse their situation and highlight what is important for them. Being in this process, the client discovers insight for being un-stuck and areas to improve.

Choosing the 'suitable' problem and keeping on track

As we have discussed above, clients often view themselves using global language. For example, *'I am not good enough for this level'*. While in sport, this may be true from a skill/physical/technical/tactical level, it does not mean the client cannot develop. Indeed, success in elite sport has been linked to consistent development ability. This sort of global language describes the image of the *whole* person through *all time* (i.e., 'no part of me is good enough' and 'never will be good enough'). This sort of global rating of self never captures the complexity of the individual. Even the best players in the game's history were not globally 'perfect'. For example, few would argue that Lionel Messi has football's greatest ever right foot. The best golfer in the world may have a less than comparable wedge game. The best cricket batsmen in the world might struggle to a particular type of delivery. This does not capture their global ability.

Practitioners should remember an attribute, a behaviour, a performance, or a trait does not equal the global person; however, clients, especially developing athletes, frequently make that error. For example, Annette says that *'I was horrible during that game. I was inferior in every shot and exchange, so that makes me hopeless'*. This type of presentation is often accompanied by client's feedback that they have 'multiple problems' that develops like a snowball. For example, Annette has a bad game ≫ negative coach feedback ≫ self-esteem concerns ≫ leading to global negative perception (inferiority statement above) ≫ low confidence ≫ poor performance. This is commonly seen when clients consult a practitioner during performance slumps, recovery periods or transitions (to name a few). The key to handling the multiple presentations of the client is picking one at a time. Think of it like *zonal defence*, where the practitioner maps out areas based on formulation and handling presentations in that area instead of focusing on each single presentation the client says. Often this is quite tricky in initial sessions because the practitioner is afraid of missing out on the primary/important issue. To navigate these, we troubleshoot each instance specifically below.

Performance slumps

Often, clients seek help during 'difficult'/'bad' times. One of the most common reasons for such a 'bad' time is performance slumps or 'out-of-form' periods. Clients often present 'multiple' problems with the common commentator's saying going, 'if it was not for bad luck, they would not have any luck at all'. For this section, we will use the term performance slumps for any explained loss of performance, including, but not limited to, yips, lost move syndrome, loss of form and performance instability.

Clients feel out of control and search for things that are going wrong because it gives them a sense of security that they are at least doing something. Performance slumps are natural and stressful circumstances that represent an unexplained decline in performance compared to their baseline level (see Stead et al., 2022, for a review evidence). During these periods, athletes typically experience stress, anxiety, friction with teammates and organisational stressors. They might also question their own self-efficacy (especially if they have been an athlete for a short period). The yips and lost move syndrome also have their own psychosocial effects (see Bennet et al., 2015; Clarke et al., 2015).

Performance slumps are accompanied by their own cognitive and behavioural consequences. Let us frame the cognitive consequences using the ABCDE model, particularly focusing on the ABC (see Chapter 7).

(A) Activating event – loss of performance compared to baseline;
(B) Beliefs triggered by the event – 'I am not good enough'/'I need to try harder';
(C) Consequences of belief – anxiety (I am not good enough)/overtraining to 'find a way'.

There are other thoughts which also accompany this process. The individual will typically think about previous times in their life when they experienced something similar or had a dip in performance levels. Athletes engage in an internal oriented pessimistic explanatory style. We see this in statements which attribute the cause of the performance dip to only internal attributes and/or self-related issues. When this happens, the internal cognitive system loses touch with the present and makes negative attributions about the consequences of this slump in the future, which reinforces the cycle of negative cognitions (see Ball 2013).

This leads to behavioural consequences at two extremes of overtraining or disengagement. Often athletes go on a search for performance enhancement hyper-focusing on technical training. This typically also leads to a disengagement from team environments, because the individual thinks they are letting the team down. The performance slump may even be a matter of perception. For example, an intrinsically motivated individual who has a core belief of *'always getting better'* may perceive that they are in a slump if they stop seeing massive gains in their developmental progress, or if they play at a higher level. In team sports, performance slumps may be relative to the team's performance. For example, a striker in football is scoring 40% fewer goals, and thinks they are in a slump. In reality, the midfield has not been working well enough to put him in goal-scoring situations.

The primary issue that practitioners face when an individual with a performance slump presentation arrives is the sense – *too much is going on*. During formulation and assessment, there may be various elements of the individual's life that the practitioner may deem to cause the performance slump. Some common examples are confidence, social support, concentration lapse issues, training methods, yips, inadequate coping mechanisms, experience and resources and cognitive appraisals of the event. Each of these causal concerns could be both the cause and the consequence of a performance slump. For example, loss of confidence may lower performance levels, which may eventually add up to a performance slump. Once the slump occurs, the confidence stays low, preventing improvements. This same vicious cycle would occur for all the potential causes and consequences listed above. This makes it quite confusing in practice.

What should we do?

When clients arrive with performance loss presentations, the key is to understand where they are in the continuum of loss (see Figure 10.1). This will provide important insights into where their cognitive interpretations of the slump are as well. For example, someone

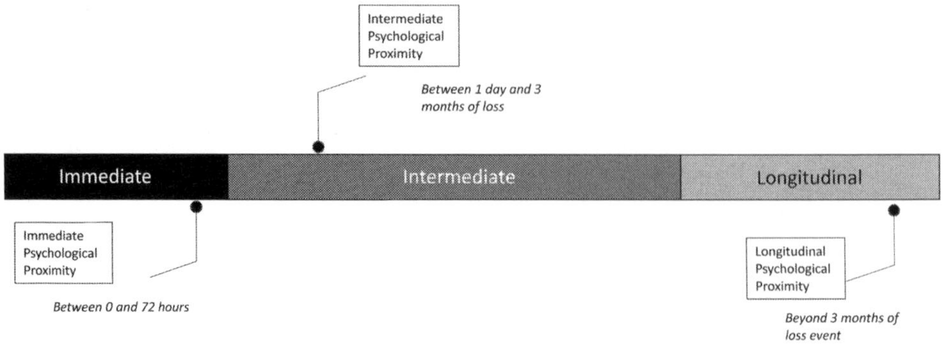

Figure 10.1 Continuum of Loss

at the beginning stages of what they perceive as a slump would have anticipatory cognitions (*'maybe I am in …'* whereas someone who has been handling the slump for a period may have explanatory cognitions *('I think it's because I am not good enough'*).

- **Assessment and formulation:** The assessment and formulation are key in all such situations. The performance slump event should not dominate the assessment and formulation itself, but rather seek a deep understanding of the way the individual's cognitive system and behavioural patterns work. This will provide key areas of understanding around how their core beliefs and automatic thoughts are operating in the situation. A key assessment test to measure the patterns of coping is the modified COPE inventory developed for sport (Eklund et al., 1998), which provides the practitioner with an understanding of the default coping mechanisms that the client has.
- **Focusing on antecedent and/or consequences:** During this work, the practitioner must begin with the focus on ***one*** thing at a time. It is extremely easy to get swept away by the vicious cycle of the client's cognitions. For example, if the practitioner is looking at the consequences of the slump (depending on where the client is in the continuum), then they should focus on what is happening within the cognitive system now that the slump is underway. It is easy to go along with the client who will naturally drift towards explaining why the slump is happening. This is not wrong; however, the practitioner should be strict and draw boundaries between these two. This is an intervention because this will prevent the client from distinguishing the cause and the consequence, which prevents NATs.
- **Maintenance factors:** A key thing that the practitioner should focus on is the identification of maintenance factors (i.e., factors in the cognition and behavioural pattern that is keeping the 'problem' going). These are typically varied from client to client. For example, a figure skater could have a perfectionistic tendency and is always trying to go for a high percentage move, which is difficult to be perfect with every time. This may cause frustration and an overall loss of points, causing a perception that they cannot accomplish their task and are in a slump. A golfer could define his game parallel to a rival. There is a negative social comparison because he thinks his rival has a better long game (which is true) but disregards that he has a better short game. Focusing too much on trying to match up to his rival's long game leads to him to neglect his own strengths. It is important to understand

these maintenance factors well because they typically feature in the consequences of what is causing the slump to continue.

- **Incremental gains:** Now that the focus is on one thing at a time, the client should be facilitated to (a) be aware of the cognitions that are arising via thought diaries (see Chapter 6); (b) understand their core beliefs fuelling this thought pattern; and (c) try to modify or negate them one at a time. Common thinking traps that are present during performance slumps are all-or-nothing thoughts, shoulds and musts, and personalisation (although others may be present as well).
- **Multidimensional view:** The performance slump (like most aspects of the sport performance) is not made up exclusively of a psychological element. There are technical, tactical and physical aspects to it as well. For example, an 18-year-old cricket batter repeatedly gets caught out in the boundary after facing 30 balls. Here, the maintenance factor was poor tactical awareness, concentration lapse and poor regulation ability (psychological), lack of physical power and poor technical position, causing him to lose shape in the shot. The practitioner should focus only on the psychological element with CBT assessment, formulation and intervention, but needs to encourage the player to work with the coaches and other support staff to develop the other areas as well.
- **Intervention philosophy and choice:** An overarching philosophy guides your process of interventions. Some key questions to ask are: Are you trying to 'fix' a slump? Are you trying to facilitate the emotional expression that accompanies a slump? Are you helping an individual with a safe space within which they can figure the way forward themselves? This guides the choice of intervention as well. Some common intervention choices are strengths-based approaches (see Ludlam et al., 2016; Wagstaff & Leach, 2017), thought-balancing, cognitive restructuring and attribution retraining (see Chapter 7); however, it is of paramount importance to choose the intervention based on the needs of the client and formulation on a case-by-case basis. See Bennet and Maynard (2017) for further evidence and directions.

These directions are not exhaustive nor prescriptive; however, together they represent good, effective CBT practice. In the following section, we look at best practices for supporting clients through injury recovery.

Injury recovery

Direct and indirect costs that are associated with major sport injuries result in the early retirement of up to 24% of elite athletes (Engebretsen et al., 2010) and have various psychosocial effects. Modern sport injury rehabilitation follows a team biopsychosocial approach that includes physiotherapists, nutritionists, S&C coaches, and sport psychologists. One-on-one psychotherapy using CBT is one area through which they support injured athletes through the course of their rehabilitation journey. While there are similarities, each injured athlete is different. We will use the cases of Mo and Annette to illustrate this and the best practice techniques.

I. **Define the outcome:** The first step of CBT for injured athletes should allow the client to describe *why* they are seeking support. Some clients might have intrusive negative thoughts on the injury itself, while others may struggle to maintain behavioural adherence to their rehabilitation program. The practitioner is not the expert in this sense, but through the space of assessment and formulation, allows the client to define the outcome and area of support. Typical negative cognitions surrounding injury are linked to the future and are directed at the self, with a low controllability element, which creates emotional and behavioural consequences. For example, when he gets injured, Mo says, 'I need help, I struggle to sleep every night because my thoughts keep banging in my head, about what will happen to my contract if I am not fit and performing by September'. Whereas, Annette has a different thought-cycle stating, 'I want to get this fixed quick. It sucks when I am not on the court. Tennis is a part of me, and right now I cannot play'. While both cognitions are related to the self, Mo is worried about the future consequences (which he cannot control), and Annette is focused on tennis as a part of her identity and self-concept, which she is missing.

II. **Select a target cognition:** As established above, humans have multiple cognitive cycles running in parallel at the same time. During injury, individuals typically experience a continued host of NATs. To practice effectively, assessment and formulation should inform selecting target cognitions. One thing to focus on is triggering cognitions which start the NAT vicious cycle. Although these may appear similar, they are often greatly different. For example, if Mo says, 'I am worried about my contract in September' his cognitions are focused on his future. This is different to if Mo says, *'I am worried that I will lose my place in the team and have to start from scratch if I am not fit by September'*, which is rooted in social comparison and can act as a separate trigger. The second area to focus on is how the NAT cycle is linked to the self-concept of the individual. Injuries threaten the athletic identity of individuals (see Brewer, 1998; Podlog et al, 2015) and these NATs may lead to maladaptive thought and emotion cycles.

III. **Select a target behaviour rooted in the present:** A common theme during injuries is the focus on the future, which the individual has little control over; however, behavioural consistency and adherence to a rehabilitation program is critical to injury recovery and return to play. Behaviours do not occur in isolation and are part of an interactive and dynamic system (Atkins & Michie, 2015), multiple behaviours may affect the athlete's ability to perform rehabilitation adherence behaviours. It is helpful to breakdown the behavioural domain into identifiable constituent behaviours using the formulation process. The assessment questions that can guide this process are: 'Who needs to perform the behaviour?'; 'What does the person need to do differently to achieve change?'; 'When do they do it?'; 'Where will they do it?' The messaging on these behaviours needs to be rooted in the present and not the future. Goal setting is one helpful mode through which this can be accomplished (see McCarthy & Gupta, 2022). Once injured, athletes show fragmented behaviour patterns because the sport behaviour that guides and dominates their life is absent from them. This needs to be appropriately replaced by another behaviour system that is adaptive.

IV. **Time and tracking:** A critical factor that individuals (and psychologists) often discount in the rehabilitation process is the importance of time. Injuries can last from three days to three months and more. We should factor the importance of time in during the formulation stage to help plan CBT support appropriately. Tracking should be done in collaboration with the support staff team including progress reports from physiotherapists, sports psychologists, gym and coaches and personal feedback from the athletes involved. Two key measures that aid the tracking process from a psychosocial point of view are (a) Sport Injury Rehabilitation Adherence Scale (SIRAS) which provides an insight into the cognitive and behavioural actions of the individuals; and (b) The Injury-Psychological Readiness Return to Sport Scale (I-PRRS) is a psychometric questionnaire that assesses the confidence levels of athletes in their own body and abilities post-injury. Psychological readiness is the degree to which the athlete is confident in their body, and abilities to return to play (Glazer, 2009), which is important because low psychological readiness to return to sport leads to higher fear of avoidance, low confidence, distracted attention, and loss of concentration which has accompanying negative emotions (Podlog et al., 2015). Each of these elements manifests itself through the vicious cycle of NATs and dysfunctional core beliefs which can be addressed using CBT.

V. **Watch out for mental health concerns:** Injury, especially long-term injuries, cause a major negative psychological influence. Nearly 53% of injured athletes display significantly higher levels of depression, anxiety and low self-esteem compared to non-injured athletes (Neal et al., 2013). This may lead to sub-clinical or clinical illness presentations as major depressive disorder, panic disorder, eating disorders (anorexia or binge eating) and substance abuse (see Gouttebarge et al., 2021). The Sport Mental Health Assessment tool (SMHAT) (Gouttebarge et al., 2021) can be used as a measurement screening tool in such cases.

When applying CBT with injured athletes, the focus should be to first maintain equilibrium and protect their mental health. By setting behavioural systems that are adaptive, we can help the individual maintain their rehabilitation goals and avoid engagement in adaptive action. Through the cognitive measurements (thought diaries) and interventions (attribution retraining, self-talk, PMR, see Chapter 7), we can facilitate the individual to gain a deeper understanding of their NATs and core beliefs. Following this we can focus on acceptance of the cognitions and restructuring of any maladaptive ones.

Seek 'hidden' or subliminal NATs in verbalisations and behaviours

Through various stages of this book, we have advocated the importance of assessment and formulation. Within that process of assessment and formulation, we have highlighted the value of the information provided by the client, which acts as a window into the internal cognitive system and behaviours. That being said, much like a detective, the practitioner should look at it from all angles. Not that you should not trust your client, but rather converge on the experience of the client through multiple avenues.

We view it through the lens of the client, but our job is also to be the objective observer. We have to examine for inconsistencies because often during sessions, the client may intentionally or unintentionally describe situations in their life. This is because the practitioner is viewing and experiencing the client's life through the view that the client is offering them. Think of it like a photograph. You only see what the camera was pointing at. Here, the client is in charge of where they choose to point the camera. How much they want to zoom in or out of specific things.

Often during sessions, clients may describe incidents in their life which may have distorted the reality a little or have examples of concealment for many reasons. A client may (a) want the practitioner to view them in a certain way; (b) have shame about their place and role in the situation; (c) their core beliefs may lead them to interpret the situation in a certain way, which is distorting reality; (d) they have forgotten the details and sequence of events in the 'heat of the moment', which is typical of high intensity, fast-paced sport settings; and (e) they might not trust the practitioner with the information yet, particularly if it is early in the therapeutic relationship. The practitioner needs 'detective senses' to seek hidden verbalisation.

Develop your detective senses

So, what is this detective sense? Detective senses are the coordinated use of auditory, visual, contextual and formulation information about a client to understand inconsistencies or hidden verbalisations. For example, did the client hesitate and fidget as they were saying something (visual), did they take a long pause and change the topic slightly (auditory), did they miss out on contextual information that you say through other areas of measurement (observation/coach feedback) or did something happen that goes completely contrary to the existing formulation?

The important thing (and often the hardest thing) here is that these detective senses should not work in isolation. Rather, all of them should operate interdependently to guide your process of discovering hidden verbalisation. Hyper focusing on one specific detective sense can often lead to skewed interpretations. Information from all the senses should converge to provide the practitioner with the full picture. It is also helpful to remember that this detective sense is measurement, because we are measuring the different 'data' that the client is providing. This allows the practitioner to acquire *patterns* in that data which provide us with an effective baseline to start off from. For example, Annette starts every session by asking, 'how are you? Have you seen any new movies yet?'. This is the baseline. But if Annette does not ask how the practitioner is nor shows any interest in their movie watching habits, that is divergent from baseline, and is something that the detective sense allows us to pick up.

This means that all clients have the in-session and outside session patterns of interpersonal and performance problems. Developing and reflecting upon your detective sense, and the 'data' the client provides you with allows the development of this sense, and also enables you to be an effective practitioner by understanding the hidden elements in verbalisations and behaviours. A key point to remember is that *'each individual has a different pattern to their internal world'*. Each individual will have different responses to all stimuli. Therefore, actively working on the therapeutic relationship, and working to discover the specific pattern of a client, is so crucial. Some major areas of work on this are:

1 **Identify personal language patterns:** Every individual has a personal language pattern. When in highly stressful conditions and during tricky phases of the intervention, always rely on using these to get through to the client. For example, a client might always greet you with 'yo' or 'all right' say confirmatory statements with 'you got it'/'that's fab'. Personal language may not be the language of therapy or even an aspect of body language (self-hug, comforting, tapping the chest for affirmation). Ensure these are noted and used them to deepen the relationship.
2 **Behavioural reference points:** Human beings always display consistent behaviour patterns. Within sessions, these are manifested within how the client takes a seat, does a handshake, their punctuality patterns. In sport settings, these are manifested within their routines (pre, during and post-performance) and their behavioural interaction with others (coaches, teammates, rivals, officials, spectators).

These reference points are crucial data points which allow the practitioner to have a picture of what is present and an understanding of what is absent.

3 **Be aware of own biases:** We all have biases. In sport, practitioners often have a prior history of being an athlete or have core experiences in sport (as a participant or from working in it). It is crucial that we do not project these biases on to clients. These may be as blind sighted formulations (the practitioner considers something not as important because it was not so in their personal experiences) or improper interventional development. Personal therapy and constant supervision are helpful processes to control these.
4 **Prepare your formulation & keep yourself familiar with it:** It is often easy to get carried away with the things that clients present during sessions. The practitioner should always come back to the formulation and keep updating it as the sessions progress. Constantly update the formulation and ensure that it is collaboratively shared with the client periodically. This ensures the changes in the client's life are appropriately represented in the formulation so that the practitioner can draw upon it if feeling stuck.
5 **Use other data sources:** Working in a sport environment allows the practitioner to draw upon other sources of information beyond the individual client. These may be coaches, video highlights, being at competition and training (see Chapter 6 for other sources). This can be used to explore alternative formulations apart from what the client is presenting or confirm existing formulations or even get new data points which the client may have missed.

What to do with detective sense data?

Now that the practitioner has collected all this valuable data with their detective sense, what should be done with it? There are numerous uses to which we might put this data. It primarily depends on the data collected and the goals of the CBT intervention that is underway. It also depends on what type of data is collected. Broadly, this can be classified into (a) concealment and (b) divergence.

Concealments are information that the practitioner has uncovered with his detective sense but the client has intentionally/unintentionally withheld. These data have been obtained by the practitioner and *have not* been offered by the client. For example, Annette and the practitioner are working on emotion regulation, because there are powerful negative emotions arising from maladaptive perfectionism; however, Annette has a public 'blowout' in the last match where she smashes her racquet to pieces after failing to meet performance standards. She does not tell the practitioner this in the session, but the practitioner has been informed by the coaches. During such concealments, the focus should be on creating a safe unconditional space for the client to have an empathetic discussion with the practitioner on this. The concealment should not be conveyed to the client in an accusatory manner such as '*why did you not tell me you got angry and smashed a racquet?*' Rather, it should be framed as an open and safe discussion,

PRACTITIONER: I have to tell you something.
ANNETTE: What? (nervously)
PRACTITIONER: I was informed by your coach about the incident in the match, and I wanted to let you know that its okay. We are humans and we don't need to be perfect every time. [*this adds onto the formulation of perfectionism that is present with Annette*]

ANNETTE: Oh! (surprised) I am sorry I did not tell you.

PRACTITIONER: That's okay (reassuring tone), it was your choice, and I respect it.

ANNETTE: It's just that ... I felt quite poor for letting you down because it was going so well and you have helped so much ... but that match it sort of happened.

PRACTITIONER: I understand. But you will never be letting me down with anything you do! [*reinforcing the unconditional safe space*]

Such a discussion often strengthens the relationship between the client and practitioner, which also increases the trust that the client has in the practitioner. While enhancing this relationship, the practitioner in the case example above also used it as an opportunity to reinforce the themes that they are working on.

The key thing to do with the detective sense data is to ground its use in the *here-and-now*. This allows the client and the practitioner to explore the implications of that data in the session at this present moment of time. This is helpful because clients often struggle with thinking traps that manipulate their view of reality with the past or the future. For example, if the client does not perform their pre-performance routine of listening to music before a match, the practitioner can ask why. The explanation might be something as simple as they forgot their headphones at home or something as deep as they had a big fight with their partner and are in 'no mood to listen to music'. This focus on the here-and-now with the detective sense data allows the client to gain self-awareness of what they do as well. It reinforces their values and adds on to the focus of CBT work at a more direct level (compared to abstract historical focus on what happened in a past incident, which is also useful). For example, in the case of Annette.

Application Time: Case of Annette

PRACTITIONER: So why were you thinking that you were letting me down?

ANNETTE: Because well, you spend so much time with me, like my parents and I want to do well and ... oh ... (trails off with surprise).

PRACTITIONER: Go on (warmly).

ANNETTE: It is what we talked about isn't it. That personalising, I think it's up to me to make my parents happy, and that's why I try to be perfect all the time.

PRACTITIONER: It could be. Does that explanation make sense to you?

ANNETTE: Gosh it totally does. I think I also get it ... like it was a high stress game already ... then I twisted my ankle in practice so my mum massaged it and bandaged it ... and I felt like I had to do more ... but I was playing well but ....

PRACTITIONER: But?

ANNETTE: They were playing better ... and I lost it ... it ... it makes sense now.

As seen above, the practitioner's use of the concealment data gathered from detective sense was focused on the here-and-now. This facilitated an awareness of the content (i.e., the words and description that is expressed) and of the process (i.e., the nature of the relationship between individuals who are expressing the words and description). The practitioner starts with working on the process after revealing the concealment that enables an unconditional positive regard, increased trust and reinforcement of the previous theme of perfectionism. This is continued with the content based Socratic questioning that allows greater self-awareness within Annette that is anchored in the *here-and-now* despite using an event that *has* happened.

When in doubt, return to simplicity (model and basics)

Inevitably, at some point, all practitioners, expert or novice, will get stuck/lost/confused within their sessions with a client. This often triggers feelings of insecurity and an imposter syndrome that pushes us to act and behave as a practitioner that we would not have done otherwise. In these times, it is crucial to ***return to simplicity***. This section is a quick navigation map of certain to-dos that the practitioner should engage in during those times of doubt.

- **Understand your client's life:** Often practitioners feel they know everything about a client. This is true if you have had 12+ sessions with them through a deep therapeutic relationship. Assuming that there has been a weekly session, the practitioner has spent 12 hours out of 2184 hours of the client's life, which is 0.005%. Therefore, check-in and get an understanding of the client's life. In sport, there may be a lot of change within these three months as well because of training and competition schedules. Discuss it in detail including sleeping habits, training, leisure and eating patterns, recreation, social life, periods/events of joy/contentment, periods of discomfort/negativity, patterns at training, social preferences, leisure preferences (Netflix, TV, magazines, Instagram and so on). By making this detailed, the practitioner learns a lot, which can be used when there are periods of doubt and getting stuck. For example, if you know the client spends a lot of time with their doubles partner, but now cannot because of the partner being injured. Some change in their behaviour and emotional patterns can be uncovered.
- **Client history:** Effective client history taking is a key part of psychotherapeutic training, one that is key to effective CBT practice. Psychotherapy training includes systematic history schemes which have items such as present difficulty, presenting complaint, health, education, social sphere etc. We recommend any practitioner to get training in this regard. Without this process, the practitioner cannot get an idea of the client's life-context. It is not separated from the CBT process but is a central part of it. How to you know that you have taken *enough* of a client history? A simple way is the **'Wikipedia Check'**- do you know enough to write up a Wikipedia page that explains who, where, what, when of your client's life, and why they are working with you? (see Chapter 5.)
- **Reinforce the four-factor model:** The four-factor model completely or partially explains most of the client difficulties and 'frames' the client presentation. When in doubt, return to it to make sense of the client's presentation and problems. Look for which of the four factors is the dominant cause that is maintaining the client's issues. Is the physiological arousal too dominant and overpowering the cognitive restructuring? - then include more physiological arousal management techniques/encourage the client to consult a physician. If the cognitive element is dominant, then focus interventions that work on NATs and how they manifest in daily life. This allows the practitioner to have a navigation guide which is important during times of doubt and getting stuck (see the section 'Getting Stuck: Dig for More Information and Varied Sources of Information' and Chapter 4).
- **Engage in metacommunication:** Metacommunication is the communication between parties about their communication patterns. It means that the practitioner engages the client in a discussion about their communication patterns and therapeutic relationship. This often offers key insights, such as is the CBT process aligned to the

client's areas of focus. Is there enough trust? Does the style that the practitioner has adopted suit the client? Is the client finding the process helpful but it is only the practitioner who feels that 'progress is not enough?' This metacommunication process is easily conducted by requesting feedback at the end of the sessions. This gives the practitioner actionables to prepare with and serves as a 'quality check' of the relationship and where the CBT process currently is with the client.

- **Supervision:** Supervision is critical. From a short-term focus, it helps secure a different perspective on a case. From a long-term view, it allows the practitioner to focus on areas of development within their professional practice. At different points of a career, one may even change supervisors to those with different areas of expertise to develop professional skills. Having regular supervision is also an ethical process because it allows self-monitoring and an active regulation of one's own biases, conscious and unconscious. When in doubt, engage in supervision (see Chapter 4).

Fluctuate the medium, stick to the message

Some clients dislike talking. Others talk too much and divert the focus of sessions. Sometimes the practitioner may be too involved or under involved during the session itself. At times, troubleshooting may be required, because the focus of the sessions seems to be stuck in the same circle. In such times, the 'message', that is, the aims and key focus of the sessions, should be consistent in line with the assessment, formulation and intervention; however, a good solution to this issue can be to *fluctuate the medium* that is used to deliver the message.

1 **Understanding types of question-response:** There are different forms of questioning and responses from the client. Typically, we engage in vertical question-response (i.e., the content of a situation or event). For example, while working with Mo's anxiety about needing a higher performance standard, the practitioner might encourage vertical question-response about the historical development of when it started or ask about the details around the experience of it. This is a fundamental skill in the practitioner toolbox, but is often overused leading to monotony. Another form of question-response is the horizontal pattern where the question-response is aimed at the experience and act of the question-response itself. For example, when Mo shares that the expectations of the new contract bring anxiety, the practitioner might follow-up with the question, *'What is the experience when you are sharing this now with me?'* which facilitates Mo to dive deeper into his insecurities and experience. Other questions, particular to high emotionality could be, *'Is there something which prompted this discussion today?'*; *'was it hard for you to bring this up?'*; *'did you want to share this earlier by any chance?'*; *'now that you have spoken about this, do you feel different to before?'* By mixing up the vertical and horizontal question-response patterns, we *fluctuate the medium.* This allows diversity in what the client is prompted to bring and also allows more authentic expression from the client.

2 **Use objects and demonstrations:** In sport, individuals are often involved in *doing* far more than they are involved in *talking*. Hence, sometimes (particularly with young athletes), it is advisable to bring more of the *doing* into the CBT sessions. Use of objects and demonstrations are suitable options; however, the objects and

demonstrations are *aids* that facilitate understanding and interaction rather than dominating the session. It is up to the practitioner to be creative and ethical while using objects and demonstrations to explain concepts or processes. For example, taking a tissue paper and spilling water onto it to trace how it spreads can demonstrate how fear and related cognitions influence behaviour. A whiteboard is also extremely useful for drawing out four-factor models and thought-emotion-behaviour vicious cycles because it *demonstrates* the internal workings of the mind to the client.

3 **Metaphors and storylines:** Metaphors and storylines are important accelerators in the therapeutic process. They have been termed as being useful to build cognitive bridges (Stott et al., 2010). Often, clients have metaphors that they themselves bring. For example, an injured footballer terms his frustrating rehabilitation process as 'climbing up a hill but having to stop many times'. This can be used both as a touchpoint to the client experience ('where are you in the hill now?') and also to measure progress ('on that hill, where are you emotionally now?'). Clients often find it easy to create narratives and storylines to frame their cognitive experiences and NATs. A golfer can explain pre-performance anxiety and the associated NATs during that time as a 'dark cloud hovering, but one which passed slowly as I tried to challenge those NATs'. Such examples can be client-led and be easy access points for the practitioner; however, the practitioner can also trial metaphors and storylines with the client to see their comfort with it. Further reading on metaphors and storylines in CBT is recommended before implementation in practice (see for further reading Blenkiron, 2011; Otto, 2000; Stott et al., 2010).

Create CBT anew for each client

CBT as a psychotherapeutic treatment and intervention form, gains much of its effectiveness as being semi-standardised (uniform in pattern of application from one client to another); however, each practitioner is different and so is each client. It is even arguable that the same practitioner is not identical to different clients. Therefore, we arrive at a paradox. How can we support and provide engagement in high-quality service-delivery by practicing CBT consistently but differently for each of our different clients?

Let us first simplify what it means to be the good practitioner that we have referred to throughout this book. (1) You need to establish a good relationship with the client characterised by unconditionality, empathy, genuineness and that forms the therapeutic alliance; (2) You need to be sufficiently accurate at assessment and formulation to capture the client experience; (3) You need to use therapeutic tools to encourage clients to explore and dive into their key presentations and moments in life; and (4) You need to design, implement and, if necessary, modify interventions to achieve mutually agreed goals.

All these four elements to good practice are spontaneous and ever-evolving with changes between sessions, within sessions and larger changes in the client's life. It is helpful to view the process as a continuous line that turns and changes, as with stimuli of various kind as the client experiences and examines the process, rather than a pre-set 'formula'. This is not to devalue the effectiveness of a 'therapy protocol' (i.e., standardised manuals which show a step-by-step prescribed sequence and exercises which the practitioner guides the client through).

We can appreciate the uniqueness of each client, their personal language, experiences, and their world. Therefore, the CBT process must also be developed and delivered 'anew' for each individual. Below are some directions to engage with this process:

1 **Go *with* the client:** The practitioner must be prepared to go where the client goes, engage in their experiences, and understand their lives. This does not mean being completely passive. Rather, it is the willingness to dive within the client experience to continue providing a safe space and building trust. The understanding that comes from going *with* the client allows the practitioner to tailor certain elements of the CBT process to that client and create CBT anew for them. Some small wins include acknowledging and implementing sport-to-sport difference, cultural differences and gender differences.

2 **Formulate patterns, not absolute truths:** It is often tempting to consider our formulation to be the final word on the client experience. There are two problems with that; (a) the client experience is changing (due to CBT and outside experiences) and (b) it does not capture the situation specific demands of sessions. Formulation as a technique should always adhere to an evidence based theoretical framework/model (see Chapter 5); however, this should be customised to each individual, even for similar presentations. After some practice and experience similar presentations look similar. For example, pre-competitive anxiety between two different athletes has similar patterns. It is tempting to have a template of absolute truths for this presentation. But practitioners should aim for patterns that duplicate across presentations to keep the individual differences. This will guide a slightly different, customised and new version of CBT for each client.

3 **Techniques and Interventions:** Following on from previous recommendations about formulation, techniques require some flexibility. Novice practitioners typically have an over-reliance on a rigid application of intervention techniques (see Chapter 7). Rigidity in technique often falls flat in sessions because the client cannot associate it with their unique NAT patterns and life experiences. To use a metaphor, an individual needs to know the technical aspects of how to execute a sport skill. But eventually, if they are to be a great athlete, they must go beyond the technique alone, trust their spontaneous reactions and application of that technique in competition. For example, SG once had a client whose father had just passed away. The urge was to use models of grief and techniques, but because of the fragility of the emotions associated, that option was dismissed. Instead, because customised formulation highlighted the key role of the father in the client's sport life, the focus was only on having a Socratic question on his cognitions regarding where he would be without his father in sport. Later on, the client mentioned that it really helped to understand why he was thinking the way he was, and could then transition to grieving the death properly.

4 **Ask your client:** Inquiring into the client's view about what is helpful is often grossly overlooked. There is research that highlights that the client's view of what is 'useful' is often different from the practitioners. To create CBT anew, feedback on what is helpful for that client needs to be worked on. Feedback can (and should) be asked for at the end of every session initially to use it to fine tune the therapeutic relationship and goals of CBT. Feedback should also be inquired for after implementing any intervention. Some example questions for feedback include (please vary according to situation); 'How was that style for you?'; 'Did you feel comfortable in that session?'; 'Opening thoughts, what was that exercise like?'

Cherish the learning curve, be aware of the stagnation hazard

In 'Thinking, Fast and Slow' Daniel Kahneman remarked that every author 'has in mind a setting in which readers of his or her work could benefit from having read it' (Kahneman, 2011, p. 1). For our readers, we would put this book somewhere on every person's learning curve. Plotting the individual's development along, and keeping them out of that hazard of thinking, that we have all the answers – we do not. Nor do we expect any psychologist to.

In some ways, all psychologists should be on a personal and professional quest to discover how the intricacies of mind and behaviour fit together. In sport, it is all too pervasive. After all, athletes we work with, and support, are continuously trying to get better. Why should we be any different? Remember that adage we often say, 'the only person you need to be better than, is you yesterday'. It is therefore crucial to remember what we have learned so far, identify what we still need to learn, and reflect on how these pieces fit within our professional practice. This book provides a thorough overview of the 'essentials' of CBT and focuses on helping the practitioner 'apply' it. But further reading, practice, training and supervision are also required to being an effective practitioner. We emphasise the idea of the learning curve in this section, and the idea of stagnation hazards. This is because it is easy to stagnate, and hard to keep committed to learning. But to be effective, that is what we must do. We conclude with certain broad thematic areas where this learning curve needs to be traced.

Learn and reflect on yourself

Every practicing psychologist will have an intra-culture of a kind, a governing system of beliefs and philosophies (both personal and professional) that is accepted as 'truth' and used to guide decisions simple and complex. This stems from our personal experiences and professional influences. Before and during applied practice, understand what these 'truths' are and how they might influence our interactions with clients. Distilled, this is the practitioner's core beliefs and rules for life.

These may even lead to biases (conscious or unconscious). At other times, they may lead to a mis-acknowledgement of our limits (taking a session when we are physically tired). Sometimes they might create pressure on us (an 'important' client where one has to prove oneself). They could also create friction and dissociation with the client (client is 'talented but lazy' but the practitioner's core belief is hard work and consistency, leading to friction in intervention). One key area to be aware of and reflect upon is *what is sport to us?* This is relevant if the practitioner has at some point in their life participated or competed in organised sport at any level. We encourage personal therapy during the training process and also at intermittent points during professional life. This allows the practitioner to (a) introspect with their truths; (b) mitigate the stress and demands of the profession; and (c) experience CBT/therapy from the client's perspective.

Negotiate with your professional philosophy

Early CBT used to be seen as rigid and only adhering to the cognitive paradigm; however, with third wave CBT, newer influences have arrived. This has opened up the practice of CBT with many professional philosophies. It is imperative that you debate, deliberate, and discuss your professional philosophy with your supervisor and in peer supervision to understand how you view individuals, their processes in sport, and your role as a practitioner applying CBT (see Borders et al., 2014). We have titled this as a 'negotiation' because practitioners typically wrestle with this debate consistently across their professional life. Regarding CBT applied practice and professional practice, some key questions to consider are:

- Who am I? The expert or the facilitator?
- How comfortable am I with deep emotions? Or are cognitions and behaviours my area of competence?
- What is my role with this client and in this situation?
- If I were sitting in the client's position, what would I expect?
- The client is presenting ______, have I been through this myself? If yes, am I too emotionally involved?
- Did I act in my client's best interests at a holistic, long-term level? (It is often easy to get into short-term performance fixes and ignore potential long-term health risk factors.)
- What other potential interventions could I have taken?
- Is this my decision to make or is it the client's?
- Do I need supervision regarding this client or issue (refer to Hutter et al., 2015)?
- Should I apply the 5Ws and 1H to myself? (See Socratic questioning in Chapter 7.)
- Am I too impersonal? Or have I let this client matter too much to me personally?
- Did I do something wrong? How can I reflect upon it and work on my professional development?
- Do I have any regrets? Am I bringing that into the sessions with my clients?
- I am just giving way to the forceful personality of my client? Are external events controlling my actions?

Simple may sometimes be better

Every practitioner, starting off, wants to be perfect; however, fortunately or unfortunately, there is no 'perfect' way to practise. Some might start as a logical thinker, with a brilliant orientation to theory, complete with an unfailing sense of insight. Others might aspire to be the master of emotions, to dive deep into those with clients. Whatever may be, we remember we are the practitioners who have read the books and the articles, attended the training programs and who reflect through supervision. *Our clients have not.*

Our clients typically arrive wanting change. It is therefore sensible to focus on the simple, which may sometimes be better. It is the job of the practitioner to know the complex interplay of formulation factors to design an elegant and intricate intervention. But to the client, this must be simple enough to engage with and adhere to in the short and long run. If you have a *precision to your purpose*, you will find *success in simplicity.*

Good luck! May you find this journey of learning and practice rewarding!

References

American Psychological Association. (2006). Policy Statement on Evidence-Based Practice in Psychology [Review of Policy Statement on Evidence-Based Practice in Psychology]. American Psychological Association. https://www.apa.org/practice/guidelines/evidence-based-statement

American Psychological Society (2017) APA Ethical principles of psychologists and code of conduct. https://www.apa.org/ethics/code.

Andersen, M. B. (Ed.). (2005). *Sport psychology in practice*. Champaign, IL: Human Kinetics.

Aoyagi, M. W., Portenga, S. T., Poczwardowski, A., Cohen, A. B., & Statler, T. (2012). Reflections and directions: The profession of sport psychology past, present, and future. *Professional Psychology: Research and Practice*, *43*, 32–38. http://dx.doi.org/10.1037/a0025676

Atkins, L., & Michie, S. (2015). Designing interventions to change eating behaviours. *Proceedings of the Nutrition Society*, *74*(2), 164–170.

Ball, C. T. (2013). Unexplained sporting slumps and causal attributions. *Journal of Sport Behavior*, *36*(3), 233-242.

Barber, J. P., Liese, B. S., & Abrams, M. J. (2003). Development of the cognitive therapy adherence and competence scale. *Psychotherapy Research*, *13*(2), 205–221.

Barker, J. B., Slater, M. J., Pugh, G., Mellalieu, S. D., McCarthy, P. J., Jones, M. V., & Moran, A. (2020). The effectiveness of psychological skills training and behavioral interventions in sport using single-case designs: A meta regression analysis of the peer-reviewed studies. *Psychology of Sport and Exercise*, *51*, 101746.

Barlow, D. H., Curreri, A. J., & Woodard, L. S. (2021). Neuroticism and disorders of emotion: A new synthesis. *Current Directions in Psychological Science*, *30*(5), 410–417.

Beck, A. T. (1964). Thinking and depression. Part II: Theory and therapy. *Archives of General Psychiatry*, *10*(6), 561–571. https://doi.org/10.1001/archpsyc.1964.01720240015003.

Beck, A. T. (1976). *Cognitive therapy and emotional disorders*. International Universities Press.

Beck, A. T. (1979a). *Cognitive therapy and the emotional disorders*. Penguin.

Beck, A. T. (Ed.). (1979b). *Cognitive therapy of depression*. Guilford Press.

Beck, A. T., Brown, G., Steer, R. A., Eidelson, J. I., & Riskind, J. H. (1985). Differentiating anxiety and depression: a test of the cognitive content-specificity hypothesis. Journal of abnormal psychology, 96(3), 179.

Beck, J. S., & Beck, A. T. (2011). Cognitive behavior therapy. New York: Basics and beyond. Guilford Publication.

Beck, J. S. (2020). *Cognitive behavior therapy: Basics and beyond*. Guilford Publications.

Beck, J. S., & Fleming, S. (2021). A brief history of Aaron T. Beck, MD, and cognitive behavior therapy. *Clinical Psychology in Europe*, *3*(2), 1–7.

Beidas, R. S., Stewart, R. E., Walsh, L., Lucas, S., Downey, M. M., Jackson, K., & Mandell, D. S. (2015). Free, brief, and validated: Standardized instruments for low-resource mental health settings. *Cognitive and Behavioral Practice*, *22*(1), 5–19.

Bennett, J., Hays, K., Lindsay, P., Olusoga, P., & Maynard, I. W. (2015). Yips and lost move syndrome: Exploring psychological symptoms, similarities, and implications for treatment. *International Journal of Sport Psychology*, *46*(1), 61–82.

Bennett, J., & Maynard, I. (2017). Performance blocks in sport: Recommendations for treatment and implications for sport psychology practitioners. *Journal of Sport Psychology in Action*, *8*(1), 60–68.

Bennett-Levy, J. E., Butler, G. E., Fennell, M. E., Hackman, A. E., Mueller, M. E., & Westbrook, D. E. (2004). *Oxford Guide to behavioural experiments in cognitive therapy*. Oxford University Press.

Bennett-Levy, J., & Lee, N. K. (2014). Self-practice and self-reflection in cognitive behaviour therapy training: What factors influence trainees' engagement and experience of benefit? *Behavioural and Cognitive Psychotherapy*, *42*(1), 48–64.

Bjork, R. A., Dunlosky, J., & Kornell, N. (2013). Self-regulated learning: Beliefs, techniques, and illusions. *Annual Review of Psychology*, *64*, 417–444.

Blackburn, I. M., & Davidson, K. (1995). *Cognitive therapy for depression. Anxiety, amended.* Oxford Scientific Publications.

Blackburn, I. M., James, I. A., Milne, D. L., Baker, C., Standart, S., & Garland, A., et al. (2001). The revised cognitive therapy scale (CTS-r): Psychometric properties. *Behavioural and Cognitive Psychotherapy*, 29, 431–446. doi: 10.1017/S1352465801004040

Blenkiron, P. (2011). *Stories and analogies in cognitive behaviour therapy*. John Wiley & Sons.

Borders, L. D., DeKruyf, L., Fernando, D. M., Glosoff, H. L., Hays, D. G., Page, B., & Welfare, L. E. (2014). Best practices in clinical supervision: Evolution of a counseling specialty. *The Clinical Supervisor*, *33*, 26–44. doi:10.1080/07325223.2014.905225

Brewer, B. W. (1998). Adherence to sport injury rehabilitation programs. *Journal of Applied Sport Psychology*, *10*(1), 70–82.

British Psychological Society (2019a) BPS Guidelines on testing and test use. https://www.bps.org.uk/guidelines-testing-and-test-use.

British Psychological Society. (2019b). *Guidelines for the use of psychological tests in healthcare research* (pp. 1–22). British Psychological Society. https://cms.bps.org.uk/sites/default/files/2022-07/guidelines_for_the_use_of_psychological_tests_in_healthcare_research.pdf.

Bronfenbrenner, U. (1992). *Ecological systems theory*. Jessica Kingsley Publishers.

Bronfenbrenner, U., & Ceci, S. J. (1994). Nature-nuture reconceptualized in developmental perspective: A bioecological model. *Psychological Review*, *101*(4), 568–586.

Burt, J. B. (2021, April 27). The show pony who became captain: How Neymar grew up at PSG. *The Telegraph*.

Clark, D. A., & Steer, R. A. (1996). Empirical status of the cognitive model of anxiety and depression. *Frontiers of Cognitive Therapy*, *18*, 75–96.

Clark, G. I., & Egan, S. J. (2015). The Socratic method in cognitive behavioural therapy: A narrative review. *Cognitive Therapy and Research*, *39*(6), 863–879.

Clarke, P., Sheffield, D., & Akehurst, S. (2015). The yips in sport: A systematic review. *International Review of Sport and Exercise Psychology*, *8*(1), 156–184.

Cone, J. D. (1995). Assessment practice standards. *Scientific Standards of Psychological Practice: Issues and Recommendations*, 201–224.

Corlett, J. (1996). Sophistry, socrates, and sport psychology. *The Sport Psychologist*, *10*(1), 84–94.

Cowen, A. S., & Keltner, D. (2017). Self-report captures 27 distinct categories of emotion bridged by continuous gradients. *Proceedings of the National Academy of Sciences*, *114*(38), E7900–E7909.

Cox, R. H., Martens, M. P., & Russell, W. D. (2003). Measuring anxiety in athletics: The Revised Competitive State Anxiety Inventory–2. *Journal of Sport & Exercise Psychology*, *25*(4), 519–533.

Cropley, B., Baldock, L., Mellalieu, S. D., Neil, R., Wagstaff, C. R. D., & Wadey, R. (2016). Coping with the demands of professional practice: Sport psychology consultants' perspectives. *The Sport Psychologist*, *30*(3), 290–302.

Cropley, B., Miles, A., Hanton, S., & Niven, A. (2007). Improving the delivery of applied sport psychology support through reflective practice. *The Sport Psychologist*, *21*(4), 475–494.

Curry, S., Marlatt, G. A., & Gordon, J. R. (1987). Abstinence violation effect: validation of an attributional construct with smoking cessation. *Journal of Consulting and Clinical Psychology*, *55*(2), 145.

Dimidjian, S., Barrera Jr, M., Martell, C., Muñoz, R. F., & Lewinsohn, P. M. (2011). The origins and current status of behavioral activation treatments for depression. *Annual Review of Clinical Psychology*, *7*, 1–38.

Dobson, D., & Dobson, K. S. (2018). Evidence-based practice of cognitive-behavioral therapy. Guilford publications.

Durand-Bush, N., Baker, J., van den Berg, F., Richard, V., & Bloom, G. A. (2022). The gold medal profile for sport psychology (GMP-SP). *Journal of Applied Sport Psychology*, 1–24.

Eklund, R. C., Grove, J. R., & Heard, N. P. (1998). The measurement of slump-related coping: Factorial validity of the COPE and modified-COPE inventories. *Journal of Sport and Exercise Psychology*, *20*(2), 157–175.

Ellis, A. (1957). Rational psychotherapy and individual psychology. *Journal of Individual Psychology*, *13*, 38–44.

Ellis, A., Gordon, J., Neenan, M. & Palmer, S. (1997). Stress counselling: A rational emotive behaviour approach. Cassell.

Engebretsen, L., Steffen, K., Alonso, J. M., Aubry, M., Dvorak, J., Junge, A., & Wilkinson, M. (2010). Sports injuries and illnesses during the winter Olympic Games 2010. *British Journal of Sports Medicine*, *44*(11), 772–780.

Garber, J., Frankel, S. A., & Herrington, C. G. (2016). Developmental demands of cognitive behavioral therapy for depression in children and adolescents: Cognitive, social, and emotional processes. *Annual Review of Clinical Psychology*, *12*, 181.

Gilbert, P. (2010). An introduction to compassion focused therapy in cognitive behavior therapy. *International Journal of Cognitive Therapy*, *3*(2), 97–112.

Gilbert, P. & Leahy, R. L. (2007). *The therapeutic relationship in the cognitive behavioral psychotherapies*. Routledge. https://doi.org/10.4324/9780203099995.

Glazer, D. D. (2009). Development and preliminary validation of the Injury-Psychological Readiness to Return to Sport (I-PRRS) scale. *Journal of Athletic Training*, *44*(2), 185–189.

Gouttebarge, V., Bindra, A., Blauwet, C., Campriani, N., Currie, A., Engebretsen, L., & Budgett, R. (2021). International Olympic committee (IOC) sport mental health assessment tool 1 (SMHAT-1) and sport mental health recognition tool 1 (SMHRT-1): Towards better support of athletes' mental health. *British Journal of Sports Medicine*, *55*(1), 30–37.

Greenberg, L. S. (2011). *Emotion-focused therapy*. American Psychological Association.

Greenberger, D., & Padesky, C. A. (1995). *Mind over mood: A cognitive therapy treatment manual for clients*. Guilford Press.

Gupta, S., & Divekar, S. (2022). A symmetry or asymmetry: Reflecting upon realities of cultural practice in sport psychology. *Sport and Exercise Psychology Review*, *17*(1), 60–72.

Gupta., S. & Duncan, E. (in review). Person-centred sport psychology practice: A framework for working with emotions. *The Sports Psychologist*.

Gupta, S. & McCarthy, P.J. (2022). The sporting resilience model: A systematic review of resilience in sport performers. *Frontiers in Psychology*, 13, pg 1–18, DOI:1003053. doi: 10.3389/fpsyg.2022.1003053.

Hanna F. J. (2002). *Therapy with difficult clients: Using the precursors model to awaken change*. Washington, DC: American Psychological Association.

Hanrahan, S. J., & Andersen, M. B. (2010). *Routledge handbook of applied sport psychology*. Routledge, Taylor & Francis.

Hawkins, P., & McMahon, A. (2020). *Supervision in the helping professions 5e*. Open University press.

Hayes, S. C., & Follette, W. C. (1992). Can functional analysis provide a substitute for syndromal classification? *Behavioral Assessment*, 14(3), 345–365.

Hayes, S. C., Pistorello, J., & Levin, M. E. (2012). Acceptance and commitment therapy as a unified model of behavior change. *The Counseling Psychologist*, *40*(7), 976–1002.

Horvath, A. O., Del Re, A. C., Flückiger, C., & Symonds, D. (2011). Alliance in individual psychotherapy. *Psychotherapy*, *48*, 9–16.

Horvath, A. O., & Symonds, B. D. (1991). Relation between working alliance and outcome in psychotherapy: A meta-analysis. *Journal of Counseling Psychology*, *38*(2), 139–149.

Hutter, R. I. V., Oldenhof-Veldman, T., & Oudejans, R. R. D. (2015). What trainee sport psychologists want to learn in supervision. *Psychology of Sport & Exercise*, *16*, 101–109. doi:10.1016/j.psychsport.2014.08.003

Johnstone, L. (2013). Using formulation in teams. In Formulation in psychology and psychotherapy (pp. 236–262). Routledge.

Jones, M., Meijen, C., McCarthy, P. J., & Sheffield, D. (2009). A theory of challenge and threat states in athletes. *International Review of Sport and Exercise Psychology*, *2*(2), 161–180.

Kahneman, D. (2011). *Thinking, fast and slow*. Macmillan.

Katz, J., & Hemmings, B. (2009). *Counselling skills handbook for the sport psychologist*. Division of Sport & Exercise Psychology of the British Psychological Society.

Kennerley, H., Kirk, J., & Westbrook, D. (2016). *An introduction to cognitive behaviour therapy: Skills and applications*. SAGE Publications.

Kocabas, E., & Üstündağ-Budak, M. (2017). Validation skills in counselling and psychotherapy. *International Journal of Scientific Study*, *5*(8), 319–322.

Kolb, D. A. (1984). *Experience as the source of learning and development*. Prentice Hall.

Kuruveettissery, S., Gupta, S., & Rajan, S. K. (2021). Development and psychometric validation of the three-dimensional grit scale. *Current Psychology*, 1–10

Kuyken, W., Padesky, C. A., & Dudley, R. (2008). The science and practice of case conceptualization. Behavioural and Cognitive Psychotherapy, 36(6), 757–768.

Kuyken, W., Padesky, C. A., & Dudley, R. (2009). *Collaborative case conceptualization: Working effectively with clients in cognitive behavioural therapy*. Guilford Press.

Larimer, M. E., & Marlatt, G. A. (2004). Relapse prevention: An overview of Marlatt's cognitive-behavioral model. *Psychosocial Treatments*, 11–28.

Leahy, R. L. (2012). *Overcoming resistance in cognitive therapy*. Guilford Press.

Leahy, R. L., Holland, S. J., & McGinn, L. K. (2011). *Treatment plans and interventions for depression and anxiety disorders*. Guilford Press.

Leahy, R. L., Tirch, D., & Napolitano, L. A. (2011). *Emotion regulation in psychotherapy: A practitioner's guide*. Guilford Press.

Ledley, D. R., Marx, B. P., & Heimberg, R. G. (2011). *Making cognitive-behavioral therapy work: Clinical process for new practitioners*. Guilford Press.

Lim, N. (2016). Cultural Differences in emotion: Differences in emotional arousal level between the East and the West. *Integrative Medicine Research*, *5*(2), 105–109.

Lochbaum, M., Zanatta, T., Kirschling, D., & May, E. (2021). The profile of moods States and athletic performance: A meta-analysis of published studies. *European Journal of Investigation in Health, Psychology and Education*, *11*(1), 50–70.

Ludlam, K. E., Butt, J., Bawden, M., Lindsay, P., & Maynard, I. W. (2016). A strengths-based consultancy approach in elite sport: Exploring super-strengths. *Journal of Applied Sport Psychology*, *28*(2), 216–233.

Lundqvist, C. (2020). Ending an elite sports career: Case report of behavioral activation applied as an evidence-based intervention with a former Olympic athlete developing depression. *The Sport Psychologist*, *34*(4), 329–336.

Mack, R. J., Breckon, J. D., O'Ha'loran, P. D., & Butt, J. (2019). Enhancing athlete engagement in sport psychology interventions using motivational interviewing: A case study. *The Sport Psychologist*, *33*(2), 159–168.

Marlatt, G. A., & Donovan, D. M. (Eds.). (2005). *Relapse prevention: Maintenance strategies in the treatment of addictive behaviors*. Guilford Press.

Martin, D. J., Garske, J. P., & Davis, M. K. (2000). Relation of the therapeutic alliance with outcome and other variables: A meta-analytic review. *Journal of Consulting and Clinical Psychology, 68*(3), 438.

McArdle, S., & Moore, P. (2012). Applying evidence-based principles from CBT to sport psychology. *The Sport Psychologist, 26*(2), 299–310.

McCarthy, P. J., & Gupta, S. (2022). Set goals to get goals: Sowing seeds for success in sports. *Frontiers for Young Minds, 10*, 684422.

McKay, D., Sookman, D., Neziroglu, F., Wilhelm, S., Stein, D. J., Kyrios, M., ... & Veale, D. (2015). Efficacy of cognitive-behavioral therapy for obsessive–compulsive disorder. *Psychiatry Research, 225*(3), 236–246.

Meichenbaum, D. (2014, May). Evolution of cognitive behavior therapy: origins, tenets, and clinical examples: Ph. D. In *The evolution of psychotherapy: The second conference* (pp. 132–146). Routledge.

Mitchell, C. W. (2009). *Effective techniques for dealing with highly resistant clients.* C. W. Mitchell.

Moorey, S., & Lavender, A. (2019a). *The therapeutic relationship in cognitive behaviour therapy.* SAGE Publications.

Moorey, S., & Lavender, A. (2019b). *Supervision and the therapeutic relationship.* SAGE.

Moran, A. *Managing your own learning at university.* UCD Press. Kindle Edition.

Muse, K., McManus, F., Rakovshik, S., & Thwaites, R. (2017). Development and psychometric evaluation of the assessment of core CBT skills (ACCS): An observation-based tool for assessing cognitive behavioral therapy competence. *Psychological Assessment, 29*(5), 542–555. https://doi.org/10.1037/pas0000372.

Neal, T. L., Diamond, A. B., Goldman, S., Klossner, D., Morse, E. D., Pajak, D. E., ... & Welzant, V. (2013). Inter-association recommendations for developing a plan to recognize and refer student-athletes with psychological concerns at the collegiate level: An executive summary of a consensus statement. *Journal of Athletic Training, 48*(5), 716–720.

Norcross, J. C., & Lambert, M. J. (2011). Psychotherapy relationships that work II [Special Issue]. *Psychotherapy, 48*(1), 4–8.

Otto, M. W. (2000). Stories and metaphors in cognitive-behavior therapy. *Cognitive and Behavioral Practice, 7*(2), 166–172.

Padesky, C. A. (1996). Developing cognitive therapist competency: Teaching and supervision models. In P. M. Salkovskis (Ed.), *Frontiers of cognitive therapy* (pp. 266–292). The Guilford Press.

Padesky, C.A., & Mooney, K. A. (1990a). Clinical tip: Presenting the cognitive model to patients. *International Cognitive Therapy Newsletter, 6*, 1–2.

Padesky, C. A., & Mooney, K. A. (1990b). Presenting the cognitive behavioural model to clients. *International Cognitive Therapy Newsletter, 61*, 13–14.

Peirce, C. S. (1984). Review of Nichols' A treatise on cosmology. In *Meaning and action. A critical history of pragmatism* (pp. 493–495). Hackett.

Poczwardowski, A., Sherman, C. P., & Ravizza, K. (2004). Professional philosophy in the sport psychology service delivery: Building on theory and practice. *The Sport Psychologist, 18*(4), 445–463.

Podlog, L., Banham, S., Wadey, M., & Hannon, R., J., D. (2015) Psychological readiness to return to competitive sport following injury: A qualitative study. *The Sport Psychologist*, 29, 1–14. https://doi.org/10.1123/tsp.2014-0063.

Power, M. (2010). *Emotion-focused cognitive therapy.* John Wiley & Sons.

Power, M., & Dalgleish, T. (2015). *Cognition and emotion: From order to disorder.* Psychology Press.

Purcell, R., Gwyther, K., & Rice, S. M. (2019). Mental health in elite athletes: increased awareness requires an early intervention framework to respond to athlete needs. *Sports Medicine-Open, 5*(1), 1–8.

Quartiroli, A., Etzel, E. F., Knight, S. M., & Zakrajsek, R. A. (2019). Self-care as key to others' care: The perspectives of globally situated experienced senior-level sport psychology practitioners. *Journal of Applied Sport Psychology*, *31*(2), 147–167.

Quartiroli, A., Wagstaff, C. R., & Thelwell, R. (2021). The what and the how of self-care for sport psychology practitioners: A Delphi study. *Journal of Applied Sport Psychology*, 1–20.

Robertson, D. (2018). *The philosophy of cognitive—Behavioural therapy (CBT): Stoic philosophy as rational and cognitive psychotherapy*. Routledge.

Roth, A. D. (2016). A new scale for the assessment of competences in cognitive and behavioural therapy. *Behavioural and Cognitive Psychotherapy*, *44*(5), 620–624. https://doi.org/10.1017/S1352465816000011.

Roth, A. D., & Pilling, S. (2007). *The competences required to deliver effective cognitive and behavioural therapy for people with depression and with anxiety disorders*. London: Department of Health.

Rust, J., & Golombok, S. (2014). *Modern psychometrics: The science of psychological assessment*. Routledge.

Safran, J. D., & Muran, J. C. (2000). *Negotiating the therapeutic alliance: A relational treatment guide*. Guilford Press.

Safran, J. D., Muran, J. C., & Eubanks-Carter, (2011). Repairing alliance ruptures. In J. C. Norcross (Ed.), *Psychotherapy relationships that work: Evidence-based responsiveness* (2nd ed.; pp. 224–238). Oxford University Press.

Schinke, R. J., McGannon, K. R., & Smith, B. (Eds.). (2016). *Routledge international handbook of sport psychology*. Routledge.

Schweizer, G., Furley, P., Rost, N., & Barth, K. (2020). Reliable measurement in sport psychology: The case of performance outcome measures. *Psychology of Sport and Exercise*, *48*, 101663.

Shirk, S., Karver, M., & Brown, R. (2011). The alliance in child and adolescent psychotherapy. *Psychotherapy*, *48*, 17–24.

Stallard, P. (2019). *Think good, feel good: A cognitive behavioural therapy workbook for children and young people*. John Wiley & Sons.

Stead, J., Poolton, J., & Alder, D. (2022). Performance slumps in sport: A systematic review. *Psychology of Sport and Exercise*, 102136.

Stott, R., Mansell, W., Salkovskis, P., Lavender, A., & Cartwright-Hatton, S. (2010). *Oxford guide to metaphors in CBT: Building cognitive bridges*. Oxford: OUP.

Treynor, W., Gonzalez, R., & Nolen-Hoeksema, S. (2003). Rumination reconsidered: A psychometric analysis. *Cognitive Therapy and Research*, *27*(3), 247–259.

van Raalte, J. L., Vincent, A., & Brewer, B. W. (2016). Self-talk: Review and sport-specific model. *Psychology of Sport and Exercise*, *22*, 139–148.

Wagstaff, C. R., & Leach, J. (2017). The value of strength-based approaches in SERE and sport psychology. *Military Psychology*, 27:2, 65–84, DOI: 10.1037/mil0000066

Walen, S. R., DiGiuseppe, R., & Dryden, W. (1992). *A practitioner's guide to rational-emotive therapy*. Oxford University Press.

Waltman, S. H., Codd, III, R., Trent, M. F., M, L., & Bret A., M. *Socratic questioning for therapists and counselors (Clinical topics in psychology and psychiatry)* (p. 30). Taylor and Francis. Kindle Edition.

Weishaar, M. E. (2001). Cognitive therapy. In Assessment and Therapy (pp. 103–112). Academic Press.

Weinberg, R. S. (2019). Psychological skills training. In D. Hackfort, R. J. Schinke, & B. Strauss (Eds.), *Dictionary of sport psychology: Sport, exercise and performing arts* (pp. 230–231). Elsevier. https://doi.org/10.1016/C2016-0-03935-9.

Wells, A., White, J., & Carter, K. (1997). Attention training: Effects on anxiety and beliefs in panic and social phobia. *Clinical Psychology & Psychotherapy: An International Journal of Theory and Practice*, *4*(4), 226–232.

Witkiewitz, K., & Marlatt, G. A. (2007). Overview of relapse prevention. In *Therapist's guide to evidence-based relapse prevention* (pp. 3–17). Academic Press.

Young, J. E., Klosko, J. S., & Weishaar, M. E. (2003). *Schema therapy*. Guilford.

Index

Made in the USA
Monee, IL
13 September 2026

62977685R10118